Portrait by Emma Freeman

Ranulf Rayner has led an adventurous life. After Eton, he served in the British army, where he captained their team on the Cresta Run, instructed on nuclear warfare, and flew helicopters. Later, he spent a year climbing in the Himalayas, experiencing the horrors of Cambodia, meeting aboriginals in the Australian Outback and witnessing the destruction of the Amazon rainforest and of the oceans with plastic, before flying to Switzerland to manage the winter sports scenes for the Bond movie OHMSS.

On returning home to farm, he started several innovative businesses including England's first computer company specialising in agriculture. He later wrote a memoir *Is Anyone Out There* by The Major, which follows a number of fully illustrated sporting books, including *The Story of the America's Cup*, presently in its tenth edition.

Based on his own remarkable experiences, and concerned about less fortunate generations to come, he decided to write a trilogy of real time adventure stories about the three most worrying issues now facing our planet—the ever-growing population, the pollution of our oceans, and in this book, some answers to galloping climate change. By inspiring readers to consider these issues and think of their own solutions rather than listen to the harbingers of doom, his intention is to give them hope so they may fight for a brighter future.

Half the proceeds from this book will be donated to ShelterBox—an international relief charity which provides immediate support to those who have lost their homes due to sudden catastrophes, many of them attributed to climate change.

To Annette, my long-suffering wife who has contributed her splendid drawings of the main characters.

Ranulf Rayner

CLIMAX

Saving Mother Earth

Susan

Best wishes,

Ranulf Rayner

AUSTIN MACAULEY PUBLISHERS™

LONDON • CAMBRIDGE • NEW YORK • SHARJAH

A CIP catalogue record for this title is available from the British Library.

ISBN 9781035826421 (Paperback)
ISBN 9781035826438 (ePub e-book)

www.austinmacauley.co.uk

First Published 2024
Austin Macauley Publishers Ltd®
1 Canada Square
Canary Wharf
London
E14 5AA

My thanks to Jan Verbeer of Sea Forester, finalists in the Prince of Wales's Earthshot competition, for supporting my imaginative ideas on carbon sequestration.

Part One

Chapter 1

The Major struggled desperately to hold the ancient Piper Cherokee straight and level as it bucked violently in the shimmering heat. Below a sea of fire stretched on for ever, half obscured by billowing purple clouds of wood smoke, until it melted into the white-hot horizon. As the smoke hit his lungs and he gasped for air, he noticed a burst of flame shooting up from the rainforest not far ahead and a sudden flash of light as a small object hurtled so fast towards him that, although he wrenched desperately at the controls, he was too late to avoid it.

As the windshield shattered with a deafening explosion, a splinter of perspex hit him so hard on the head that he passed out. It was only the blast of hot air rushing through the cockpit that brought him back to his senses and to the realisation that his engine had seized and his plane was plunging like a shot bird into the blazing trees now less than a hundred metres below him. On finding it impossible to claw his way back to the pilot's seat from where he had been flung against the rear bulkhead, he tucked himself into a tight ball, thought of his dog back home, and prepared to die.

**

The Major. Bob's ruthless mercenary

Bill Buckmaster, known better as Bob because for years he had earned a few "bob" selling nuclear material around the globe, had been so impressed by his personal mercenary and his ideas for implementing a humane method for controlling the world's burgeoning population, that he had summoned him to his Elizabethan mansion overlooking Lundy Island, a granite rock rising sheer out of the Atlantic not far off England's North Devon coast, to discuss plans for putting an end to the baffling increase in the number of fires afflicting the Amazon rainforest.

'We are both agreed, Major, that the population explosion, plastic pollution, and now climate change are the greatest threats to have ever faced mankind. We are now doomed unless we use all our powers of innovation and creativity to do something radical about them.

'The increasing numbers of storms, floods, and fires already afflicting our planet are frightening enough, but more so is the ice melt; for apart from causing a catastrophic rise in sea levels, should the Himalaya be left without glaciers and India without fresh water, which will soon become the most precious commodity on earth, the people will start to die of thirst, or starve to death.

'The cause of climate change is clear. Due to our fast-rising population and their insatiable demand for electricity, the amount of fossil fuel being burned is loading our atmosphere with too much CO_2. In the past our forests, like the oceans, would have sequestered some thirty per cent of the carbon poisoning our atmosphere, but their wanton destruction is causing the planet to heat up so fast, that should fossil fuels continue to be burned at the present rate, there will be no turning back.

'Major,' he continued, standing legs akimbo in front of a blazing log fire with an expensive cigar jutting from his mouth like a torpedo. 'Do you realise that while I stand here enjoying my Montecristo, one and a half acres of virgin forest is being mindlessly destroyed on the Amazon every minute, just to fill farmers' pockets with the excuse of feeding more and more people.

'Deforestation on such a scale is not just happening in Brazil but elsewhere in the world, such as in the Far East, where the canopy is being destroyed to grow countless plantations of oil palms, which are of no more use to the atmosphere than your father's blotting paper. Meanwhile, an increasing amount of coal is being mined, particularly in Australia, and more coal fired generators are being built, principally by the Chinese. So, Major, what happens in thirty years' time when there is not enough oxygen, and perhaps, two billion more mouths to feed?'

'Bob, I am beginning to understand your deep mistrust of the human race, but before you continue with your tale of woe, there must be a word for the increasing number of fires and deforestation.'

'Do you mean the word greed? For more than twenty per cent of the Amazon rainforest has already been lost because of farmers wishing to graze more cattle and grow more soya on ground which, once the trees and vegetation are gone, will quickly erode and become worthless. Because of their selfishness and the world's increasing appetite for beef, in less than fifty years' time the rainforest, which also provides us with many of our important medications, will cease to exist!'

'I agree,' the Major replied, taking a step forward to speak into his left ear, the other having been destroyed by too much game shooting. 'Our minds always think alike, Bob. Greed is certainly part of the problem but the more appropriate word I see on your lips is blackmail!'

'Yes, blackmail, Major, but on a huge scale. Something that must be dealt with immediately. It is said that should our climate continue to heat up at its present rate, by the end of this century, much of our planet will be under salt water and life as we know it will cease to exist. Before that happens, people will panic to escape the heat with many more migrants seeking sanctuary in Europe, for instance.' He puffed even harder at his cigar while thumping the mantlepiece with his fist.

'I am just as worried about that as you are, Bob, noticing your greying hair. It is a terrifying prospect but, surely, a preventable one?'

'Major, as I am approaching sixty, and you are only half my age, it is far more of a worry for you, and should any girl someday dare to marry you, think of your children. Just take a look at this!'

Turning on his heel, he pressed a button beside the fireplace and the magnificent 18th century painting of British warships assembling under canvass off the Devon coast became a map of the world. Standing there in his immaculately tailored tweed suit and brown polished shoes, Bob much resembled the model of an English gentleman about to point out his favourite grouse moors. But that was only for a fleeting moment.

When he used the keypad, which he had picked up from the mantlepiece, his great forehead began to pucker, and just as a chameleon changes colour when it takes aim at a fly, his face started to glow like the forest fires he was so keen to eradicate. Having made squillions during his lifetime from nuclear fuel, after his wife had left him mainly for that reason, his determination to save the world instead, made him appear like a wartime general planning a vital mission of life or death.

'As I now enlarge the continent of South America,' he continued, 'and the area covered by the Amazon rainforest, you will see that it is not only owned by nine different nations but it is so vast it is said to be more than 25 times the size of Great Britain. But what you don't know is that GCHQ believes there are gangs of arsonists who are setting fire not only to the forests in Brazil but also to other parts of the world, including the Arctic, while demanding considerable sums of money from national governments to stop them doing so.

'The situation is already so dangerous that unless we act fast and governments refuse to pay them, climate change will heat up the world to double its present temperatures in just a few years. And I don't mean local governments like that of Brazil, which, although possessing the lion's share of the Amazon rainforest, may be encouraging the arsonists.

'No, I am talking about countries like the United States, India, and China, the criminals not only responsible for burning most fossil fuels and polluting our atmosphere, but also those who have done little, or nothing, to prevent their forests from being destroyed. Forests are the world's lungs, for God's sake, and should be protected from farmers and arsonists in every way possible.

'Major, when it comes to beef production, as neither of us would expect farmers to relinquish their main source of income any more readily than those growing coke in Columbia, or when it comes to forestry, for men to stop harvesting timber, when there is such a burgeoning world demand for it, the only alternative is to tackle both problems face on.

'Therefore, I am setting you two missions; firstly to eliminate the arsonists who are increasing the amount of deforestation dramatically, and secondly, to conceive and then put into practice an alternative method of carbon sequestration at the receiving end on such a scale that it will remove the poison from our atmosphere for ever.'

Bob had hired his mercenary through a company called Sentinals, interested only in employing ex-servicemen and policemen who had served their country at the very highest level and were ready to face any situation, however difficult and dangerous. Apart from intelligence and skills training at Sentinals' secret location in the Outer Hebrides, they had to endure weeks of rigorous field work supervised by instructors from the Special Air Service.

This included the use of clandestine radios, the professional handling of every type of weapon and explosive, practicing the subtleties of surprise and learning the art of close quarter fighting including the ability to kill with their bare hands. They had assured him that their man, who, because of his past reputation wished only to be called the Major, was the most imaginative and ruthless operator they had ever put in the field.

As the Major stood waiting patiently in front of him like a coiled spring, Bob admired his physique, his height of two metres, his dark swept back hair, and his finely chiselled features. But what struck him most was his apparent eagerness to take on any task set, including murder.

Bob had spent so many years peddling uranium around the globe, largely to its detriment, although he acknowledged the huge strides made in renewables, he calculated that should the world population continue to expand at the rate predicted, all forms of green energy such as wind and solar plus hydrogen and hydroelectric power, although of great importance, would never replace more than half its insatiable appetite for burning fossil fuels.

'Before I give you your final orders, Major, once you have dealt with the arsonists, who I understand from the foreign office may be Indonesian, your more important task, I repeat, will be to trap the carbon no longer sequestered by the great forests of the world, while my own job as a nuclear physicist, is to prevent the wretched stuff from being released in the first place.

'So, as you carry out your own demanding mission, I am embarking on a campaign to market such a novel form of nuclear power, that, unlike those who moan about climate change and do nothing about it, you and I by working closely together will prevent the catastrophe happening before it escalates.

'Tomorrow evening, Sam, the young pilot of my Gulfstream, will fly you to Cuiaba, which I visited twenty-five years ago when prospecting for uranium. Situated about a thousand miles in from the Brazilian coast, and once full of guys looking for gold and precious stones, all flourishing six shooters while pretty Indian girls hung around to tie their horses to hitching rails, it is now capital of the Mato Grosso. Blessed with a new international airport from where you will be able to hire a small aircraft, you will be able to search for the arsonists in one of the worst hit areas of the rainforest being set on fire.

'The flight out to Cuiaba may take at least twenty-four hours, as Sam will need to refuel in the Cape Verde islands, but you will be well looked after by Macey, my brilliant stewardess, who is Sam's fiancée. He met her when he was flying with the RAF in Afghanistan, where she was serving as a US Marine Corps nurse looking after our wounded soldiers. You will find her intelligent and a delight to talk to, indeed she has already become an important member of my team.

'I know that you prefer using your hands to defend yourself, but this time, you must carry the submachine gun she will give you on my aircraft. Meanwhile, I am transferring a million pounds to your account, which I will double when you succeed in the first of my two missions.'

Bob had homed in on the Xingu National Park, a small corner of the Amazon rainforest, which, before the internationally backed farmers and loggers arrived, he explained, had once stretched to nearly seven million square kilometres with some six thousand varieties of trees.

'But, as you see, the whole area is now so pock-marked with the red spots of forest fires that it appears to have suffered a violent attack of smallpox. Situated about five hundred kilometres north-east of Cuiaba and north of Rio das Mortes, it is where I would like you to start your search. As it is a protected area, where the indigenous tribes were once guaranteed to live their lives unmolested, it is just the sort of place for the arsonists to raise maximum publicity about their horrifying activities.

'But it will not be hitting the headlines for the first time. In 1925, the explorer Colonel Percy Fawcett together with his son and a companion went missing in the same part of the forest, never to be seen again, and later in July 1961, a budding English doctor called Richard Mason, who had been exploring the region with Robin Hanbury-Tenison, a young British adventurer, was speared to death by indigenous tribesmen while looking for the Iriri, a tributary of the Xingu River.

'Although, it is one of the most dangerous parts of the rainforest, as long as you remain airborne, it is the best and safest area for you to investigate. Meanwhile, you should leave your weapon and your satellite telephone behind at the airport in a secure locker and let me know what you have discovered about the arsonists the moment you return. They must be behind the majority of the fires burning there, as you will soon discover. That is all. Happy hunting!'

**

When his plane crashed down into the trees, he had been flung forward onto the instrument panel together with a pile of leaking jerrycans, now filling the air with the menacing fumes of aviation fuel. Although he was alive, the reality of his situation only hit him when he managed to get to his feet. Staring down through the jagged remains of the windshield, to his horror, he saw the smouldering undergrowth on the forest floor still lay more than ten metres below him.

Fortunately, the plane had stuck fast in a lacework of blazing branches, but knowing that the petrol fumes would ignite any moment, he had little time to decide how to save himself. It was only because of his survival training with the SAS and his dogged will to fight his way out of the many desperate situations he had faced during his adrenaline-soaked career, that he was still alive to tell the tale. Stripping off his flying gear apart from his boxer shorts, while leaning back against the instrument panel, he quickly tied them altogether.

But it was taking too long, and as he joined the sleeves of his bush shirt to those of his light flying jacket before attaching them to one trouser leg, he could already see flames licking their way towards him along one of the aircraft's wings.

He was well aware of the fact that, despite all these efforts, he still had no idea if the cloth rope he had made would hold his weight, and even if it did, how high it would leave him still hanging perilously above the ground. So rather than fasten it to the control column, he decided to climb through the shattered windshield and by holding onto its broken rim, to lower his feet onto a propeller blade and secure the rope to that.

But just at that moment, a branch snapped off causing the stricken aeroplane to lurch so violently that he lost his hold and went sliding relentlessly over the side of the engine cowling, knowing that only a miracle would save him. But one did.

As he fell past the engine, it was lucky that he managed to get his left hand into a narrow gap where the cowling had been sprung open on its latches. But as he did so, he felt the flesh tear and blood started running down his arm as he tried desperately not to cough and dislodge it due to the suffocating clouds of wood smoke. Remembering everything he had learned while climbing in the Alps, he quickly swung his body like a pendulum in an attempt to get one foot on the propeller. But the moment he managed to do so, the blood caused his hand to start slipping from the cowling, making it difficult to hold on for a moment longer.

His mind was racing to find a solution, when, just in the nick of time, he remembered the knot he had tied in the sleeve of his shirt, which he was holding with his other hand. By jamming the knot into the small gap still left in the cowling, he was then able to remove his injured one and go for it. Gripping hard on his rope, he seemed to drop for ever until the knot held, leaving him dangerously suspended six metres above the ground as he heard the branches, which had been holding the plane, starting to break.

A sense of foreboding was beginning to creep over him. This was unknown territory and for all he knew, although he could see no one, there would be a reception committee waiting below to finish him off. But he could do nothing about it. He was not wrong, at that very moment, a bullet ripped past his left ear, followed by the unmistakable sound of a rifle being re-loaded high up in the towering canopy directly in front of him.

As the stricken plane started to plummet down from above, it was the exploding jerrycans followed quickly by the fuel tanks that must have saved him. Hidden by the smoke and falling debris, he began to drop so fast that the marksman had little opportunity to take another shot at him before he hit the ground. It was lucky that because of his parachute training that not only was he able to land on his feet, but to run without hesitation into the burning undergrowth before the Piper smashed heavily into the red-hot embers behind him.

Finding he was still masked by the smoke, he sprinted quickly towards a clump of monkey brush and on a further ten metres to hide behind the trunk of a massive red cedar tree.

Ahead of him he could see a small clearing obviously cut out recently by loggers, and beyond, between some freshly sawn tree stumps, a large green "cherry picker" with FOREST RANGER painted on its side. The machine, he noted, had four supporting legs splayed out around it, and one of the longest articulated arms he had ever seen. At its head, just proud of the canopy, a man in khaki shorts was standing in the bucket with a rifle pointing directly down at him.

Just as dramatic was the green towing vehicle hooked on to the cherry picker. The rear doors were hanging open and although, he wanted to take a closer look, there was no need. Clearly visible on a metal shelf was a sinister black drone with a livid red dragon painted on it.

As he rolled back behind the tree and lay there as a second shot kicked up the soil not a metre in front of him, realising that it was a drone that had brought him down, it also gave him time to recall the man's instructions when he hired the plane in Cuiaba.

'If you are investigating the fires, senhor, the best way to see them is by flying over the forests bordering the Xingu River north-east from here. First, you must fly over Paranatinga and then keep directly on towards Tangura, a forest village, which is not only in the worst affected area, but also within range of my aircraft, although not for the flight home. On heading back it will be necessary, therefore, to land on the savanna and re-fuel the aircraft from these jerrycans.'

He remembered the sallow looking guy with dreadlocks then giving him a marked map to show him the route to his initial search area, realising, much to his annoyance, that he had been duped. He was certain that the villain who must have been well insured, had been paid good money to get rid of anyone trying to stop the arsonists, and had hired him an old aircraft with sufficient extra fuel on board to make certain that when it was brought down both he and the plane would be incinerated.

Nor could he have flown it back to Cuiaba, for he had seen from the air that the area was covered in thorn bushes and the savanna did not exist. It was obvious now that a lookout had been left in Paranatinga to warn the arsonists of any unwanted aircraft approaching, which, being at the junction of several forest roads, he deduced, had to be the gang's Brazilian headquarters.

As he crept forward, tanned by the smoke and blackened by the burning undergrowth, much resembling a local Indian, the camouflage may have helped him, as did his knowledge of fieldcraft, for the marksman with the rifle momentarily lost sight of him as he managed to reach one leg of the cherry picker without another bullet being fired. By crawling along some waste deep ruts caused by soil erosion, he was then able to skirt round the machine, again without being noticed, to find the hydraulic bleed valve.

Giving it a mighty blow with a heavy spanner, which he found lying beside it, he watched as the gantry dropped out of the sky to crash to the ground with such force that the drone he had seen in the back of the van, fell out and burst into a ball of white, incandescent flame. The man, however, who should have broken both legs, leapt out of the remains of the bucket with such alacrity that as the Major watched him throw away his rifle and run as fast as a cheetah into the green wall of still verdant forest, he decided not to chase after him.

Instead, believing, as Bob had suggested, that he was likely to be one of a gang of Indonesians, he climbed up into the tow vehicle with the intention of driving it back to Cuiaba as fast as possible to hire another aircraft and go looking for them. But the keys were missing. With not a moment to lose, he realised that the only option left to him was to follow the man into the forest, grab hold of him plus his keys and then find out who he was working for before throttling him. If successful there would, at least, be a slim chance of dealing with the rest of them.

His hand was still bleeding profusely, but although he realised that his fingers had been badly lacerated by the metal engine cowling and were likely to become infected, he decided that before searching for some water and something to bandage them with, his first priority was to find the man's tracks before they disappeared, unaware of the ordeal which was to follow.

On reaching the trees, he was hit by such a heavy curtain of pungent humidity that he could have been entering a sealed greenhouse. All around him the din of countless insects mingled with the throaty burps of bullfrogs, the distant chirps and squawks of countless parrots, and the hoots and howls of other hidden creatures almost deafened him, while in front was such a mass of tangled vegetation that he realised it would be near impossible to catch up with the man, who, as he feared, seemed to have left no footprints, or broken greenery, and appeared to be as nimble as a monkey.

The jungle is never neutral, and when to his relief, he saw the distant glint of water, he found it more exhausting than any of the ordeals set him by Sentinals to reach it. Pushing aside the thorn bushes and clinging lianas with his only good hand while trying to hold the man's discarded rifle with the other had become so difficult that he was soon forced to throw it away into the undergrowth, knowing that it would be impossible to shoot anyone in such close surroundings.

He was already being plagued by flies, bullet ants and tiny stinging bees, and although he hoped the stream, in which he had been able to wash his injured hand, would give him a reference point, he was unable to tell its direction due to leaving his compass behind in a trouser pocket.

Attempting to see the blazing sun through the dense smoke and layers of green foliage above his head soon defeated him, so believing the stream was probably heading north to join the mighty Amazon, and hoping that the arsonist would have followed it as well, he waded on knowing that if it was indeed a tributary, it would soon be teaming with flesh eating piranha fish.

Coming upon a family of capybara, the world's largest rodents, sitting on the bank preening their whiskers, it reminded him of a story he had once been told of the fish stripping an injured one to a skeleton within minutes. Any hint of blood dropping into the water and he knew he would suffer the same fate. So stopping to wrap his still bleeding hand in some more leaves, he waded on downstream until it met a wide, lazily flowing river, hesitating only when he saw the eyes of some caiman weighing him up from the surface directly ahead of him.

Perhaps his calculations had been correct. This must be the headwaters of the Xingu which flowed fifteen hundred kilometres north towards the Amazon. If so, he was standing at the edge of the famous National Park Bob had shown him on his map, home to no less than fourteen tribes of indigenous Indians.

Just at that moment, above the increasing din of the forest, he thought he heard a cry for help, or was it just a howler monkey, the noisiest of all forest animals. He stopped, cupping his good hand to his ear and listened for ages, but the cry was not repeated. Knowing that the it had come from somewhere downstream, he was denied a further chance of locating it when it started to rain so heavily that not only did the surface of the water become a hissing fury of bouncing white beads, but an angry toucan bird began complaining so loudly behind him that listening became impossible.

Beginning to feel increasingly frustrated by not being able to see far enough ahead, he spied a waterlogged tree to climb up on, which had fallen part way across the river. But when, after considerable effort, he managed to lever himself onto a rotten limb, the sight which confronted him made him almost let go again. Not thirty metres away, where the reeds had been flattened close to the water's edge, was a giant python doing the job for him.

The anaconda, which measured at least eight metres long, must have grabbed the Indonesian's leg when he stepped on it thinking it was a log. It was not, and because the Major had thrown away his rifle, there was little he could do about it but wade forward as fast as he could to search for a stick and beat the serpent off with it. But he was too late, and when he heard the man's bones cracking and starting to break, noticing the narrowness of his shoulders, he knew he had to kill the reptile before it started to consume the wretched fellow and any useful evidence with him.

But there was no need, for as the man gasped his last breath, unfortunately not his truck keys but a sheet of yellow paper fell from his pocket into the pool of green slime surrounding the grisly scene.

JAMASHI FIREWORKS, Jakarta, the heading stated. And below scrawled in biro: To Dragon 6: 100 sticks of white phosphorus in 20cm copper tubes with wax stoppers.

The Major had learned all about white phosphorus from his time in the military where it was packed into smoke grenade launchers on the turrets of armoured vehicles, such as his former squadron of Centurion tanks. First known as "Fenian Fire" when used by Irish nationalists during the 19th century, it had the unique properties of bursting into flame when exposed to air. Subsequently, it had been used to fill bombs and hand grenades in both world wars, then and later on in Vietnam, Iraq and Afghanistan.

Although, it was being employed here for a different purpose, the image of Phan Phuc, the badly burned girl running towards the camera at Trang Bang during the Vietnam war, remained indelible in his and many other people's memories, for much like the napalm used on that occasion, white phosphorus causes such dreadful injuries that he wished it had been banned a long time ago.

It was a useful find, but apart from discovering the nature and source of the material the arsonists were using and the fact that there must be at least five more of them setting fire to the rainforest, it had disclosed very little apart from confirming that the fireworks company was indeed Indonesian, a part of the world he had not yet visited.

The note also confirmed that they were dropping phosphorus sticks from drones, which they must be flying from wherever they were able to find sufficient views over the canopy. Once the sticks hit the ground, he knew that the heat would quickly melt the wax and cause the phosphorus to set fire to the forest floor around it.

Having carefully folded up the note and shoved it into the small security pocket, which he had previously asked a shop attendant to have sewn into a number of boxer shorts, while leaving the anaconda to enjoy its meal in peace, he waded back into the river determined to return to Cuiaba as fast as possible in order to retrieve the Heckler & Koch submachine gun which Macey had handed to him, and contact Bob on his satellite telephone, both of which he greatly regretted leaving behind at the airport.

After getting hold of him, he would then hire another aircraft and after removing the pilot's door, fly back to locate as many of the arsonists he could see from the air, hoping to shoot them dead if the smoke allowed him to do so. But because of the size of the area to be covered, he knew that it would be more difficult than "looking for a needle in a haystack".

Having passed the fallen tree, he cursed himself for not taking more notice of the way he had come. Then, convinced that he had entered the river from the first stream he came across, he waded slowly up it.

But it was not!

Forests are notorious for getting lost in unless you have marked your route on the trees, just as any sensible person would mark the rocks when exploring a cave. To him, everything was beginning to look different, but then it would do, he thought, looking at the trees from the opposite direction. Then, glimpsing a shaft of sunlight penetrating the canopy not far ahead, and believing that it was the same clearing from which he had set out, he gave a sigh of relief and waded on even faster.

But it was not!

He was well into the clearing when finding no fresh tree stumps or the cherry picker, he realised that he must have followed one stream too early. He was standing on a bright green crust of moss, but on searching for his footprints and the direction of the stream flowing beneath it, let alone for the gap through which he had just come, he quickly began to question his sanity and the hours of field training already beginning to fail him. Worse still, the light was fading and when he took a step in any direction, he found himself sinking into such a bottomless bog that he knew that he would never be able to extricate himself before nightfall.

It was then he heard the saw-like growl of an approaching jaguar.

Chapter 2

Bob. Multi billionaire strategist

It was a glorious morning. As Bob strode out with Storm, his Rottweiler, along the cliff path which ran close to his North Devon house perched high above the restless Atlantic Ocean, he noticed a seal lying on a black rock sunning its tummy and a school of porpoises twisting through the waves before leaping high into the azure blue sky, while gannets dive bombed around them for fish. In May, the cliffs were alive with activity and as he watched the black-backed gulls marauding the nests of furious guillemots, he began to feel much like them himself.

If only, he thought, the people of Brazil would get equally furious about the destruction of their rainforest, where ninety-nine per cent of the fires were now being started deliberately either to clear more land for grazing beef cattle, growing crops of soya beans, or, worse still, for far more criminal reasons. Just like the nests of the guillemots, which once destroyed were abandoned to wind and weather for ever, the destruction of the Amazon rainforest was no less terminal.

Despite its amazing biodiversity, its lushness and its rich canopy of trees, he knew that once they were lost and the ground beneath them laid bare, the rain would cause such leaching and rapid soil erosion that the land would become less fertile than anywhere else on earth.

During 1995, while investigating a new uranium find in southern Brazil, a country since providing five per cent of the world's total, Bob had seen this for himself. Also interested in conservation, he had visited the Amazon rainforest with the famous Villas-Boas brothers, the only people in Brazil who seemed to care about the disastrous increase in deforestation and its effect on the indigenous Indians and the world in general. They were brave pioneers who defended the forest in a frighteningly hostile environment, which had grown many times more dangerous since.

It infuriated Bob that so many thoughtless people should be clearing the rainforest in order to give themselves two- or three-years income before the land gave up on them completely. So on meeting the two brothers, he had sworn that he would help them do something about it. Now, many years later, when news reached him that the number of fires had increased by eighty per cent in just one year, thus causing a catastrophic loss in carbon sequestration, he was determined to hunt down the arsonists concerned and eliminate them. But that was going to be up to the Major, his mercenary, who he hoped was already hot on their trail.

So when he returned from his walk to be met by Jenkins, his butler, it was a shock to be told that there was a message on his telephone from Cuiaba stating that the aircraft the Major had hired from the airport had gone missing.

'Do you know who sent the message, Jenkins?'

'No, Sir, but it sounded like a foreign voice, although not an official one.'

'So did you get his telephone number?'

'No, Sir, and when I pressed the recall button it failed.'

'This is very serious, Jenkins. Get hold of the British ambassador in Brasilia immediately, who may have finished his breakfast by now, and ask him to investigate who sent the message from Cuiaba and what other information he has on the lost aircraft plus what he is doing about it. Then please ask him to let me know the answers as soon as possible.'

He walked back to his office faster than usual, hoping that his butler had misunderstood the call, but on picking up his satellite telephone and ringing the Major, as he feared, there was no reply.

In normal times, he would have jumped into his jet, which had now returned from Brazil, and gone looking for him, but as he had an appointment with the vice president of the United States in Washington in two days' time, he decided that the Major would have to wait. Meanwhile, he cut another cigar and lay back in his deep Moroccan leather armchair confident that should his mercenary have crashed, or been forced to land in a remote area, he was able to look after himself.

'Sir,' interrupted Jenkins again, as Bob woke up with a snort. 'The ambassador has just rung and not wishing to disturb you sends his compliments. He says that there are some unscrupulous individuals hiring out aircraft in Cuiaba and he has been told that when the Piper Cherokee flown by Mr Major failed to return, an operator in the control tower immediately telephoned you as it had been logged out with your telephone number.

'He says that the current owner of aircraft PP-BALB cannot be traced, and as the pilot did not file a flight plan, or land at any airstrip within a thousand miles of Cuiaba, he cannot be found. It is also known that he took some extra fuel on board, so in that vast area he could be anywhere. Should he discover more, the ambassador says he will ring you immediately.'

'Not my kind of ambassador, Jenkins. It sounds as if he has not sent out a search party or tried very hard to find him. Thank goodness, he did not ask you about the nature of the Major's mission, for the house telephone line here is not secure, and the less we talk about his disappearance the better. I believe we are dealing with some very unpleasant people, and if we are not very careful, we could be in trouble ourselves.'

'Do you mean, Sir, that because of his disappearance we may be next in their line of fire?'

27

'That's a good way of putting it, Jenkins, for I should have been more cautious about asking him any questions as it may have compromised our position here already. But unfortunately, we have no way of knowing. At the time I employed you, I stressed that due to my company, Nuklin, dealing in the past with some very nasty people, we must be constantly on our guard. It was only after hearing about your conspicuous gallantry while you were serving with the Special Air Service, that I employed you to replace my last butler, who I had discovered to be a Russian spy!

'Sometimes I regret only spending two years National Service with the Grenadier Guards, although I did learn about looking after the Queen. Now it is more about looking after myself. But I would be much happier if all those cameras surrounding my place were fixed line machine guns. However, Jenkins, I worry most about anyone approaching from the sea.'

'Why so, Sir?'

'Because, Jenkins, approaches from the sea cannot easily be protected, and since my wife left me, the Briny is all that I am now wedded to. That's why I like to take my daily exercise along the cliffs with Storm, although only guarded by black-backed gulls, a particularly useless bird of prey!'

'Right, Sir, I will always keep my eyes trained on you when you are out walking in that direction.'

'But first, let's concentrate on getting me ready for Washington, where I am likely to get involved with a different type of problem as I try to put the world to rights. The mission may be almost as dangerous as chasing up those bastards who are setting fire to the world's forests. So if I make it back here afterwards, I will need my Smith and Wesson forty-five calibre brought from the safe, Jenkins, and hidden under my pillow.'

**

The flight to Washington two days later was without incident but became much less tedious when his first pilot came back from the cockpit to have a word with him.

'Sir, do you want me to take the usual precautions when we land at DCA?'

'Sam, we live in an increasingly fragile world where, largely due to climate change, everyone who is trying to balance nature with greed is becoming vulnerable to abuse. Nuklin has always generated a considerable amount of flak, but what I am about to embark on will make both my life, and the lives of those who work for me, more dangerous than ever. That is the reason I have just upped all your salaries.

'So my answer is yes. I want you to increase your vigilance and arm the sensors just fitted to my aircraft, every time we land so that anyone approaching it, including ground staff, are monitored day and night by you or your co-pilot.

'I expect you have already warned the crew that this is no ordinary mission, for after my meeting with the vice president, all hell may break loose. We are not, therefore, going to hang around in the American capital for long, but fly on to San Francisco, where there is more dangerous work yet be done.'

'Thank you, Sir. Perhaps you should take a lesson from the USAF A10 Warthog ground support aircraft and equip your Gulfstream with an Avenger, or what was once called a Gatling Gun. After what you have just told me, it appears that we are about to go to war!'

At that moment, Macey joined them with three cups of coffee. 'I could not help overhearing what you were saying, Sam, for you will remember what happened when we were both together in Afghanistan, you flying a Chinook helicopter with the British RAF, and myself serving as a nurse with the US Navy, looking after all those horrifying casualties we had on board.'

Then turning to Bob, she continued, 'It was soon after the Taliban attacked Fort Bastion where they managed destroyed several Marine Corps Sea Harriers and at least five other aircraft. Why? Because it was evident that the risk management decisions taken by the man in charge were found to be totally lacking and no attention had been paid to the fundamental requirements of defending the camp.

'It was later discovered that the Taliban had been transported to a de-bussing point very close to Bastion where they had all changed into US Army uniforms before approaching the Fort up a ravine and breaching the perimeter fence with simple wire cutters. It is true that several of the them were neutralised, but if the fence had been kept under surveillance and the lights had been left switched on, the attack would never have happened.

'At Washington airport, I know from previous experience that there is no perimeter fence worth talking about, and although nothing is likely to happen while you, Mr Buckmaster, is in charge, no one is infallible and nor is our aircraft's new security system. Sam, I remember you telling me, after the attack on Fort Bastion, that, however secure an airport was supposed to be, you would always start your pre-flight checks by walking around the outside of the aircraft twice before also searching the interior twice for explosives.

'May I therefore suggest,' she said turning to Bob again while collecting the empty cups, 'that despite all the surveillance equipment you have had fitted, both Sam and Eliot, your co-pilot, should be asked to do that every time we take to the air as it will make you feel far more comfortable, Sir.'

'Macey, you are a star,' replied Bob. 'Of course, we shall follow your every command.'

At Washington's DCA airport, Bob was immediately escorted to a waiting limousine which he was told by the driver had been the presidential state car known as Cadillac 1, until it had been superseded with a machine known as The Beast.

'That car,' said the driver, 'is nothing more than a mobile fortress, but you are just as safe in this one, mister, for it has five-inch-thick bullet proof glass!'

'I am happy about that, driver, but will be happier still when we get back from the White House.'

'Except, mister, even if we were allowed to exceed the speed limit when being followed by Al Capone, this junk heap of armour plating would be unable to do so! And sorry to disappoint you, boss, but we are not bound for the White House. The vice president's home and office are situated within the grounds of the US Naval Observatory, known as Number One Observatory Circle, just down the road from here. He normally greets his guests in the library.'

The Queen Anne style house turned out to be unspectacular and no better defended than his house in North Devon, but that was only an illusion, for the first thing the man at the door told him was that should there be a problem, there was a nuclear bomb shelter built deep underneath it.

'Welcome, Mr Buckmaster, or may I call you Bill,' stated the vice president as he was ushered into the library. 'I hope that it is not a threat of nuclear attack that you have come to warn me about?'

'It is, Sir, but I would prefer you call me Bob. I am here to warn you that even should your president change his tune about global warming, the world is soon going to heat up to such an extent that only the latest form of nuclear energy, which I am about to describe, will save us!'

'What do you mean, Bob? I thought you and your company, Nuklin, had stopped trying to sell us any more of your bloody uranium?'

'No, Vice President, the world is fully aware that coal and natural gas remain your preferred option in the United States for both private and commercial reasons. Apart from renewables and hydro power, I agree that they may still be the cheapest means of generating electricity, but not the safest. However, the reason that your president will not acknowledge climate change is because he considers any assault on your coal mining industry, which indirectly employs over half a million people and provides twenty-five billion dollars' worth of export sales, would cost him his job.'

'That is a very aggressive statement!'

'I meant it to be. Apart from China, by burning seven hundred million tons of coal a year, the USA is the most irresponsible country in the world for feeding the atmosphere with CO_2, which, if not stopped, will lead to an irreversible decline in life on Mother Earth.'

'Aren't you getting too emotional, Bob? So what then are the alternatives?'

'To satisfy a growing demand for electricity, America and the rest of the world must now turn totally away from burning fossil fuels, not just by installing more renewables, but to follow China in developing the most radical transportable power plant's fed by a safe nuclear fuel, yet created.'

'Ah, I thought you might be coming around to that again.'

'If you think I am looking for even greater personal reward in the future, Vice President, you are mistaken. It is true that Nuklin has profited for years by flogging material which threatened the world with disaster. But now, by introducing this remarkable new form of energy, our intention is to save the world from disaster. Although, electricity produced in this way may initially be more expensive than coal, oil or gas, the situation will change quickly.

'Meanwhile, your ongoing mistrust of nuclear reactors, largely due to Chernobyl in 1986 and Fukushima in 2011, must be banished forever. At Chernobyl, which was passed its sell-by date and poorly managed, although the resulting fallout caused later mayhem, only thirty-one deaths were recorded at the time, all but two being firemen. At Fukushima, there was just one fatality. How can you compare that with the tsunami which killed almost a quarter of a million people during that same year!'

Bob, leaning forward, continued, 'I repeat, Vice President, my future aim in life is no longer to make any more money but with my knowledge of nuclear physics to save us all from Armageddon.'

'What against an ante-nuclear lobby, which is not only politically motivated at the highest level, but also the public's strongest ever attempt to throw out nuclear and return to natural gas instead?'

'Yes, Vice President, but tell me, how are you personally intending to survive climate change?'

'It all sounds to me like sheer fantasy, Bob. I am sure my dear wife will see to that.'

The vice president, moving swiftly to a table, rang a bell and a man in livery entered the library.

'Please escort Mr Buckmaster back to his car, Hudson. Thank you, Sir, for flying over the Pond to discuss your ideas with me, which have been recorded. But I'm afraid that you are suggesting the impossible and it will only stir up a hornet's nest here in the United States. Once Ban the Bomb was the cry in our great country, but now it is Ban Nuclear.

'There are plenty of nuclear nuts about too, Bob, so because your aircraft, I am told, is easily recognisable and the aim of your visit obvious, please tread very carefully. Good day, Sir.'

'One last question, Vice President, do you know of anyone who has been attempting to blackmail your boss over the issue of setting fire to the Amazon rainforest?'

But the door was already closing and Bob was soon back in the limousine heading for the airport having failed to obtain the result he was hoping for, or even the sniff of a glass of whisky!

He had always feared that the meeting would be a nonstarter, but his razor-sharp mind had already decided how to deal with the lack of help from the government of the USA. Until they were forced into his way of thinking by more sensible Americans, he would first fly to California and attempt to lobby the most rebellious ante nuclear state of all. Then, should he fail to divert them from their love of natural gas, for a time he would concentrate his efforts on helping his mercenary, should he still be alive, in order to create the most innovative method of carbon sequestration ever attempted.

But on returning to the airport and sensing all was not well, he thought it must wait until later.

Beside his aircraft stood a man looking like an American paratrooper, but on closer inspection he was not so sure, as he appeared to be carrying a WWII

German carbine strapped over his shoulder. So he rang through to Sam and asked him, 'What the hell is going on?'

'Not too much right now, Sir, but I talked to that idiot standing by your plane when I boarded it just a minute ago. He had little to say except that he was just point troops. Meaning, I presume, that more of the buggers are on the way here. Would you like me to call the airport police, Sir?'

'Not yet, Sam, leave that to me.'

After checking in at the desk of the private aircraft terminal, he asked the duty officer to let him know if any more protestors turned up. Then striding out onto the tarmac, he confronted the man.

'How you managed to get through airport security surprises me, soldier, particularly as you are carrying an old German Mauser that should be in a museum. You don't look much like a military man to me and I am surprised that you are able to get any ammo for it, even directly from Hitler!'

'Well, I won't be needing much ammo to blow your aircraft's tyres to pieces, mister!'

'Perhaps, Private Ryan, but as you smell strongly of drink, before you demonstrate your skill at marksmanship, however inaccurate you may be, why not tell me what elite military unit you are benefiting with your fighting experience, as I would like to meet your commanding officer?'

'Yep, he'd like that, mister. His name is General P. Horatio Stickleberger, who is sitting this very minute on the steps at the White House flying the Union flag.'

'You are right, Sam.' He called up from the tarmac 'The fellow is a crank. Yes, please ask airport security to get rid of him. You will not be surprised to know that nuclear protestors have been constantly sitting on the steps of the White House since the early 1980's, totally ignoring the difference between nuclear bombs and nuclear energy. However, if I now join them there, they will, no doubt, skin me alive and roast me on their barbecue. As you are finding out, not only is there a ludicrous lobby against nuclear energy in the United States, but also against my company.'

Bob was not in a hurry, so he returned to the airport desk and telephoned Jenkins to find out if there was any news of the Major.

'No, not a squeak, Sir, but the British ambassador has rung again to say that it is believed that the guy who hired him his aeroplane is one of the most notorious crooks in the whole of the Mato Grosso. Rumour has it that he may be involved with a gang of arsonists, who are setting light to the rainforest while blackmailing countries to stop them doing so in exchange for big money.'

'Well, at least the ambassador is catching up with us, Jenkins, but the Major is obviously out on his own now, if he is still alive. Nothing is going in the right direction for us at the moment, for not only has Congress here in America again failed to pass any legislation on climate change, but because the president of Brazil is also shutting his eyes to it, he is actively supporting the arsonists by doing nothing whatsoever about the growing number of fires on his patch. The Major is up against it and I doubt if we will hear from him for some time.'

'I understand then that all we can do is pray that if he is still with us, he manages to find out the latest on what is going on in the rainforest so that you may inform the world about it and also the mistake the presidents of Brazil and the United States are making in not putting a stop to it.'

'Right on the button, Jenkins, but that is only the start of three major actions necessary. Firstly to prevent the forests being further destroyed, secondly to change the world from burning fossil fuels to installing a new type of nuclear reactor, and thirdly to create an impressive method for sequestering the CO_2 still poisoning the atmosphere. Please note that my next port of call will be San Francisco, for the State of California has recently placed a death warrant on every one of its nuclear power stations.

'Meanwhile, they think it's clever to make up the deficit by burning natural gas, pretending it is organic and harmless, although it produces almost the same appalling level of carbon as coal!'

Bob checked out and found Sam waiting by the steps of his Gulfstream with Macey, who was looking more beautiful, standing beside him in her Nuklin uniform, than ever.

'So are we off to California, boss, for I need to file a flight plan?'

'Yes, Sam, having just escaped from mad Unionists, we are now off to Frisco to face a load of crazy Confederates, which is going to be even more demanding. When we arrive there, however, I am first meeting up with a nice lot calling themselves the Environmental Progress Group, who are valiantly opposing the decision of the California Public Utilities Commission to close down their nuclear power plants, which is total lunacy. It was quoted in Forbes magazine that the failure of the US nuclear power programme ranks as the largest managerial disaster in business history.'

Chapter 3

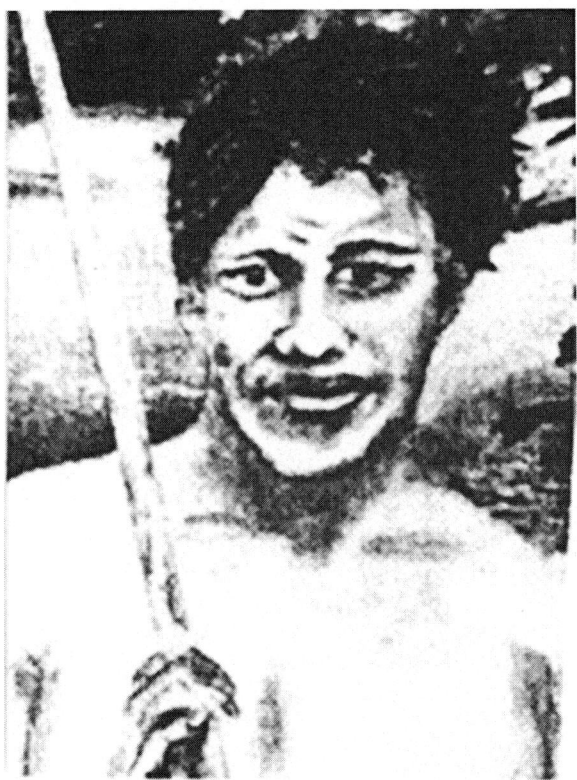

Napoleon. Amazon Indian rescuer.

It had started to rain again but although, it was only mid-afternoon, the heavy cloud combined with the smoke from the countless fires burning in that part of the forest, was turning day into night as the Major's situation became more serious by the minute. Knowing that he could neither climb a tree or run away from an animal as large as a lioness, he had sensed the jaguar was almost upon him when he jumped out of his skin. Was he dreaming, or was it the light touch of a human hand on his shoulder?

He tried to spin around but with his feet stuck in the bog, there was no need. He was looking into deep brown eyes set in the scarlet painted face of a curious indigenous Indian.

As the man tried to speak to him in a language removed from anything he had heard before, he felt relieved but confused. Had he come to help him, or was he about to magic him away like Colonel Fawcett, never to be seen again. But, although the Indian held a sharp spear, when he pointed it towards the narrow gap he had missed between some trees, he prayed that he had been saved.

The Indian beckoned him to follow and as he did so, wearing no more than the man who had rescued him, he started to sweat so much in the hot evening air that he became prey to every type of flying insect, including some determined mosquitos. As they progressed fast down the stream to where it joined the river close to the fallen tree, he tried to swat them with his good hand while they dived at him relentlessly, screaming like squadrons of German Stukas.

Although, the anaconda gave them a nasty look as they waded past it, he reckoned that it had such a large bulge in its green and yellow scales, that it must have been suffering from constipation. The Indian, although saluting the reptile with his spear, gave it barely a glance, and striding on did the same to a crowd of tamarin monkeys chattering furiously at them from some overhanging branches.

Although, his hand had stopped bleeding it had now started to swell, warning him that it was badly infected. He wanted to show it to the Indian, hoping that he would be able to make a sling from some tall reeds, but as the river also began to swell and the caiman become more numerous, he found keeping up with the fit man he was following was difficult enough in the chest high water.

He had just slipped on a rock when at last the canopy opened up ahead of them and what light was left in the sky illuminated a wide circular clearing with a floor of red dusty earth. Scattered around it were some reed thatched huts each about six metres long by half that in width. The Indian, whom he had named Napoleon because of his imperious manner and crooked nose, then strode towards one of them, beckoning him to enter the open doorway before pointing to a hammock slung beneath some bamboo poles, which he climbed into, falling at once into a deep sleep.

It must have been close to dawn when he woke to see a bat flying above his head. His swollen hand was by now so painful that nothing else seemed to matter, but heeding Bob's warning about the jungle vampires, as he tried to find out if he had been punctured and had lost any more of his blood, he felt something prodding him in the back. Already knowing about the need of all indigenous Indians to share the forest with every living creature, he was not surprised, on leaning over the side of his hammock, to find a brown, hairy, monkey eagerly trying to climb up and join him.

'Va! Va!' A woman was shouting, but hardly had the monkey scampered away than he was surrounded by a gaggle of bare-breasted, dark haired, girls wearing only minute yellow G strings. One of them was offering him something to eat, but when he turned over to take it from her and she saw the state of his infected hand, she quickly took the food away again and after a hushed discussion with her girlfriends, they all vanished.

He was grateful that it was not a bowl of sago, or manioc, they brought back later, but instead, two large fruits one looking like a bright orange pineapple and the other resembling a massive, half metre long, green pea pod. A young girl then sliced them open for him, the first fruit producing a white foamy substance that tasted of vanilla, and the second revealing a line of juicy kernels that were like large, flat sided, grapes, which popped inside his mouth as he bit into their sweet, delicious, centres.

He had never known such fruit existed, but neither did she, or the rest of her friends, know that such a man existed. As they gathered around him again bursting into fits of giggles, they were, no doubt, comparing him with their own sinewy forest warriors. Not only did they notice the stranger's rippling muscles, but that his pale skin and dark swept back hair made him look like a god.

Then there was then a sudden hush as a tall man, he was later to name Bonio, appeared. Looking serious through a mask of red paint, he bent so low over him that the string of white bones strung around his neck, he hoped were not human, brushed against his chest.

'Bem-vindo,' he said surprisingly in Portuguese, offering him the shell of a large nut containing such a foul-smelling liquid that it almost caused him to vomit. Then taking his injured hand he soaked it in the goo before wrapping it up again in some leaves and tying it all together with a thin length of vine, pointing towards the fringe of tall trees that for them was the only world they knew.

Hardly had he left him as swiftly as he had appeared, when Napoleon, his hero from the previous evening, turned up again. He clapped his hands on seeing him, and holding his arms out sideways like aeroplane wings, somersaulted around the floor before pretending to fall down dead. Ever since he had woken up that morning, the Major, embarrassed by the way his fellow tribesmen were being treated by the white man, had been wondering about the extraordinary manner of his rescue by an indigenous Indian. But the fired up fellow cavorting in front of him explained everything.

Napoleon had obviously watched the whole incident from the time the arsonist had driven into the forest behind the illegal loggers, to the time he had raised his gantry and started launching his drones, first to set light to the forest and then to knock his plane out of the sky. But one thing still puzzled him. Why was he not being regarded as enemy? Surely, he could have been on yet another mission to map their forest kingdom from the air with the sole intention of grabbing hold of it?

As he pondered over his dilemma for a while, he noticed that an increasing number of the tribe had joined the women gathered around him, as if amongst the thousands of species, such as giant anteaters, anacondas, tapirs, jaguars and poison dart frogs that lived in their forest, he was an exciting new discovery. Perhaps they were all waiting for their cannibal pot to start boiling? No, this was not New Guinea, he reminded himself, for with so much forest food on offer, there was no need for them to eat human flesh.

Perhaps, on the other hand, they were the tribe that had murdered Colonel Percy Fawcett, possibly for no more reason than he was an intruder like himself. He and his small party had disappeared in precisely the same area where he was now lying, and suddenly, he felt more helpless and exposed than at any other time in his life.

It then dawned on him that after the Indian had seen his plane crash into the trees and fall to the ground in flames, he would also have noticed how the forest floor had become strewn with its debris. So he must have returned to search among the dying embers for the dreaded camera, which was always carried by white men intent on mapping the forest that so rightly belonged to them.

He was almost correct. But as Napoleon lifted a small metal object high above his head, he noticed that it was not, after all, a camera, but the one item he had needed more than any other throughout his recent ordeal getting lost in the rainforest, his compass.

Bonio, who must have been both their leader and camp doctor, then arrived with a flourish. Walking towards Napoleon and taking the compass carefully out of his hands, he brought the precious instrument to the side of his hammock and then slowly turned it over. He must have examined it already for on the back were inscribed just two words—STANLEY. LONDON.

'Igles,' he crooned grinning from ear to ear. 'Igles—good, good.' Whereupon the crowd of onlookers clapped their hands and stamped their feet.

He had been told by Bob that since the disappearance of Fawcett and the unfortunate murder of Richard Mason, although there were tribes living in the Amazon rainforest yet to be discovered, most were now known to be largely peaceful. But what Bob had not told him was that even in the Indian villages protected by Brazilian law, loggers and farmers were continuing to drive out the indigenous population and move them to other less productive areas, totally without mercy.

It was well known that, since 2002, when the second of the Villas-Boas brothers, who had championed their cause, died, the future for the endangered Indians living in the Amazon basin had become so uncertain that a number of well-meaning Englishmen had set out into the rainforest determined to protect them and their tribes, still numbering about four hundred, against any further exploitation by the white man.

Many of these invaders, they had discovered, were backed by unscrupulous multinational companies trading in timber, gold, or Brazilian beef, who were all as indifferent to destroying the Indians' traditional way of life, as to stamping on a colony of forest ants, or kicking over a mound of termites.

While the Major recovered in his hammock, constantly watched over by a few excited maidens, some of whom had bosoms any young girl would have been proud of, he thought first about how to get back to civilisation, and then about the difficult decisions he must take if he was to accomplish the second part of the important mission Bob had set him.

Having discussed Bob's second task with his brilliant young stewardess on the flight to Cuiaba, she had told him that replacing just the trees lost to the Amazon rainforest, would require more mental courage and physical effort than she believed was possible. Bob would never have suggested such a daunting task, Macey had continued, knowing that horticulture and engineering were not part of his training, unless he had great confidence in him due to his legendary drive and professionalism.

So, as he pondered over her words while recovering from his ordeal among some of the most threatened people on earth, he was grateful that he still had time to put his frightening task into practice.

With so much of the forest being destroyed around him, he knew that the only way to replace the serious losses already incurred in carbon sequestration, was not to attempt to re-plant trees on ground which would no longer be able to support them, but to cover the last of the world's empty spaces with billions of plants, or trees, wherever soil conditions would be suitable. As a result, not only would such areas benefit from greater precipitation, but they would sequester carbon on such a grand scale that the world was never be able to step so far backwards again.

He had already ruled out the use of men or machines on the ground to plant them, for while flying over the canopy before he was shot down, he had decided that the only way to accomplish such a mighty task was from the air. But to do so, it would not only mean inventing flying machines large enough to plant hundreds of square kilometres per day, but also a method of reproducing the plants, or trees, in numbers beyond anyone's wildest dreams, or his own powers of innovation. But with Bob behind him, all was possible, he thought, unless climate change galloped past everything.

Macey, whose dazzling personality continued to fill him with confidence and admiration, was correct. Unknown to him, far away in California, Bob, who must have previously asked Sentinals for his final report on leaving the army, although recognising his remarkable ability for dealing with every situation he had been trained for, but not this one, was already working with her on the case.

At that moment, the Major, who had been deep in thought on these more important matters, was annoyingly interrupted by a maiden inviting him to climb out of his hammock and help lift a wooden bucket from a well to make some tea. But when he tipped the brackish water into an old tin pot, likely to have once belonged to an invading logger, he found it full of tarantula spiders the size of soup plates.

Making a brew with some leaves, as the spiders scattered into the shade of his hut, he had pretended to start drinking it when Napoleon arrived outside his hut again. Although, not head of the tribe, he must have been one of their leaders, for he had noticed him ticking off a man for not carrying a spear as he always did himself. Now he demanded the Major's full attention.

He had brought a fish along with him, which he proceeded to gut and then place on a torn shard of metal which he must have found at the crash site at the same time he retrieved the compass. As they picked at the barbecued fish with their fingers, although delicious, he was so distracted that, momentarily, a bone became lodged in his throat. For it was not the fish that attracted his attention but the metal shard beneath stamped into the alloy was a serial number becoming clearly visible.

It takes a sprat to catch a mackerel, he thought, but these were not mackerel but sharks about to rip the world apart for no other reason than to fill their fat bellies. Indeed, the metal shard was such an important addition to the Indonesian delivery note already stuffed in his pocket, that he grew more determined than ever to present it to the Brazilian police as soon as possible.

It was shortly before dawn after his third night spent with the Indians, when, feeling something tickling his feet, he stretched down from his hammock only to feel the hairs on the back of one of the errant tarantulas. If his injured hand was so much better, he thought, it was time to return to civilisation and tackle the first task Bob had set him again, which he had not started to complete.

His one hope, as it had always been, was to persuade Napoleon to guide him back to the cherry picker. For if he was then able to hot-wire its towing vehicle, he was sure he could get it running again without the key. But when he managed to find him again, he was waving his spear towards the river making it obvious that his one and only intention was to take him fishing.

He thought Bob would have been a better choice for he remembered him saying that he had once travelled around Europe with his fishing rod looking for trophies. But not to the Amazon, which had the greatest variety of fresh water fish in the world. Some, he had been told, were as much as three metres long, weighing over a hundred and fifty kilos. But as Napoleon lunged his spear into the peat brown water, the first two fish he caught were nowhere near that size, although equally extraordinary.

The first, weighing only about ten kilos, had all its fins bunched up by its tail, and the second of about twelve kilos, was coloured such a bright yellow that it looked as if it had been living on a diet of buttercups. He wished he had a piece of paper on which he could illustrate the fish and scrawl the part number on the shard of metal Napoleon had brought back with him, but now it was his turn, and before he realised it, the spear had been pressed firmly into his good right hand.

With Napoleon standing behind him hissing every time he saw a flash of silver passing his feet, although he struck as accurately as possible, all of them swam on regardless. Worse still, when his spear finally began jerking, he found he had caught nothing better than one of their ferocious piranhas, which he was about to wade ashore with when Napoleon shouted, 'Ato! Ato!'

Grabbing the spear before throwing the gnashing fish onto the river bank, he showed how the piranha was determined to bite everything in sight with its razor sharp, backwards sloping, teeth. But if that was not enough, the fish let out such a terrifying series of grunts, that the Major lost his footing, and to the applause and shouts of joy of all those watching, fell headlong into the river.

It was then he spotted the caiman swimming fast towards him.

First alarmed, he was then astonished when the man, who he had seen stalking it from the far bank, leapt onto its back and, steering it by the head, landed it directly in front of him. Hardly had he scrambled to his feet when two other men appeared from nowhere, one armed with a cudgel and the other with a machete, with which, once the wretched caiman had been dispatched, he lopped off its tail. It had happened so quickly that he would have soon forgotten the grisly scene if they had not chucked the remains of the beast into the river below him. In an instant, the piranhas had launched themselves on such feeding frenzy that the water became a boiling broth of blood.

When he sat down on a log with Napoleon to roast the tail for their breakfast, at least he felt grateful that he had been spared the delights of eating capybara, parrot, giant centipede, howler monkey and anaconda, or any other forest food that the Indians may have included on their menus. If only Macey could have been with them, he thought, for she had produced such excellent food while flying to Brazil on Bob's Gulfstream, he knew she would have turned "Tail of Cayman" into a tender delicacy, worthy of any five-star Michelin restaurant, but instead, it almost took his teeth out.

Worse still, for some obscure reason, he started to shiver so violently that he could no longer eat it.

Then, just as he realised how ill he was suddenly becoming, he was scooped up by a posse of screaming women wanting to daub him with face paint and join them in some kind of a ceremony. He tried to persuade Napoleon, who was about to lead him back to the crash site, to stop them in their tracks, but when he failed to do so, he had to pluck up courage and join them.

During the 16th century when Christopher Columbus and the Spanish Conquistadors began colonising South America, the population of indigenous Indians was so decimated by Pizarro's brutality and their own lack of immunity to the diseases they brought with them, that their ranks were reduced to a paltry few thousand. Thus, the group looking after him, he presumed, were among the proud few remaining, some Indian tribes now numbering only two, or three, hundred in total.

He had been instructed to sit on a wide tree stump in the centre of the arena near several strong men who were adorned with red painted stripes across their chests and bands of brightly coloured feathers around their heads. Holding heavy branches, they started thumping them down on sheets of bark when a crowd of bare-chested maidens appeared from the fringe of the forest, some with good figures, others not, to dance forward and back in ragged lines, stamping their feet in unison.

When one of the girls came across to crown him with a band of feathers, his heart sank, for as the Indians swarmed around and started clapping their hands again, he realised that that the occasion was being staged entirely in his honour. So he rose unsteadily to his feet, saluting them as if he was their king. But king of a dying kingdom lit by an orange sky, tainted by smoke and ringed by fire.

He was by now sweating profusely in the humid air, but there was one last duty he knew was unavoidable. The men had started blowing fanfares through long bamboos, and as he was taken by the hand and lead by a phalanx of singing woman in a wild snake dance, their loud discordant voices almost caused his head to burst. They danced like dervishes through every hut until they finally came to one, he just managed to recognise as his own, where the men lit torches and lifted him, shaking like a leaf in a thunderstorm, onto the sanctuary of his hammock.

As he lay there becoming increasingly delirious, he realised that he had contracted malaria, and unless the fever could be treated within twenty-four hours, he would be dead. More frightening was the fact that the Indians, like those before them, knew nothing about malaria and certainly not how to treat it. Through a haze of fleeting images, he thought he could see Bonio leaning over him again, but before he was able to suggest what was wrong with him, he had vanished. Meanwhile, he felt for the metal shard he had hidden under his body, determined not to lose it.

The following morning, Bonio returned accompanied by two women, who, holding bowls of hot water, washed him all over without a towel in sight. Afterwards, they offered him another foul potion, this time for him to drink. He prayed that it would taste bitter like quinine, but when he tried his best to swallow it, to his growing dismay, the dark yellow liquid tasted nothing like it.

He had been taught all about quinine when undergoing survival training with the SAS and had been assured that it was the only cure for malaria. He knew that during the war in the Pacific, so many American servicemen had been catching the disease that when quinine became scarce and thousands of men began dying like flies, they sent a party of farmers to Costa Rica with the object of establishing plantations of the South American, quinine producing, cinchona tree.

But they were too late. Subsequently, his instructor told him, that although American deaths were far too high, they were nothing compared to those experienced by the Japanese, who ignored quinine altogether.

'Quinine!' He tried impressing on Bonio. 'Cinchona, Chinchona!' But the man only looked puzzled and perplexed. Either there must have been a different name for the trees, native to the very forests they were living in, or the forest Indians had never found a use for them. 'Cinchona,' he repeated yet again and then "ciona", "cinona", and every other name for the tree he could dream up, but to no avail. Yet all they had to do was find and then tap into one of the trees most likely growing within sight of their clearing.

It made him feel frustrated and furious, for it was the third time within a week that he had been faced by a situation totally out of his control, and this time, he was going die without a shot being fired—just because of a ruddy little mosquito.

**

He was gazing at two bamboo poles twisting above his head, but this time, there was no thatch above his hammock to look through at. Instead, there was an occasional glimpse of a starry sky, often obscured by dense foliage. There were moments when he thought he was lying helplessly on a raft in a rough sea, which made him feel increasingly nauseous.

But powerless to anything about it, he sensed that his fever was getting worse, and through brief periods of consciousness that he had never been so ill in his life. Indeed, should he be so remarkably fortunate that the Indians were carrying him out of their forest kingdom to see a doctor, he knew he would never make it.

It was when he heard the men swearing, he realised they were trying to force their way along a trail continually blocked by lopped off branches. Knowing he was in one of the most protected areas of the rainforest, which had been wantonly destroyed by loggers out to fell the most valuable trees they could find, he struggled to keep his eyes open, for should his bearers be following the river where he found the dying Indonesian, they were taking him in the wrong direction. He fumbled for the compass now stowed away in his boxer shorts, thinking they would not be able to use it.

On another waking moment, he thought hazily about Bob, who was attempting to stop the Americans abandoning clean nuclear energy. Then again, about his own project and the emptiness of the wilderness he would have to find as the best place to start planting the carbon eating trees, or plants, yet to be chosen by experts. Also, there would be the wildlife to consider, like the birds and many animals not dissimilar to those he was trying to help in the rainforest.

It would also be difficult to find water in deserts and the last great areas of wilderness, let alone get permission from governments to plant over their land before they considered any consequences. Or, if he was still in the land of the living, with so many countries already suffering from extremes of heat, violent storms, flooding and forest fires, would they all welcome his attempt to combat climate change and his determined efforts to save them from even greater disasters in the future.

He drifted away again before his ever-active mind returned to imagine a vast, aerial, planting machine. Was it a dream? Would the construction of such behemoths ever be possible? It was all spinning around in his head like a hundred aeroplane propellors. Yes, it must be a dream because he was dying and knew that whatever crazy invention he thought up, it would be derided by every decent engineer and agriculturist on the planet. But before he died, his last wish must be to get back to Cuiaba somehow, and then deal with the bastard who had stopped him in the first place.

As he lay there worrying about how his stretcher bearers would reach civilisation, he wondered if those on duty in the control tower at Cuiaba had bothered to read his flight plan and call Bob's telephone number to report him missing. Perhaps the Brazilian police were out looking for him at that very moment, but he doubted it. So his last thoughts, before he lapsed again into unconsciousness, were not about being saved, but of being allowed to die peacefully before the Indians became hopelessly lost, or blocked by fallen trees, and dropped him into a shallow, unmarked, grave.

Chapter 4

There was the sound of a tractor starting up and the bleating of sheep, or was it goats, when he opened his eyes. Then, as the mists cleared for a fleeting moment, he thought he saw the face of a very beautiful girl looking anxiously down on him. Thinking he had, at last, tasted something bitter that made his tongue curl, he shut his eyes again and still swimming in sweat disappeared from the world for several more hours until it was dark again, unaware of the fact that his chance meeting with a young doctor was not only to save his own life, but ultimately, the lives of others.

Rick, the owner of the facenda, was a man in his mid-fifties, who had seen it all. He had been farming on the boundary of the Xingu National Park for over thirty years, ever since he had run away from school in England, aged fifteen, and been employed on one of the largest cattle ranches in Argentina. But importantly, he had also met the Vilas-Boas brothers, who during the early sixties had been responsible for founding the "resguados" to protect the forest and all those living there.

Because his farm was right on the edge of what was acknowledged to be the most threatened rainforest in the world, he had joined the two brothers in championing the cause of Brazil's tiny indigenous population more than any other person in the whole country. Although, the brothers had died almost twenty years previously, he continued to lead a determined fight against the government and those setting out to destroy their unique habitat and traditional way of life, particularly their leader.

So, when the stretcher party appeared out of the jungle on a path which some illicit loggers had just cut to extract stolen timber, he was astonished when of all people, the man they were carrying turned out to be a fellow Englishman. He stood back in amazement and welcomed the semi-conscious stranger, realising that the Indian in charge of the party was his friend from the forest with the necklace of bones around his neck.

He had met the tribe's leader only once before when sorting out an issue concerning the Indians and the same band of wretched loggers, who, despite his protests, had pushed on regardless with one of them being shot dead, but not by the Indians, who had never seen a firearm in their lives. He hated all such skirmishes over their protected territory, but as he was not a policeman, he had decided that finding the person who had killed the man was none of his business.

Before the stretcher party departed, he thanked them for their "gift", giving their chief a bottle of Scotch. Knowing that he would translate his words of thanks into their own language, he wished them luck with their fishing, for the tribe lived not off forest food, but only on a diet of fish.

The "gift" was in a very bad way and was, obviously, suffering from the bite of a pit viper, the shock of an electric eel, or from the venom of a poison dart frog. So he summoned his wife, Francisca, and asked her to quickly make up a bed for the dying man.

'No,' she said, 'whoever he is and whatever he was doing among those Indians, he is not going to die on my watch. All that man needs is plenty of water and the correct medicine.' Then noticing his six pack and the fitness of his half naked body, she continued, 'I am sure Ana will see to that.'

When Ana was summoned to his bedside, she recognised malaria immediately. Then, having marvelled how handsome the stranger appeared, but fearful about his shaking and that he might drown in his own sweat, she exclaimed, 'I'm afraid, Francisca, from what I have learned about malaria, the speed in providing treatment is crucial. In this case, the poor fellow has been suffering for too long. All I can do now is give him a hefty dose of quinine and hope for the best.'

It took him a long time to come round again, but when Francisca offered him a bowl of chicken broth, he sat up and gratefully accepted it. Then, as his head started clearing, he realised, with luck, he was no longer going to die after all. However, as he began to take in the room and its surroundings, his crisp white sheets and the softness of his pillow, rather than dwell any more on his past desperate situation, he stupidly became more concerned about the shard of metal he hoped the Indians had brought with him, for it was nowhere to be seen.

But all was forgotten when his vision was suddenly realised and Ana re-appeared complete with a flannel and towel. Then, he forgot the problem altogether.

She looked like the guardian angel he had always hoped to find in heaven. Her honey-coloured skin, superb figure and light brown hair turning to gold as it was touched by the rays of bright sunshine, made her seem more wonderful to him than any girl he had ever clapped his eyes on. When she examined him again with her anxious, searching eyes, he noticed that they were more beautiful than the purest Brazilian aquamarines and the scent she was wearing more intoxicating than he believed possible.

Even in his shattered state, he felt such a sense of longing creeping over his fevered body that he could not help saying, 'With you looking after me, nurse, I will now live for ever!'

'I am going to slip away now,' whispered Francisca, who had remained at the head of his bed. 'You have been very lucky, wild man, for Ana, who is training to be a doctor at a hospital in Brasilia, is not only becoming particularly clever at her profession, but luckily for you, she always carries some quinine in her medical bag. You were so ill that she emptied the whole bottle of it into you!'

'Thank you for your kind words, Francisca,' Ana replied in perfect English. 'You should have become a doctor yourself, for what you have done to save him is truly remarkable, but did you not notice the poor man's hand? His fingers must have been cut to ribbons.'

'Please forget all that, nurse,' interrupted her patient. 'But before I nod off again, please tell me why I have not only been blessed with your loveliness, but with someone who understands this horrible disease, which I knew I had from the outset, but could do nothing about. Do you think you have permanently killed it, or do you think it will return to haunt me again one day?'

'Well, it does tend to rear its ugly head again depending entirely on the mosquito that infected you.'

'What a pity, in that case, I was unable to examine the blighter at both ends. What I do know about mozzies, nurse, as you seem to be hinting at rather than admitting, the only mosquitos known to give you malaria are the voracious females!'

'Do you consider then, wild man, that all females are voracious? If so, I hope I am the exception!'

'The word is not exception, Ana, if that is your name, for you are exceptional. No, it is now recognised by most men that the female species rule the world, which has become far too dangerous for us to live in without female supervision.

But how the hell did you come to be on duty here when I was brought in half dead by Rick's friend, Bonio, and his tribe of Indians?'

'Because I am staying on the farm with Francesca and Rick, my uncle, who runs everything here, and has always been my father's best friend. You see, my parents have a grand house in the hills behind Rio, set amongst all those druggy people living there, which is not and never will be my scene. So, I often spend my short holidays helping them out here, such as milking their house cow, or feeding the chickens and collecting their eggs—all the nice things one does in the countryside.'

But he had dozed off again, without hearing half of it.

The following morning, Rick gave him a razor and, as he got rid of his beard and put on a blue shirt and some khaki shorts Rick had lent him, he began to feel more like himself again, while Francisca started preparing a full English breakfast of bacon and eggs.

'This is a real treat,' he said on joining the three of them in the kitchen. 'Those Indians never even gave me one of their monkey sausages for breakfast!'

'Ah, that is because the Kalapalo tribe only eat what they are able to catch in the river with their spears and bows and arrows,' responded Rick. 'But first, please will you tell us your name and why you are here. It seems you have had an experience which only a very few white men have been able to experience and, possibly, enjoy?'

'Enjoy, Rick, is not quite the right word! I arrived in the rainforest in a miserable state after the plane I was flying while trying to spot where the fires were being started, was brought down by one of a gang of arsonists, whom I believe to be Indonesian. And I left their community being carried out in a hammock by those splendid Indians who rescued me, possibly without the piece of hard evidence I had collected.

'The bastard Indonesian was operating with five or six others, setting light to your forest with sticks of phosphorus which they were dropping from drones. It is all part of a foul attempt to extract money from any country in the world bold enough to stop them. As if the fires started by your beef producers, soya growers and gold diggers were not bad enough already.'

'You mean that you are here to investigate why all these new fires are destroying our forest?'

'Yes, Rick, not just to investigate the growing crisis, but also to find the bastards who are starting the new fires and eliminate them.'

'Crikey! Francisca, at last we have a man here after our own hearts! I don't know your name yet, wild man, but Francisca will tell you that we have taken it upon ourselves to act on behalf of all those Indians being poisoned with mercury due to illegal gold mining, those being evicted without mercy from their traditional villages, and all those others who recognise that further destruction of our rainforest will not only cause the planet to heat up out of control, but create such a drop in annual rainfall that all our crops will fail.

'It is not only farmers in the Mato Grosso who will go bust, but the whole country with us. For although, some consider Brazil to be like America, the bread basket of the world, it is not true. Our shaky economy is as fragile as a feather.'

'I am entirely on your side, Rick, and already at one with you on your endeavours, hoping to do something about it. And please just call me Major. The reason being that during the short time I have been a mercenary, I have created so many enemies that I never dare give my real name away, nor even to you. My employer also insists that I must remain anonymous.'

'So, Major, tell us about your employer? Then we are all then itching to hear what happened after your aircraft was brought down in the forest?'

'OK, believing I may trust you as I have only just started on the task I was given and am nowhere near completing it, my extraordinary tale goes, briefly, like this. I am a British mercenary employed by a mega-rich businessman called Bob, who, through his company Nuklin, is the world's leading purveyor of weapons grade nuclear material to international governments such as North Korea and other organisations not involved in terrorism but prepared to pay through the nose to acquire it.

'I would never have taken on the job, except it is very well paid and more importantly, Bob has now renounced all his previous work and although, retaining his company, has decided to change direction totally and invest in saving our world rather than blowing it to pieces. He is currently in North America attempting to persuade the Yanks to change from relying on generating their electricity from natural gas and renewables, to installing new types of nuclear reactors called SMRs. After doing so, which he admits is going to be a struggle, he is then determined to get the rest of the world to follow suit.

'Meanwhile, here in Brazil, I have been commissioned first to eliminate those responsible for setting fire to your forest, and then to locate and destroy the organisation behind it, which I now believe to be based in Indonesia. My second task, which is going to be considerably more demanding, is to conceive a method for replacing all the sequestration lost to your rainforest, followed by those vandalised in other parts of the world, and then arrange a massive planting scheme.'

'Jeepers!'

'You seem to be impressed, Rick?'

'We are all hugely impressed, Major. For a long time, living out here miles from anywhere and knowing how little attention is being paid to the destruction of our environment and the very air we breathe, terrifies us. Where it will end?'

'Your rainforest has always been described as the lungs of the Earth, Rick, but no one is more aware of those lunatics burning the breath out of every living creature here, than Bob!'

'However, you must agree, Major, that the magnitude of the problems facing our world are not generally understood. Some may help by reducing air travel, others by driving cars powered by gas, or electricity, but although they mean well, they have no concept of the disaster awaiting us.

'Only photographs of starving children, melting glaciers and hungry polar bears, seem to be making people think more positively about climate change. But nobody has a clue on how to solve the problems, or should they have a realistic solution, do anything about it. At times, although we are armed with sensational new technology, we are wedded more to finding out about our friends on Facebook and Instagram rather than planning for the future lives of our children.

'Because of such complacency, it is shameful that in a single generation, we are witnessing the collapse of an eco-system, which has held life on earth together since the beginning of time.'

They had gone out into the garden where the Major, lying back on a wicker rocking chair, was now listening to Rick congratulate him on his remarkably recovery. All around him he could see modern farm buildings and signs of a well organised work force, while the farmhouse itself, painted a pale pink, was covered so much by bougainvillea, ranging from bright orange to burgundy, that its design was hard to make out.

But it was not the house but the sharp outline of the forest behind that grabbed his attention, for not a kilometre away he could plainly see an ugly gap in the trees where they had been felled by the vandals Rick had told him about. So it must have been through there, in full view of the farm, that he had been carried out by Bonio.

'I have been listening to every word you have said, Rick, but you have not yet expressed you anger at seeing all those trees being stolen on the edge of the forest right in front of you. Blast the ruddy loggers and all who support them, for they don't give a damn about anyone trying to stop them, or the effect deforestation is having on our planet. Their sole aim is to fill their pockets at the expense of the world in general.

'Do you think, Rick, that the people who sit on wooden chairs and dine on smart wooden tables, ever consider where all that magnificent hardwood came from in the first place?'

'Major, now your blood is beginning to boil again, it is obvious that neither of us has spent a sheltered life. Nor, I hope, will those arsonists much longer due to your intervention. But, forget them and the loggers, we wish to know about your crash and time living with the Indians?'

'To continue. I was flown to Cuiaba in Bob's jet and at the airport, I hired a small plane from a man who gave me a map marked with his suggested search area, saying, as I would have to land in the savanna to top up the plane before returning, he would load some extra fuel in jerrycans. But he never expected me to return, his intention being to turn both his Cherokee and its pilot into cinders.

'A lookout must have been positioned at Paranatinga, which I had been told to fly over, who informed an arsonist operating only a short distance from here, that there was a snooper coming his way who needed fixing. The arsonist then directed one of his drones to hit my aircraft and bring it down. The drone shattered my windshield and threw me so hard into the back of the cockpit that I was no longer able to fly the plane, which fell out of the sky and crashed into the branches of some blazing trees.

'Somehow, I managed to escape down a rope I had quickly made from my clothes, before the plane fell to into the undergrowth directly behind me. Covered by smoke and the dust kicked up by the falling debris, I was able to locate the culprit standing on the platform of a cherry picker from where he was flying drones far out over the canopy to drop fire sticks, before directing one of them at my plane.

'Then, as he tried to shoot me with his rifle, I managed to creep under the cherry picker and drop him heavily to the ground, before chasing him into the forest, where I found him being crushed to death by a giant anaconda. That was when I saw a delivery note fall out of his pocket, which I stowed away in my pants—the only clothes I had left.'

Then, it dawned on him. 'Oh, I must be going crackers, Francisca, why did I not tell you about the note when they brought me here. I bet it has now been destroyed in your washing machine?' He held his breath for a moment, but when she failed to reply, he continued without hesitation.

'When I tried to retrace my steps, I became so lost that I had almost giving up hope when I was rescued by an indigenous Indian holding a spear. He took me back to his village where my damaged hand was treated by your extraordinary friend with bones around his neck.'

'Stop there, Major, for one day that man may be extremely useful to us. He knows most of what goes on around here and although not a witch doctor, he is a man of influence. Not long ago, risking retaliation both from my fellow farmers and the loggers, I visited him in the forest myself.'

'Well Bonio, as I named him, did a great job on my hand by dipping it in some foul-smelling potion, but not knowing what was wrong with me when I started becoming delirious, thank God, he brought me here. You must have pointed to where you lived when you met him.'

'Poor fellow,' Ana interrupted. 'It looks as if your hand was very badly injured. It is extraordinary how Bonio managed to heal such deep lacerations in such a short time. He has also helped many others suffering from burns in this unusually hostile environment. What happened to it?'

'Getting out of the crashed aircraft, which was a long way above the ground, was not easy and when it was chucked sideways due to a branch breaking, I cut my hand on the engine cowling.'

'Ana is right about your wound,' interrupted Rick. 'But forgetting all the humidity and those dreadful mosquitos, the effectiveness of the potion that Bonio used to heal your injury will not surprise her. You should know that ninety per cent of all human illnesses, injuries and diseases are treated with medicaments originating from the Amazon rainforest, so should deforestation be allowed to continues at the present rate, we will not only loose most of them, some of which have not yet been investigated, but many well-known health cures as well.

'Deforestation is so advanced here that it has already caused serious flooding together with many other problems effecting our agriculture. That is why I have started a joint venture with the Carrefour Foundation in France, now known as the Sustainable Trade Initiative.'

'Tell me about that, Rick?' But before he could reply, there was such a loud clap of thunder. They ran for cover as heavy rain turned the farmyard into mud.

Once back in the house, the Major was starting to feel so unwell again that he collapsed into a deep armchair and covered himself with a poncho.

'Major, I am, obviously, alarming you but do you realise that beef animals in Brazil far outnumber our human population, which, surprisingly, numbers over two hundred million people, most of them living along the Atlantic coast. It is calculated that if just one of them gave up eating beef, it would not only save a considerable number of trees, but because our cattle farming is so hopelessly inefficient with too many animals being allowed to graze ad lib, it would also free up the land for other forms of agriculture, of equal importance to our economy.

'Just in the Mato Grosso alone, where I am strictly an arable farmer, by reducing beef exports by a quarter, it will release millions of acres for other profitable enterprises, while halving the rate of deforestation and land erosion. Meanwhile, we are lobbying the government hard to turn their minds from exporting beef, to creating better and more sustainable opportunities for the whole country. If they do not do so, before long there will be nothing left for the beef cattle to feed on.

'However, that scare tactic does not work, which may already be happening in a very small way, I have one more card up my sleeve, although I am loathe to use it.'

Ana was back wiping his fevered brow, and as he looked up at her shapely long legs and slim figure, he had to resist an overwhelming desire to kiss her. 'Just between us, what is that, Rick?'

'No one living will forget the 2001 outbreak of foot and mouth disease in England which was blamed on infected meat being fed to some pigs. Not only were over six million animals slaughtered as a result but, because the finger was pointed at Argentina, beef imports from South America were banned for a very long time. So just consider what would happen to their beef exports now if there was an outbreak of the disease in Brazil, for the animals are often grazing cheek by jowl with hardly a blade of grass between them. It would certainly solve the problem.'

'Rick, it is my turn to say jeepers! But do you think that is ever likely to happen?'

'It could be arranged, although darling Ana here and Francisca are dead against it.'

'Of course, Rick, but forgetting all that please could you drive me back to the crash site. Since losing not only the shaft of metal with the drone's serial number stamped on it, and now the delivery note destroyed in Francisca's washing machine, I must look for some more evidence. If I fail to find any then I will drive the tow van left there back to Cuiaba where I will collar the bastard who hired me the plane. Having extracted everything he knows, I will then break his bloody neck.'

'So why did you not copy the serial number down before?'

'What with my precious blood and a small stick? No, the number would never have survived.'

'OK, then let's go.'

So they set out together in his Land Rover, arriving before long at the sandy track he had spotted from the air.

'This is the track, Rick, carved out by more of those bloody loggers. We should now be able to find what we are looking for through those burned trees you see several hundred metres ahead.' But the scene which confronted him was not what he had been expecting.

Both the cherry picker and its towing vehicle had been burned to skeletons and were barely recognisable. He could only imagine that when the drone he had noticed in the back of the van caught fire, it had ignited a pile of phosphorus sticks hidden behind it and turned both machines into a blazing inferno.

'Damn and blast,' he swore. 'I was hoping to return here later to drive that van away from here.'

So they began searching where the charred remains of the aircraft were scattered among the burned undergrowth, before turning to where the drone must have ricocheted off the plane's windshield.

But although they found a few more bits and pieces, nothing was marked with a serial number. Worse still, when they broadened their search, all they discovered were the rotting bodies of the two loggers the Indonesian must have shot before commandeering their van and the cherry picker.

'Leave those to my men, Major. At least it means there are two less of the buggers. It is not the first time, and not the last that this will happen to those encroaching on the Xingu Nature Reserve.'

Before they left the scene, they went looking for the man's rifle which he had thrown into the undergrowth. It turned out to be an old British army Lee Enfield with open sights.

'No wonder he could not hit you with that old fashioned fowling piece,' Rick remarked. 'I wonder just how organised these "Dragons", as you call them, really are?'

'Rick, if Bob is correct, they are not only setting light to the rainforest in Brazil, but to other forests as well. They don't need to be efficient, for they are making such a killing from any government prepared to stop them, they will soon be able to arm themselves exactly as they like. Both Bob and I agree that what they are doing is speeding up climate change, but neither the Yanks, or anyone else Bob is talking to, have done anything much about it. So being unable to return to Cuiaba, I have no other option than to deal with the bastards closer at hand in what must be the Dragon's base camp at Paranatinga.'

It was still raining heavily, turning the burned-out vehicles, the bodies and the trees around them into a scene from hades. The sun was beginning to set when they drove back out of the forest and as they reached the farm gate with the acrid smell of the smouldering trees filling their lungs, they were surprised to find Ana waiting for them jumping up and down with impatience.

'What the hell's biting her, Rick?' Rick was a fine-looking man in his fifties, who exuded confidence, merely shrugged his shoulders.

But when he asked her what was wrong, all she could blurt out was, 'I've found it, Major!'

Thus, began one of the most testing experiences in his precarious lifetime.

Chapter 5

Sam. First pilot of Bob's Jet.

Sam was not just an accomplished aviator with several years of flying experience in the British Royal Air Force behind him, but soon after Bob had taken him on as his first pilot, he showed himself to be a perceptive judge of character when he informed him about his fiancée, Macey.

'I know she is American,' he said. 'A race you always regard with suspicion, but understanding your interest in SpaceX and the amazing rocketry happening at Vandenberg Airforce base, plus the fact that you are looking for a stewardess, if you take her on, you will find her no less charismatic.'

'So where did you meet her Sam and how old is she?'

'Her age is 24, just five years younger than myself. I met her while I was stationed in Afghanistan. She was serving with the American Marine Corps and was only nineteen at the time. I could not believe that such an inexperienced and fragile young girl, I thought, could have been recruited by the Marine Corps to work amongst all the horrors in the front line. However, you may know that no non-combatant personnel are ever accepted by them and that all medical staff are normally provided exclusively by the US Navy. Macey was their one and only exception.'

'How extraordinary. But for what reason?'

'Her father was a celebrated doctor and having always wanted to be a nurse, she had just passed out top of the University of California medical school in Los Angeles, one of the finest anywhere, when she noticed a Marine Corps recruiting station near the gate. So being Macey, she just walked in saying that if they needed a skilled doctor to look after their wounded soldiers fighting in Afghanistan, they should employ her before she went to work for the Afghans themselves. The colonel in charge, who happened to be a friend of her father, was so surprised and delighted that he agreed, and so she won yet another first!'

'She sounds as if she is an outstanding choice then?'

'You bet, Sir. 2014 saw the end of the battle of Nawzad which, because of lack of men on the ground, had prevented our coalition forces from eradicating the Taliban from Helmand Province for almost eight years. I was flying Chinooks out of Camp Bastion. Then one day when the US marines arrived, it all changed, just as my whole life did. Macey, who had been seconded to us, was dealing with the such horrendous casualties in the back of my chopper that when we returned to base for the last time, I hugged her, begging her to keep in touch with me when she returned to the States.'

'So what happened next, Sam?'

'Well, luckily she did, and when, two years ago, I was posted to a flying school near Vegas in California to convert to flying jets, as she lived just outside Salt Lake City, not too far away north of the Nevada desert, amazingly she was there waiting for me.'

'So that's when you became engaged before returning to fly Typhoons in our British air displays?'

'Yes, Sir.'

'So where is Macey living now?'

'When you took me on, Sir, and asked me to arrange for your aircraft to be based at Exeter, Devon, England, Macey came over to join me there. So we now share a house I bought by the river, which has suited her brilliantly. Without even trying she landed a job working for the Royal Marines next door.'

'OK, Sam, bring her to see me. She sounds not only delightful but also intelligent.'

**

Macey was waiting for Bob at the door of the Gulfstream, holding out a slim, beautifully manicured, hand to welcome him back on board. As he gave her a quick glance, he noticed that her dark hair was tied back in a chignon with a blue ribbon and that his former choice of a pale mushroom coloured pleated skirt and beautifully cut jacket with white trimmings suited her admirably. He thought she looked terrific. He had always believed in the best and Sam's fiancée was proving to be yet another excellent addition to his small staff.

Once he had settled down in his deep armchair covered with the finest white buffalo hide, Macey came to strap him in and serve him with a plate of ginger biscuits and a cup of his favourite chamomile tea.

'Macey, tell me, do you know how long the flight is going to take to San Francisco?'

'Yes, Sir. Flying in your beautiful aeroplane at a cruising speed of eight hundred kph over a distance of six thousand six hundred kilometres, it will take us about eight hours and fifteen minutes. As we are flying over night, there should be little delay at the other end before landing.'

'I like flying at night, Macey, do you know why?'

'No, Sir, except that most important businessmen like yourself prefer not to waste the daylight hours looking down on our fractured earth.'

'You have got it in one, Macey, particularly if that businessman is trying to put Humpty Dumpty together again. During daylight, when I look down on all those patches of concrete being poured over the countryside to build more houses and factories, I am only able to think of them as giant cow pats, which do little else than release more carbon dioxide into the air! Also, Macey, when I look down on the vast areas of savanna and parched desert, I try to think of means of planting up those empty spaces with something sensible to replace all the trees currently being destroyed in world's forests. But I get nowhere!'

'Surely, it's not cows pats creating the gas, but the cattle, Sir. But everyone agrees about the trees.'

'I know that, my dear, which is why you should not be bringing me that beef consommé later, which I see written on your smart menu card.'

'So, do you agree with those who say that we should not be eating beef anymore?'

'No, Macey, absolutely not. I know how much my own farm, which has no land suitable for growing crops, and the whole country would suffer as a result. All in life should be balanced, but because of the world's increasing demand for beef, it is hard to believe that in Brazil, their president is encouraging farmers to burn the Amazon rainforest for a few years grazing. Once the trees are gone and unable to trap the carbon in our atmosphere any more, we will ourselves go up in flames!

'So that is why, Macey, I am hoping it is still dark when we fly over the Nevada desert. Not being able to think of a way of restoring the balance to life on earth, just as it was not many years ago, is driving me bananas!'

'Sir, there must be an answer to global warming somewhere. I believe that Sam told you that my father was a doctor. But did he tell you what kind of doctor?'

'No, as you were so keen on becoming a nurse at the time, I presumed he was a doctor of medicine?'

'Wrong. You see my father, Doctor Gregory Fildew, having gained a PhD in Plant physiology at the University of Geneva and studied plant genetics for two years at the Institute of Science in Luxembourg before teaching plant biotechnology at the University of San Francisco, where we are now headed, then started the world's top laboratory in cell tissue culture at Salt Lake City. So the whole family went to live there. Do you know about tissue culture, Sir?'

'No, Macey, I don't have a clue.'

'Well, it is an exciting new method of plant propagation, employed to create millions of clones from a single specimen, or tiny slither of a plant, in no time at all. My parents live just south of city overlooking lake Utah under Eagle Mountain. I am sure that my father would tell you much more about it, if you are interested. So why don't we drop in at the airport there on our way home and stay with them for a night? I know how much they are looking forward to meeting Sam, who I have only been able to tell them about.'

'Of course, I am interested, Macey! Or perhaps I should call you Eos, Greek goddess of the dawn. For already I feel the sun, which is still far away in the east, starting to light up the night's sky!'

Bob did not say any more as he polished off the rest of his dinner of seared scallops and rosti followed by wild strawberries with coconut ice cream. Then, disappearing behind a curtain, he quickly got into his lavender coloured silk pyjamas, before wishing Macey goodnight and diving between the finest Egyptian cotton sheets money can buy.

Waiting by the private air terminal when they arrived in San Francisco, there was a gun metal grey limousine waiting for him with Nuklin written in discreet orange lettering on the door, as on his jet.

'Good morning, Matt. Great to see you again. Surprisingly, I am not on a sales trip this time but much more likely on a suicide mission. So we are heading for Berkeley to the East of the city. Have there been any earthquakes recently?'

'No, Sir, but as you know, we sit like birds on a high-tension wire and should that wretched San Andreas Fault get angry again, anything could happen. But it has largely behaved itself over the last hundred and fifty years, so life carries on regardless. However, guessing what you must be up to, we will no doubt suffer one now, for although the boss of Nuklin may not be so well known around here, the name of his company sure is.'

'Why, Matt, is there so much heat being generated by nuclear power in California so suddenly?'

'Heat, Sir! California becomes like a furnace whenever the subject is mentioned. As you will soon discover when you talk to the president of the Environmental Progress Group, who you are going to meet shortly.'

'How did you guess that?'

'Although, you are supposed to be a stickler for security, when your man rang me from England, I knew that you were coming to join him in telling those dumbheads who are shutting down our nuclear power plants to think straight and stop doing so. And that sure is not because we have always had the exclusive right to provide them with uranium.'

'That is correct, Matt, and the man I am about to see is probably the only guy I know among all the short-sighted Californians and other Americans, who is capable of changing their minds.'

They had drawn up in front of what appeared to be a long line of shops. Somewhere in the centre of them and almost unnoticeable, was a door with a four-figure number written above it, matching that, which he had scribbled on the back of an envelope. Bob could easily have been disappointed for this was not the skyscraper, or even the contemporary office block he was expecting, and it was only when he stepped inside and found an ultra-modern office buzzing with activity, that he rapidly changed his mind.

'Hi,' said a lean looking 50-year-old wearing a pressed white shirt and blue jeans. 'I am Michael.'

His well-trimmed hair, greying at the temples, close clipped beard, high forehead, and brown, intelligent, eyes, let alone his apparent fitness, impressed Bob immediately.

'So good to meet you, Michael. As you know, I have flown a long way to come and talk to you.'

'You sure have, Bob. Because nuclear has become such a dirty word right now, I guess you are here not to sell us any more of that stuff, but for a more important reason?'

'So important, Michael, that I believe the future of civilisation largely depends on it.'

'Bingo! You and I are going to get along fine, or as they say in England, like a house on fire.'

'Better to forget the fire, Mike, for at this moment, I have one of my operatives lost in the Amazon rainforest who was trying hard to find out why there has been such a sudden catastrophic increase in the number of fires being started there, but not all by farmers. So while you and I try to do what we can to stop the burning of fossil fuels, I am equally determined to save the forests which sequester so much of the carbon from our atmosphere.

'As governments, particularly those of Brazil and Borneo, remain unable to halt deforestation, and the situation gets further out of control, I am intending to replace the lost trees with such a vast area of carbon fixing trees, or plants, that the issue of burning fossil fuels becomes superfluous for ever.'

'But will that not take far too long, Bob?'

'Not on my watch. There has not yet been sufficient reaction to America shutting down its nuclear facilities and turning back to natural gas while waiting for more renewables to save the situation, which, of course, they never will. So the time has come to take more immediate action. I understand, Mike, that your crunch moment came after the Californian Public Utilities Commission had voted unanimously to shut down the Diablo Canyon Nuclear Power Plant.

SMR Small Modular Reactor

Artists impression

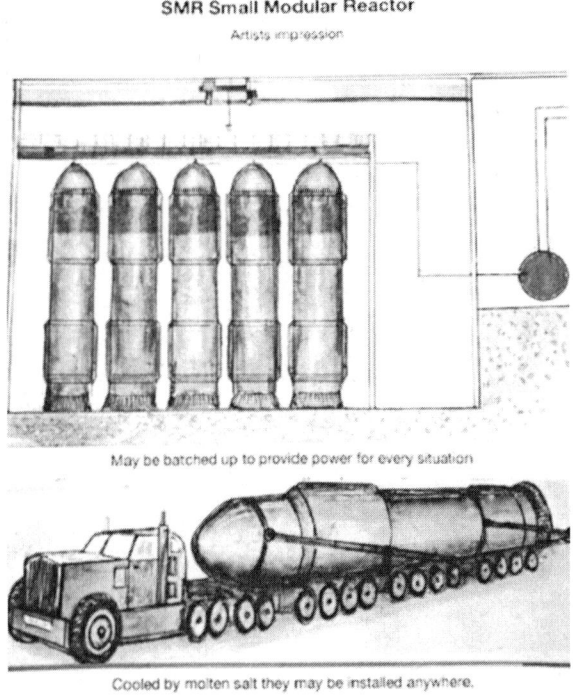

May be batched up to provide power for every situation

Cooled by molten salt they may be installed anywhere.

'As reported in the San Francisco Chronicle, I was amazed when a commissioner stated: We all agree the time has come to get rid of the last remaining vestige of nuclear energy production in California. How stupid is that from a state considered to be the top innovator in North America!'

'Bob, remind me of the objections the majority of Californians plus a large number of American citizens, in general, have to nuclear power. I will then answer them for you.'

'To start with, Mike, I have just discovered that even the vice president talks about a greener America without nuclear, which, although he may be backing up his boss, is nonsense.'

'Bob, the whole argument is based on old data. We are all agreed here that without nuclear energy, our planet is doomed, so it is up to us to see that it is not allowed to happen.'

'Of course, but the case against nuclear, which has probably been put to you a thousand times, needs to be fought not just tooth and nail in America, but everywhere. Nuclear peaked in the 1990s by providing some eighteen per cent of the world's electricity, but as cheaper methods of generating the stuff gather pace, that figure is now history. One of their main objections, Mike, is that nuclear waste is causing huge storage problems and will result in its remaining dangerous for thousands of years.'

'For starters, Bob, it is a fact that solar emits forty times more radiation per unit of energy than nuclear. But to knock them off their perch, it has been said authoritatively that should all the nuclear waste ever produced by our country be buried safely underground in 50-foot-high silos, it would occupy only the size of one football pitch. And the new type reactors produce almost none. Next, Bob, they say that nuclear energy has led to the further proliferation of nuclear weapons.'

'What bunkum, Mike, do those idiots have a single case to prove it?'

'They also say that Chernobyl and Fukushima demonstrate a high risk of cancer-causing accidents.'

'What an exaggeration, Mike! It is estimated that over seven million people are dying of cancer caused by air pollution every year as we make pathetic attempts to clean it up. Do you know how many people died directly, although others did later, as a result of Chernobyl, an accident that happened because of a stand-in crew operating an outdated nuclear reactor? The figure is only 31, 19 of them being firemen.

'When in 2011, there was a further outcry after the Fukushima nuclear disaster, it was later admitted that only one Japanese operator, who was actually standing on the reactor, may have died afterwards due to radiation poisoning!

'The opposition states further, Mike, that unlike renewables, the price of fuel and future decommissioning costs, plus expensive delays when building new plants, demonstrate that the nuclear alternative is totally uncompetitive.'

'Bob, an article in Forbes magazine stated recently: We don't need Solar or Wind to save our Climate. Of course, we don't. Because renewables produce electricity for only about thirty per cent of the time, they will always need a substantial back up. So when California's Public Utilities Commission tell me that instead of coal to supplement their renewables, they are going to use natural gas, are they just trying to outwit their customers, for what the hell's the difference?

'Furthermore, I have proved to them that despite the high cost of the uranium your company sells them, modern nuclear plants will ultimately cost them far less in real terms than any realistic alternative. So why, I keep asking myself, does more than half our population believe that renewables are now king. Have they not thought it through? Do they not realise that wind turbines and solar panels together take up one thousand times as much of their precious land as plants burning fossil fuels, while small nuclear plants will barely take up any of it.'

'So how do you propose to change their minds, Mike? For that is why I have come to see you.'

'Only through raising considerable sums of money from people who believe that without more nuclear power, which God introduced to us less than a century ago, we are not going to survive another hundred years. You will understand that the brilliant people I employ here are all striving to raise finance not just from individuals but from many of the world's top businesses. Only then may we be able to pay for the mighty effort needed to convince mankind that, although renewables will play a useful part, only nuclear will ultimately save us.'

'Mike, I am so glad I came to see you. What you are doing here inspires me to even greater efforts. But at the same time, we both realise that facts and figures are not enough. In California, they talk about nuclear's death nell, but remember that the Diablo Canyon plant, which currently provides California with ten per cent of its electricity, was installed way back in 1985. Since then, there have been opportunities for installing smaller, cheaper and more efficient plants.

'The decision to close down the last of California's nuclear generators has undermined what should have continued as an inspiring example for the rest of America. Not only will hundreds of skilled workers now be laid off and the state faced with heavy decommissioning costs, but people's electricity bills will soar—all for what purpose?'

'I agree, Bob, it is sheer lunacy largely stoked up by a load of zealots here in San Francisco who like to be known as the Armageddon Movement. They are a nasty bunch, well known to the police and best to be avoided at all times, but sadly, for that reason they have had far too much exposure in the media recently. They are even thought to have abducted some of those who have objected to the closure of our nuclear plants, and in one case, the poor fellow has not been seen again.'

'I am grateful to you for warning me. Since I was last in America, I have noticed a considerable change in the people's attitude to nuclear, which I find depressing. As in most cases nowadays, it only needs a few people to express their views on the social media, for the young in particular, to follow them like sheep. But television is not much better and when they get their teeth into something sufficiently controversial, they often become equally dangerous.

'It is obvious that the Armageddon lot are just playing on that fact, which is something we must knock on the head. But thanks for seeing me and giving me such an enlightening report on why California, of all States, have it in for nuclear. It confirms that if we are to stop the madness already influencing the rest of America, we must snuff it out in every way possible, before the rest of the world follows suit.'

Bob, casting caution aside, then made his way out of the door, asking Mike not to worry about saying goodbye, later confessing that he thought he had smelt a rat before walking across the pavement to where his company car was waiting. The street seemed remarkably empty, he thought, as though others were feeling the same way, and just to add to his forebodings, he noticed that all the shops had closed their doors, although they were wide open when he arrived to let in some fresh air from what remained of a hot but glorious day.

He thought of turning back to ask Mike what was going on, but instead strode on hoping that there had been some kind of police action in the street while they were talking.

'Matt,' he said to the driver. 'Sorry to have been longer than expected, but it has been thoroughly worthwhile and so, working closely with the Environmental Progress Group, I hope that we will be able to stop all this nonsense and throw those madmen into their own pot of boiling, bloody, oil!'

But it was not Matt!

Chapter 6

No sooner had the driver started opening his door than Bob was grabbed from behind and a bag put over his head. His arms were then wrenched forward, he presumed by the driver, and his wrists tied together in front of him and fastened to one leg. Finally, the other man holding him shoved him into the back of the limo, jumping in after him before poking a pistol into his ribs.

'Now don't you give us any trouble, mister, while we take you on a nice little evening trip down to the seaside.'

'So what's going on?' Bob asked in as calm a voice as he could muster. But there was no reply.

They seemed to have travelled only a short distance steeply downhill when, as the ground levelled out, the brakes were jammed on so abruptly that he was slammed forward against the front seat.

'We are in a hurry, man. Get out and shut up, or we'll throw you into the drink. Now, once I undo your manacles, get into the boat which you will find in front of you and make it snappy!'

'Who the hell are you?' He asked once more without a response.

Having been pushed unceremoniously over the side and into the bottom of what must have been a small dinghy, he then heard an outboard motor being started.

'Where the hell are you taking me?' He shouted in vain.

Almost an hour must have passed as he listened to the sound of water rushing past and then, as the din of the outboard motor diminished, he could hear the two of them arguing about a landing place. At least, he thought, they were not taking him out to sea with an anchor tied to his feet.

'Get up, we're here, you ruddy criminal!' The man with the pistol commanded, poking him in the ribs again as the boat slowed rapidly to a halt and began grating against some rocks. 'Stand up, you bloody man, and get out. Then keep walking as we take you down to your nice holiday apartment.'

He heard a door clanging open, then, as a rag was shoved over his face, he recognised the sickening smell of ether before drifting away into darkness.

He woke very slowly to feel some broken metal springs biting into his back. In the gloom, he could vaguely make out a small barred window, while behind the remains of the iron bed he was lying on were bars stretching across the width of what must have been one of the dingiest cells ever created. Only one thing seemed to brighten it up, the livid red lettering sprayed across the damp stone wall opposite, which obliterated many of the frantic scribblings of past murderers, who were once incarcerated there.

NAF OFF YOU NUCLEAR NOBODY

He discovered that his hands had been tied together again with some strong twine and the Hublot Tourbillon watch his former wife had given him was missing, as were the notes he had taken previously and then shoved into the pocket of his jacket, now cut to ribbons and used to tie him to the bedstead. After freeing his hands by rubbing the cloth endlessly on the bed's rusty metal frame before undoing a second tight knot tying him down, when he rose stiffly to his feet, staring him in the face and smelling of chloroform, was a crumpled T shirt printed with the word Armageddon.

He must have been knocked out for hours and as he struggled to shake off the drugs he must have been given, he was finally able to stagger towards the barred slit in the wall, which pretended to be a window. Wondering why his cell was so damp and miserable, peering through the wisps of fog streaming through it as the stuff rolled in from the Pacific, as happened in the bay during the summer months, he tried hard to get his bearings. Then, for a brief moment, he saw a flash of orange through the fog. It meant everything, for what he made out was paint on a span of the iconic Golden Gate bridge.

'You bastards,' he yelled out into the late afternoon air. 'You have thrown me into Alcatraz!'

**

Back in a small house in Sausalito, across the water not far to the north of the city, which was said to be the most attractive place in the bay area to live in, Macey, who, with Sam, had been staying the night with her favourite aunt,

Sophie, were watching the lunchtime news on CNN when they heard it announced that an Englishman visiting San Francisco with the object of selling nuclear material to the Diablo Canyon Nuclear Power Plant, the last reactor in California due to be closed down, had been abducted the previous afternoon by a group of local protestors and had not been seen since.

Although, the police had been informed immediately, because of poor visibility at the time, they had decided to delay their search until early the following morning when they were again hampered by Karl, as name the sea fret was known by.

'Sophie, you remember we were talking at supper about those ante nuclear demonstrators, they have now got hold of Bob!' Sam shouted to her in the garden. 'Come quickly, for Macey says that you may have an idea where they have taken him. We must find Bob before the police do.'

'What?' She said, as she joined them holding some gardening shears. 'You mean that some bloody terrorists, most likely that wretched Armageddon lot, who have been making such a nuisance of themselves in Frisco recently, have now captured your boss. They are a rough lot and one person known to have abducted by them has never been seen again.'

'Dear Sophie,' Sam explained, 'we must find Bob quickly. Once in the hands of the police, he will have to answer so many questions that it will stop us leaving from here. We were expecting to stop off for a night in Salt Lake City with Macey's parents, but will no longer be able to do so if there are any further delays. Knowing what those dreadful people have done with their captives in the past, do you have any idea where they may have taken him?'

'It could be anywhere, Sam, but if I was them and wanted to give him a rough time, I would take him by boat to that filthy old prison on the island out there, which you are now able to see emerging from the fog directly in front of us.'

'You mean Alcatraz, the notorious prison from which no one has ever escaped?'

'Yes, my friends. If he is locked up in that terrible place, we will have to move fast before anything else happens to him. How lucky my next-door neighbour has a small fishing boat.'

Picking up her cell phone, Sophie quickly called her friend, Jake. 'I have a niece staying here who has heard on CNN that her boss has been abducted by demonstrators, who may have locked him up in Alcatraz. Would you please take us over there in your boat so we may try and rescue him?'

'Sure, Sophie, but why have the police not already been informed about this?'

'Of course, they have, but it was said on the news that they were not prepared to act until this morning and Karl has meanwhile been swirling in from the sea again.'

'OK then, but landing there, I have been told, is mighty difficult, and there must be a countless number of cells to search. Furthermore, those bastards may still be on the island and we have nothing to defend ourselves with apart from a couple of oars. But let's stop messing about. Jump into my jeep and we'll go down to the boat straight away and give it a damn good try.'

The boat was only ten metres overall but it had a decent inboard engine, which took them steadily out across the bay.

'Tell me, Sam,' Jake enquired. 'How did you get over here yesterday. Via the bridge?'

'No, Macey and I took the ferry so that we could admire your famous bridge and was horrified by seeing that formidable prison of Alcatraz so close to us on the way over here. Back home, the grey walls of Dartmoor prison set in the centre of the moor where they ring a bell if you manage to escape, has always haunted me, but Alcatraz is something else!

'Somehow those great slabs of concrete dotted with tiny cell windows, rising high above rocks as sharp as shark's teeth set in a cauldron of swirling water, makes me shiver, and finding poor Bob in a place used previously to incarcerate some of the world's most violent criminals, may be extraordinarily difficult.'

'You are right mentioning the tide, which is particularly strong here, Sam, for like the wildness of Dartmoor, that is why, in 1934, the island was chosen as a prison. It is said that the few inmates who ever managed to escape from Alcatraz and reached that violent water, all drowned.'

**

Bob tried opening the door to his cell the moment he returned from looking out of the "window", hoping that if he could get himself out before it became dark, he would be able to wave to a passing yacht and somehow get ashore in time for his next appointment. But the door would not budge. Why not, he thought, for there was no chain and surely his tormentors did not possess an ancient key.

Then at the top of the door, just out of reach, he noticed a strong length of cord, attaching it to the bars. But although, he pulled the bed across and stood on it, as hard as he tried, he was unable to loosen the knot, which appeared to have been glued. Worrying about what had happened to Matt, his driver, he realised that his predicament was not going to end at any time soon.

'Bob, where the hell are you?' A faraway shout came, which he recognised as Sam's.

'Down here in these bloody cells,' he yelled back, having rushed to the window. Far below, he could just make out Sam standing in the bows of a small fishing boat shouting up to him through a megaphone. But before he was able to put an arm through the bars to wave at his rescuers, he began to feel so faint again that he fell back onto the wet stone floor exhausted.

Macey with her medical skills was onto the case the moment they had cut the cord above his head and broken into his cell. 'Bob,' she told Sam, anxiously, 'is suffering terribly from the after effects of his ordeal. No doubt the poor man has been injected with an overdose of drugs, and before then given a strong whiff of ether, reacting as many people did after visiting the dentist.'

'Then let's get him out of here as fast as possible and tuck him up in Sophie's other spare room.'

Having thanked Jake for all his kindness, that is what they did.

'We have just heard from the police,' Sam informed Bob the following morning, 'that Matt, your driver, reported into them just a moment before we rescued you, saying that he had been grabbed by the same two men as you yourself were afterwards, when bringing a cup of coffee back to your car. He was also blindfolded and led at pistol point to a bench in the park opposite, before being chloroformed and securely tied to it.'

'Well, it's all been quite a saga,' admitted Bob. 'And I'm afraid it is typical of what is happening in the United States due to their ridiculous attitude to nuclear energy, and needless to say, their lack of any sensible gun laws. We must not be complacent and with all of those who are like-minded, we must revive their enthusiasm for nuclear energy as fast as possible. Lunatics, like those who choose names like Armageddon, must be brought on side before they do any more damage.'

'So shall I try to get hold of Matt to drive us back to the airport, Sir?'

'Yes, but without stopping for a cup of coffee this time!'

Eliot, Sam's second pilot, was waiting for them by the aircraft. 'Jenkins rang from England yesterday evening, Sir, to say that there is still no news of the Major. But shortly afterwards, I did have a problem, just as you said might happen, but it was quickly dealt with by the airport police.'

'Why, what happened, Eliot?' Bob enquired, looking concerned.

'At five minutes before midnight, two guys appeared on our infrared cameras walking towards the plane, each carrying what looked like a bomb. So I rang the police immediately and they were after them before I had put the phone down. When they were arrested, however, they were both found to be carrying not bombs but cans of yellow and red paint, with which they were about to spray graffiti all over your beautiful Gulfstream in support of their ruddy anti-nuclear campaign.'

'The same bunch of hooligans, I presume, who locked me up in Alcatraz, Sam. What an extraordinary country it is for going that far against the only method devised by man to save us all from frying. They were lucky that the Major was not with you, for he would have strangled them with his bare hands!'

They took off into a golden sunset and banking away towards the east, it took them less than two hours before they circling for a time while waiting to land at Salt Lake City, known throughout the world for its large population of Mormons.

'As you see, Eliot,' Bob remarked entering the cockpit after they had been parked. 'Salt Lake City is a busy airport. But while you guard my plane it is just as well that you will be unable to buy a drink here for, we are not out of the firing line yet. Nor will you have any luck with the ladies while we are away staying with Macey's parents for the night. The Mormons keep the women very much to themselves, indeed their founder once bagged more than twenty of them as his wives!'

'Your aircraft is a good enough girl for me, Sir, and we never drink while we are on duty. However, there must be some excellent skiing here looking at those snow-covered mountains I see in the distance. But don't worry, while you are away with Sam and Macey, for after what happened in Frisco, I have already checked all your security devices, which I can assure you are go.'

'OK then, Eliot, but stay alert. Remember there is a nuclear weapons test site just north of here in the Nevada desert, which once attracted the greatest number of protestors in the States.'

Bob, Sam and his beautiful fiancée then jumped into a taxi and headed south to spend the night at Macey's home, standing proudly on a promontory overlooking Utah Lake under Eagle Mountain.

But, as it turned out, it was not to be for one night only, for early the following morning when Greg, Macey's father, took them to see his research centre just north-west of the city, Bob was so impressed that for a moment, he was speechless.

'Great Scot!' He exclaimed. 'It is like a scene out of Quartermass, once on British TV. What the hell's going on here, Greg, we will have to stay here longer to take it all in. It looks astonishing.'

'It is, Bob.'

Everything the eye could see was white. The ceiling, walls and floor of the long building were all white. Only the black faces among the hundred or so plant microbiologists working there stood out. All of them, clad in white gowns with white hair nets, white masks and white gloves, were sitting two at a time leaning over narrow tables in four rows of brightly lit white painted booths, each fitted with glass screens. Only the plants stacked up on snow white trolleys looked different.

'Heavens, the place looks like the North Pole and with all that air conditioning feels like it as well! Why so much white, Greg?'

'Tissue culture is the multiplication of plant tissues under strict environmental conditions. Each of these pairs of microbiologists are highly skilled in their individual operations, which must never be compromised. The tiniest transfer of material from one booth to another would make our experiments totally worthless, so everything here is tightly regulated and coloured white so that the tiniest movements may be constantly monitored by cameras while the tables are kept spotless.'

'But what is all this effort leading to?'

'Possibly the greatest advance in plant propagation that man has ever undertaken, which, if properly managed, will provide many other advantages. Where plants are concerned, we are not only concentrating on eliminating disease, but producing drought resistant and other improved varieties over a very wide spectrum. Then, with our son, Jeb, we will be multiplying them as clones on a scale never before attempted, producing seed pods in almost limitless numbers.'

'So, Greg, are you the sole innovator, or are many others propagating plants in the same way?'

'Many of my methods have been copied elsewhere, but not all of them. What I am about to show you is also unique and totally secret. The only reason I am prepared to describe the process to you is because Macey has impressed me with the nature of your own courageous undertaking. We live with nuclear all around us here, not only with weapons tests, but also with several outmoded reactors, powered, no doubt, with your uranium, Bob?'

'Not so, Greg, Nuklin no longer supplies u-235 for making bombs, or feeding power stations. If we are to defeat climate change, they must change to a new type of nuclear fuel based on thorium.'

'Do I understand then, Bob, that you are one of the few people doing anything sensible about it?'

'Sensible, but I am often met with scepticism, derision and, too often, defiance when trying to get my voice heard.'

'Before we go next door, come to my office, Bob, and explain what you are trying to achieve.'

Greg's office was impressive by any standards. Computer screens were everywhere, as were thousands of specimens in glass jars, all clearly labelled on a countless number of shelves. As he stood there pointing out the different experiments being undertaken in his lab, he cut a fine figure in his cream silk shirt, grey summer suit and polished black shoes.

His dome of a forehead seemed to burst with intelligence and his carefully groomed blond hair, greying around the temples, confirmed that he was as immaculate as his laboratory. Bob thought he had made a friend for life. 'So, Bob, let's hear what you are up to, for Macey tells me she is still very much in the dark.'

'Climate change, or global warming as some prefer to call it, needs to be tackled on two fronts,' Bob started off. 'The first of these, which I am finding remarkably difficult, is to persuade the industrial world commencing with the United States, to give up their insatiable appetite for burning fossil fuels, not just by turning to renewables, which will never fill the gap, but to accept the impressive new forms of nuclear energy I mentioned, ridding our atmosphere of CO_2 forever.

'My second intention, Greg, which is equally important, is to stop the frightening amount of deforestation being carried out by those disregarding the resulting loss in carbon sequestration and the effect it will have on future generations. Then to replace all the trees lost, not over time but as fast as possible with the most advanced method ever conceived for planting vast areas of wilderness, including deserts, with a sufficient number of carbon eating plants, or trees, to ensure that sequestration is no longer an issue.'

'Sir, not only have you grabbed my attention, but also, need I say it, my admiration.'

'But both these projects, Greg, will require substantial backing from every national government and sane person on Mother Earth. And that will only happen, and our children and grandchildren left a life worth living, if we are able to defeat the lack of inertia pervading our world at the moment. We must banish all feelings of hopelessness and get stuck in to sorting out the problems of climate change with every practical method we can devise. Some of these, it is true, may require eye watering amounts of money, but aa was once the challenge of our infamous British highwaymen, Money or your Life!'

'So how do you propose planting those vast inhospitable areas, often subject to intolerable heat?'

'I have absolutely no idea, Greg!'

'Of course, I don't believe that, but I now realise why you have come to see us in Salt Lake City. It was not just for Macey to introduce us to Sam. After discovering who I was, you must have flown here looking for ways to propagate plants, or trees, in vast numbers. Trees, are not our speciality, as they take too long to grow, so we must find you some fast-growing plants that need little water.'

'Correct, that would be a huge help, Greg.'

'What goes on here may generally be described as asexual propagation which in layman's terms means identifying and selecting desirable traits in the genes of various plants, which, by manipulating their different chromosomes, allows us to combine them all into one perfect individual. But the difference here, which is right up your street, is that we are already learning to do this for drought resistant plants on a monumental scale. Of course, being able to demonstrate our results here in the Nevada desert gives us considerable advantages.'

'That all sounds impressive, but I am not so interested in succulents such the many varieties of cactus, which hold water within their hairy skins, or those low, spiky leaved plants, which save on evaporation. For neither of them will provide enough ground cover for my purposes.'

'Understood, Bob. You are correct in excluding the succulents with fleshy leaves, but there are some exceptions. You must also not exclude those with deep root systems trying to penetrate to where there is water, or those with shallow, widely spreading roots, that depend more on an occasional shower. In California, we also have a very different kind of plant once valued by the indigenous tribes for medicinal purposes, which they named yerba santa, the holy plant.

'It grows and multiplies from rhizomes lying just above, or just below the surface of parched earth, or sand, but is not what you may be looking for. All these plants depend on some water for photosynthesis, and most of them have a thin veneer of wax on their skins, or leaves, to limit evaporation. However, there is one unusual plant which exists with none of those things. Hated by those visiting the desert, they are generally known as tumbleweed.

'This may break off from different plants in the form of a ball of hay-like material, which then bowls along the ground in the slightest breeze blocking roads and annoying vehicle drivers. It also has another name—the resurrection plant. That's because it can live in its desiccated state for as long as a hundred years, one variety bursting into life after all that time by dropping roots when it rains.

'Our job here is to create plants for many different purposes and if your ideas are realistic and your project achievable, then I will set aside time to improve the drought resistant qualities of any plant we choose. But there is one other plant you may like to consider, being grown not far from here, which has most of the qualities you are looking for. So I will now tell you about it.'

'That would be invaluable, Greg. How exciting. What is the plant called?'

'Its Latin name is sansevieria, but it is otherwise known as snake plant or as mother-in-law's tongue. Bought usually as a pot plant, old people in California place them by their beds to purify the air without looking after them. But when planted outdoors in hot sunshine, it will grow rapidly to a diameter of over two metres, still not needing much water. Because it is one of the only plants that absorb carbon at night, once we have tinkered with its genes to make it even more drought proof, the possibilities for the Snake Plant are mind-blowing.

'Stay another night and we will look at it tomorrow. But first, I must to show you the spectacular machine I am working on next door. Do I understand, Bob, that you are a nuclear physicist?'

'Yes, I trained in nuclear sciences at the University of British Columbia in Vancouver.'

'Did you ever see their unique cyclotron then, used for studying the nucleus of atoms among other experiments. Ours, which we have named the multiplier, is tiny in comparison and only a poor man's attempt at copying it, for I was not able to see the cyclotron before it was finally dismantled. But one important feature it had in common is that it spins!'

They all laughed and Bob remarked, 'Well, at least you are not splitting atoms!'

'No just rhizomes,' he replied. 'However, they may need to be contained by root barriers eventually.'

'But you have not yet explained precisely what your people are doing in those booths.'

'First of all, we call the booths laminar flow cabinets as all our experiments are conducted in filtered air which largely involves slicing off segments from what we call explants. These may be taken not just from rhizomes but from several parts of the plants we wish to divide including shoots, leaves, flowers and roots, after which the tissue is immersed in a nutrient culture medium before being transferred in sterile containers to what is called our growth room.

'Known also as micropropagation, this not only allows us to produce fast growing clones of genetically modified plants, but to market them as being identical and free of disease in considerable numbers.'

'But how are you ever going to market them, Greg, it sounds virtually impossible'

'I will be showing you that shortly. Although, I first set up this laboratory entirely for research purposes, when our son, Jeb, joined me six months ago, we decided to expand the business into a commercial enterprise. However, if you come up with something visionary for saving mankind with our plants, Bob, I will be able to persuade the tax man that we have changed our business into a charity!'

'Now let's go and have a look at my new baby.'

Bob glanced across at Macey, who was seemed to be as intrigued as he was.

'You have no idea how switched on my brother is,' she said quietly after taking him aside. 'Dad has only just realised Jeb's potential for turning his small business into something sensational, able to deal on a far larger scale than he ever anticipated.'

But just as they walked towards Jeb's office door, it burst open and a tall young man in white dungarees strode into the centre of the room and ordered them in a firm but measured voice, 'Stop right there, all of you!'

Chapter 7

'It's not your baby, Dad!'

'Sorry, boy.' Then, looking suitably embarrassed, he said, 'Jeb, please take over.'

'Hi, Macey, my beautiful sister. Who are your friends then?'

Turning to Bob, she explained, 'This is my brother, Jeb, who studied engineering at Stanford and has since taken a masters in the subject. And this is Bob, who is the owner of the jet, which Sam here, who is now my fiancée, flies for him. Bob is here to save the world from self-immolation!'

'Good man. Then, like our Mormon friends, do you believe in repentance if you fail, Bob?'

'I'm not going to fail, Jeb, and if I started repenting, I would have no time left to save the world!'

'So apart from "saving the world", Dad, what is Bob really up to?'

'Saving the world, just as Macey has told us, son. For as Bob will explain to you, unless we crack global warming pretty soon, our temperature here will become so unbearable that every metal object, including your multiplier, Jeb, will melt into a puddle. However, Bob may well consider your machine to be invaluable, for he wishes to seed the empty areas of the world with more plants than he previously believed possible. But, as yet, he has no idea of how he is going to plant them, which, I am sure, you will be able to help him with in due course.'

Jeb, looking across at a man of over twice his age who, as far as he was concerned, had once lived with the dinosaurs, thought that he was not going to be impressed very easily.

'Bob, you had better have a look at this, which may, hopefully, be one step in the right direction.'

He led them to a smart new circular building with white walls about four metres high and a conical roof. The interior, which had no windows but extensive lighting, was nearly ten metres in diameter and had two small openings, one a narrow sliding door and opposite it an equally narrow, three metre high, vertical slit, fitted with rollers, which, once the newcomers had cooled off in the air conditioning, Jeb explained was for his new design of plant trays to be led through the building.

Most prominent was the three-metre-long rotating arm which reached out from the centre to gently stroke one of six hundred explants, or mother plants, which, Jeb indicated, had been clamped between two, horizontal, stainless-steel rings. Set every few centimetres between the explants were narrow stainless-steel tubes pointing outwards towards a three-metre-high metal cage fitted from top to bottom with more steel rollers. It all looked very mysterious.

'You will wonder what I have been up to here, if my father has not already told you. But he will have outlined his own research being carried out here and that, as a side line, we are already providing identical, certified, plants to local nurseries. But he may not have mentioned the more exciting wholesale plans we have been working up together ever since I joined the company. Before long we are intending to supply our plants throughout the whole of North America.'

'What, in those small plastic trays my gardener buys?'

'No, not plastic or small. But you have touched on one of the multiplier's advantages as it fires tiny slices of plant tissues into three metre wide by ten metres long megatrays made only of fibre.'

He pressed a button and the arm started turning as the first of three trays slid through the aperture.

'You will see that at the end of the arm, there is a razor-sharp blade and once the rings have been loaded up with explants between the small tubes I have pointed out, it will shave off minute slithers, which an air jet installed directly behind the cutter will blow down the tubes into the flexible megatrays mounted on the cage. Once the arm completes a circuit and a line of pockets in the megatrays has been filled, both it and the rings move up in 60-minute stages until all of them have been filled.'

'How ingenious, Jeb, but why have you stopped it operating so quickly?'

'Only, Bob, because my amazing sister, Macey, had already tipped me off about your plans so I have therefore had to re-designed the trays accordingly. You will see that half of the pockets have no bases. Into these I have inserted a few close-fitting pods, or pod darts, as I have called them. Here are three of the darts for each of you to examine.

'The darts, made from plant fibre, are five centimetres long and you will notice that the sharp ends hold the plant fragments, while the rear ends are pleated so that when the darts are shot into the ground by compressed air, their tails fan out like funnels to catch the morning dew.'

'They are inspirational, Jeb. But please tell us, will the trays be air transportable?'

'Of course. They are extremely strong but feather light, designed to fit neatly onto lorries and aircraft alike. But before stacking them, we fill the front end of the pod darts, already holding the plant fragments, with jellied fertiliser, sealing them with a thin, porous, membrane, much the same as bees close the cells in their honeycombs. If twenty trays, each carrying twelve thousand pod darts, are stacked onto a lorry, we will be shifting a quarter of a million plant pods at a time.'

'That is a spectacular number,' remarked Bob. 'But how does your father's team in his laboratory keep up with supplying so many explants?'

Jeb, who was three years older than Macey, had impressed Bob from the time he had first clapped eyes on him. For he was not only a successful innovator but a first-rate engineer, and with his confident manner and firm grip of his subject, Bob thought he would go far and was someone he should bear very much in mind for the future, as he recorded in his encyclopaedic memory.

'To answer your question, Sir, once we have found a suitable explant, then our workforce will be turned to producing several thousand of them per day. On average, each explant is capable of being sliced more than a hundred times, so there is unlikely to be a supply problem!'

'I am dumbfounded. Then we must find the right plant, and once your father has improved its drought resistance, think up a way of drilling millions of its clones produced by your multiplier.'

'Of course, and it will be no surprise to you after what Macey told me, that I am eager to have a go at creating your super drilling machine. It is not going to be easy as no land driven vehicle will ever be large enough, or capable enough, of planting more than a miserable area of land per day.'

'Time to go, boys and girls,' announced Bob. 'Thanks, Jeb, and also please thank your father for showing us around his side of the business. But we still don't know the company name.'

'For security reasons, we never flash that around too much. There are many competitors after our secrets, and should they find out too much about what we are up to would be disastrous. But the name for you to forget is PlantX. That's only because Dad is such a fan of Elon Musk's SpaceX.'

Bob would not forget the name, and as they were driven back to Macey's family home by Greg's driver, he asked her to note down all Jeb's contact details.

They were welcomed back to the house by Rosie, Greg's wife, a fine-looking lady in her early fifties with cornflower blue eyes and a figure almost as good as her daughter's. The sun was just beginning to dip behind the mountains opposite, and the house, backed by a vineyard and fronted by the shimmering lake below, were quickly being turned into a molten tableau of pure gold.

'You have a beautiful place,' Bob remarked. 'Thinking about our land speed record attempts on the Bonneville salt flats nearby, I had thought your lake would be similarly saline, but I was wrong. Your driver tells me that it is barely salty and full of plump carp, which he catches for his supper.'

'Well done him, but we are lucky enough to have our own pool, so we don't need to go down there. However, many people also swim in the lake, or go out in their boats on it.'

When Greg returned from his office, he mentioned to him how fertile the soil looked and how laden with grapes the vines were on the far side of his garden wall.

'This is a land of contrasts,' he explained. 'Up in those mountains it gets very cold at night while, although it is hotter than your English summers down here, it is always bearable and the soil is reasonably productive. Tomorrow, we will leave Macey and Sam to get on with their canoodling while we take a look at those snake plants, which I mentioned earlier, in a place where it only rains once, or twice, a year if they are lucky! It is just north of Las Vegas, three hundred miles away to the south west, so we will fly there in the plane I keep in my garden shed.'

The following morning dawned with a cloudless blue sky disturbed only by some white fronted geese and a number of blue herons taking noisily to the air.

'Before we set off Rosie, will give you some of her excellent waffles soaked in the maple syrup we collect in the fall, when we fly to our home in Vermont to celebrate Thanksgiving there later. The East Coast colours are the best anywhere and it gives us all a break from the plant business.'

They walked over to his "hangar", and Bob, who was preparing to see an ancient Tiger Moth was delighted when Greg's plane turned out to be a replica of a German Fieseler Storch, similar to the one Hitler used when visiting Berlin throughout the war. The aircraft had also been made famous by pilots such as Hermann Geiger, for his precarious mountain rescues in the Swiss Alps.

'This is my plane,' announced Greg, with the shortest take-off and landing capabilities of any machine flying. In the Alps, they are equipped with skis, but here in Utah, I have fitted my own aircraft with balloon type tyres so I may land it safely in the desert.'

They were airborne well before they reached the garden fence, then, as they climbed steeply over Eagle Mountain, all they could see ahead was a rash of blue sage bushes dotted widely over a sandy desert until they became lost in the distant heat haze. 'Not much to see yet,' Greg said over the intercom as he pointed to a place on his map marked as Death Valley.

'Early in the last century, at Furnace Creek, the thermometer one day reached nearly fifty degrees centigrade, which, at that time, was the highest temperature ever recorded on the surface of the earth. That record has already been broken and it will continue to get even hotter as the earth heats up due to climate change, unless someone, like you Bob, does something dramatic about it.'

'At least I, and hopefully many others, including you and your son, Greg, are now on the case. But if I had known we were headed for Death Valley, forget the waffles, I should have stowed away some bacon and eggs on board, I could have fried them to perfection on the wing!'

'You stick to Rosie's maple syrup, my boy. It sure is going to be hot, but the plant nursery we are visiting is some way short of Death Valley and not far from a watering hole you may have heard of called Indian Springs.'

'Hi,' said a lanky looking type wearing a stetson on the back of his head of wild, yellow, hair, after they had taxied up to a wooden shack half concealed by a stand of Judas trees. 'Welcome to the land of milk and honey, folks. Only there ain't no cows, or bees in this goddam hole—just cactus!'

'I'm told that Jesse here,' Greg said, placing a hand on the fellow's shoulder, 'who I have never clapped eyes on before, and may never wish to do again, will tell you that he has the best desert nursery anywhere, which we are about to find out. So take us around, cowboy.'

'Folks, tell me what you're after and we'll go a lookin for it. My place is known on the planet as Hot House Heaven, for it has every variety of desert plant known to man, as I am about to show you.'

'That's right, Jesse, but there is only one particular plant we are interested in. I know very little about it but one of our customers told me that you can show us one or two of them.'

'What's its name, pilot?'

'It's called sansevieria, or more commonly known as snake plant.'

'Damn that bloody varmint, for I was trying to keep those plants secret. You see it is normally considered only as a house plant, but I'm no ruddy groundhog like the rest of 'em try'n to pinch my ideas, who are fast asleep most of the year. The first time I saw one of 'em snakes sitting in a pot in my granny's house in Reno, it got me in the guts. You see old ladies depend on the plants. Apart from look'n pretty, they say that the snake takes all the impurities out of the air.

'That is why, its other name is mother-in-law's tongue. But on further research, pilot, I discovered that it not only chews up carbon dioxide but is about the only plant that does so at night. How's about that!'

'It's the very reason we have come to have a look at it, Jesse.'

'What, all that way from Salt Lake City, you said, just to look at a wretched little house plant?'

'No, come clean,' Greg growled. 'You know why we are here, Jesse. Where are you hiding them?'

'OK, pilot, so what are you going to pay me for all that know how I have gathered about the plant. You understand that I flew all the way down to Nigeria to find out why in West Africa it grows in their hot climate like a mad thing.'

'Then show it to us, cowboy.'

'Not before we do a deal, pilot. If I show you the plants, whatever your name is, first you must tell me why you are so interested in it, and second, mister, you must agree to spend five thousand dollars on promoting the snakes for me in Vegas, once I have cultured a hundred decent specimens to sell 'em.'

'It will not surprise you, Jesse, that I am one of those dreadful microbiologists experimenting with tissue culture. So why don't we say after a hundred of the plants, which if you let me have one or two to take away, I can arrange for you before the moon is full!'

'Cripes, you mean that, mister. Let me write this down on paper and then get you to sign it for me.'

'So where the hell are they in this crazy place of yours? All I can see from here are the cactus you were talking about, and with them so many types of succulents it is impossible to count them. Then there are the agaves, aeoniums, aloes, crassulas, saguaros, spurges and those yuccas over there, let alone your grove of Joshua trees plus all those beautiful adenium obesum, or desert roses, and countless varieties of grasses.'

'Crikey, pilot, you certainly know your plants then!'

'You asked me why I was so interested in sansevieria and the answer is straightforward, Jesse. It was because Bob here, who had heard of your aspirations to become the saviour of mankind from the other side of the Pond. He is out to mop up the CO2 rising from all those coal-fired factories and generating stations fouling the air down south.'

'So I've been blown out of the water already?'

'You have, Jesse. But perhaps your granny spilt the beans long ago?'

At the far end of the crowded nursery, there was a pile of boulders and beyond that only sand and a cleared area of the sage where Greg's aircraft was parked.

'So here we are,' said Jesse, skirting around a low wall of rocks above which they noticed just the tips of some dark green, spiky, leaves showing. 'This is my secret army preparing for war.'

'So tell us about them?'

'Well, there are no less than twelve different varieties of sansevieria, all grown from rhizomes and all largely indestructible. But my experiments were only with those I thought suitable for growing to a decent size and surviving in the battlefield for long periods without water.'

'So which variety have you now gone for?'

'There is one called dracaena trifasciata, which may fit your purpose perfectly. It already has various cultivars, which you, pilot, will no doubt be able to improve upon. Trifasciata, which thrives in Nigeria, is linked with Ogun, the African spirit of war, and used in their rituals to remove the evil eye. The plant exchanges oxygen for carbon dioxide, allowing them to withstand long periods of drought.

'Because I am talking to someone posh, I'll tell you why this plant is so exceptional, for exposed to hot sunshine it will grow to more than two metres in diameter from a simple rhizome fast, spreading just under, or above the ground, quite freely. It also yields bowstring hemp, folks, useful one day for replacing plastic with plant fibre. The natives made their bow strings from it.

'Look at my young plants here and you can see the microscopic pores on the leaves of the snake, called stomata, which, unlike other plants, open at night to prevent any moisture evaporating when the sun comes up.'

It was just at that moment, Greg thought he heard a muffled rattling noise. But Bob, by craning over the plants, failed to see the reptile's head poking out of a crevice, and as it struck, moved a fraction too late. 'Dam,' he shouted, jumping back, 'that ruddy snake has bitten me on the shin!'

'Stop where you are!' Jesse yelled, kicking the snake away, but too late. 'That rattler is a killer!'

Chapter 8

Ana. Beautiful Brazilian doctor

As the rainforest came bursting into life, the Major plucked up courage to tell Ana he was leaving.

'Ana, the time has come for me to drag myself away from your uncle and aunt's hospitality and somehow return to Cuiaba to ring my boss and explain why I have not dealt those arsonists yet.'

'Do you mean that you want to hitch a lift with me?' She queried with her eyes twinkling.

'No, of course not!' He joked. 'If Bob was here, he would have been so furious about my hopeless lack of progress that he would have left me to walk.'

'I doubt that, sunny Jim. From here to Brasilia, where I work, is approximately eight hundred kilometres. or say five hundred miles, which driving Esmeralda at her favourite speed normally takes me the best part of eight hours. But with you on board, Jim, it is bound to take longer!'

'What is Esmeralda then—a miserable old three wheeled jalopy?'

'How I wish I knew your real name, wild man. No, she is a beautiful emerald green Porsche Carrera 911. But I know you will complain about my fast driving on these terrible roads.'

'Great Scot, do bring her around to show me the lady at once, Ana. I thought I noticed something flashy parked in the barn at the far side of your uncle's farmyard.'

When Ana, telling him to keep his eyes shut, fetched Esmeralda, he found the car astonishing.

'What a speed machine and certainly no lady, Ana. I know only too well that the 911 GT3 is tested to reach over one hundred and ninety miles an hour. But why is it finished in that livid green, for even the forest birds must be scared by it! Did you choose that colour yourself?'

'No, it wasn't me. My father chose the colour when he gave me the car as my twenty-first birthday present. My dear parents had not seen me for ages as I was away studying at your Cambridge University. But sadly, after they had organised a party for me in Rio, I had to leave Esmeralda behind for several months while I completed my degree course in England.

'When I returned, I asked my father the same question. He put his arm around me and explained that with my looks, I was bound to get into trouble. As it was probably the only car painted like that in the whole of South America, he said that he would, therefore, always be able to keep an eye on me.'

'You realise, Ana, that in England green cars are often considered to be unlucky?'

'Well not Esmeralda, Jungle Jim. Perhaps emerald green is different and more appropriate for this part of the world whatever you say. She has since made me feel so happy that when I returned to England, I won a double first in biology and medicine!'

'And you have never looked back since?'

'No, since meeting you, Jim, and Esmeralda now has only one gear and that is fast forward!'

She did not look like Fangio, but he watched spellbound as she sat down behind the wheel in a pale-yellow cotton dress with her hair blowing in the breeze, knowing her driving would be no different.

'OK, having thumbed a lift I suppose I will now have to risk my neck with you. And as I have nothing to bring with me apart from Rick's clothes I am wearing, I may just be able to squeeze into your rocket ship given several tranquillisers. However, I have one last request, Ana?'

'Of course, tell me what it is, Sir Jim, before I drive you to the scaffold.'

'There is a problem, Ana. Instead of heading straight for Brasilia, due to the fact I am no longer able to deal immediately with the man who rented me his flying bomb at Cuiaba airport, please may we drive via Paranatinga, for I am convinced that the arsonists behind the frightening increase in the number of fires destroying your forest, must have their South American hideout there.'

'Once we have said goodbye, let's do that, and if they get hold of you and try to kill you, I will just have to leave you there.'

Rick had come out of the farmhouse with Francisca to wave them goodbye.

'Rick, I am so unhappy about those poor Indians who carried me here. Everything you are doing for them and everyone here is hugely important and we must keep closely in touch. And, Francisca, thank you for helping to save my life, which Ana will, no doubt, have to do again.'

'What does he mean by that, Ana?' Francisca asked, looking decidedly nervous.

'We are about to embark together on what may be an even more dangerous mission than the wild man has just survived. Keep your fingers crossed for us and should we manage to make it back to my flat in Brasilia, I will let you know what happened immediately I get there. It seems that he is asking me to drive him into the jaws of death! Goodbye and look after yourselves until, if all goes according to plan, I will be back to see you again on my next break from the hospital.'

But there was no plan and as she stretched her long elegant legs under the dashboard and her slim brown arms over the wheel, she let out a whoop of joy as they disappeared into the unknown in a boiling cloud of red of dust.

'So to war in a Porsche!' He enthused.

'You must have told Rick about leaving yesterday. How did you two get on together?' She asked.

'He is one of the most inspiring characters I have ever met, Ana, and should be rewarded for his defence of the indigenous Indians and the Amazon rainforest. His rapport with the tribes in the Xingu National Park is remarkable, and by stressing both the value of the forest and the importance of them holding on to all their territory, he seems to be making some progress with members of the government, but not the president.

'It is unbelievable that he is now saying that because the Indians own too much of the forest, they are preventing agriculture from expanding. Does he not understand the damage he is also doing to the world outside? Rick told me he is using words like past protected about the Xingu National Park so frequently that it had almost driven the Indians to fight for their freedom. However, as their weapons consist largely of spears and bows and arrows, he admitted they did not stand a chance.

'Their only defence, he told me, are their darts, dipped in toxin from the bark of curare vines and then shot through long blowpipes, which I noticed while I was with them. If only the so-called farmers, Rick stated, would manage their grazing better.

'As you know, Rick is also trying to encourage more research into regenerating the forest which, at the moment, is being farmed to exhaustion, or as he says to extinction. Once the topsoil with its humus has gone, it makes it impossible to re-plant the bare land with trees. Instead, the farmers the loggers and, worse still, the unlicensed gold miners, care little about laying waste to the extraordinary biodiversity for which the Amazon rainforest is so famous.

'No one realises, as much as he does, the importance of the tree canopy, for without it, as we know, the rain will stop falling and what remains of the forest plus all its exotic flora and fauna will be no more.'

'And with it the vitally important role it plays in the world for sopping up all that deadly carbon!'

'Precisely, Ana. That is why the Indian reserves are also so important and Rick, rightly, is so determined to stop any further violation of their protected territory by ensuring that the indigenous tribes throughout the rainforest have better security of tenure. Did he ever tell you about the dreadful massacre perpetrated in the twenties by a rich rubber baron near Manaus, who ordered his men to throw sticks of dynamite into an Indian village and then to slaughter those still left alive with their machetes.

'Such brutality was not uncommon and still continues today, but in a smaller and far more surreptitious manner. He tells me that some tribes in the Xingu Reserve and others, which may not yet be known about, have seen their land being stolen from them every day that passes and the government, led by their president, is wickedly encouraging that.'

'Although, Rick has been brilliant with his Sustainable Trade Initiative, Jim, I'm afraid that if this and all his other ideas fail to halt the destruction of our rainforest, he will enact something terrible to sort the problem out for good and all before it is too late. He may have already told you about what he has in mind for it may be the only way to bring the Brazilian government to its senses.'

'So, Ana, forgetting your uncle for a moment, perhaps we should concentrate on the job in hand. When I flew over Paranatinga before my plane fell out of the sky, I noticed the town was situated on ground well away from the fast-receding river. As I flew over it, right on the grid reference the crook gave me, I noticed a building perched on the old river bank with a drive running to it. It seemed to be a small guest house and is likely to be from where the arsonists are running their operations. No doubt it is also from where they ordered that bastard to shoot me down.'

'So what will be your plan of attack, Jim?'

'I will not have one until I have crept up on the place to take a closer look. Initially, you will have to hide Esmeralda as close as possible to the building but from where you are able to get back onto the road in a hurry.'

They had been driving for about three hours, when he said, 'Ana, stop right here. Over to the right of the road, you will see the building I spied from the air. So best to hide behind that derelict barn over on the left, while I crawl forwards to take a closer look from under the river bank.'

The area was not ideal for a military operation. Due to most of the region's rainforest being destroyed, the diminishing amount of rainfall had caused the Rio Paranatinga to dwindle to a trickle, leaving its bank to crumble away to nothing in places while all around were flat expanses of red sandy soil with hardly a tree visible with the building standing out like a sore thumb.

'Do be careful, Jim, if that neglected looking guest house is where the arsonists are operating from, crossing all the open ground surrounding it will be extremely dangerous.'

'Unfortunately, Ana, because the delivery note I found on the man strangled by the anaconda disintegrated in the pocket of my boxer shorts when Francisca washed them, all I have left as evidence of these criminals is that shard of metal you found for me. But as tracing them through a part number may not be possible, I must now obtain more proof. So my intention is to cause as little disturbance as possible while I do that. Rick has warned me that should I not succeed, the police will take no notice of us whatsoever when we go to see them in Brasilia.'

'What sort of evidence are you looking for? There's no room in the boot for a stiff, Jimbo!'

'A dead Indonesian would have been best, but since I stupidly left my weapon in a lock up at Cuiaba airport, probably too difficult, even should be able to use my hands. No, just what I can grab plus some telling photos on your cell phone if you will be kind enough to lend it to me?'

Handing it over, all she was able to do was wish him luck and wait in trepidation for his return.

Shoving her phone in his trouser pocket, he started moving swiftly across a small field before jumping down over the dry river bank. Although, being forced to crawl at times, it did not take him long to reach the building standing twenty metres back from the bank beyond two abandoned sun terraces. HOSPIDARIA TUCANO it read in flaking red lettering above a row of missing windows, with a pile of rotting deck chairs stacked below.

He took a quick photograph, then cursing that the entrance must be on the far side of the building near a car park, he returned to give Ana a quick thumbs up, before jamming the battered straw hat Rick had given him well down over his eyes. He then walked along the road and strode through a pair of rusty iron gates, he had noticed previously, down a short, deeply pitted, drive as if looking for somewhere to stay.

Before arriving at the entrance, he noticed that the car park was empty apart from three sinister looking black vehicles parked directly outside the hostel, one appearing to be a truck with cross country tyres fitted, and the others unmarked, black vans shod similarly. So he took several more photographs before entering the building, where he found the hall deserted apart from a sallow looking female in a purple jumpsuit sitting behind an empty rattan-faced desk fiddling with a pen.

'Can I help?' She asked, languidly.

Thinking fast and pretending that he knew no known language, the Major indicated that he was waiting for his wife to join him and, pointing at a chair, sat down on it, with his hat still hiding his face. For although, he did not expect to be recognised, throughout the length of his clandestine career as a mercenary, he knew that he could always be picked out in a crowd later.

Almost an hour had passed before two men armed with Pindad revolvers, he recognised, appeared from a back room, both, much to his satisfaction, appearing to be Indonesian. Then one of them, probably the boss, after making a crude gesture at the receptionist, threw open the front door to allow his mate, who was carrying a heavy metal box, to pass through.

So far, so good, he thought, taking a quick photograph of them, but although he had caught the bastards red-handed, fearing they were off to do more damage, he decided to act immediately.

Creeping out into the car park, he hid behind the truck as they opened one of the vans' doors. Then moving swiftly forward, he accosted the men. 'Greetings,' he said, lunging forward at the man he thought was the boss with a straight left, who crashed to the ground in a heap, not realising what had hit him. Then, before his friend had time to react, he also clobbered him so hard that he fell into the back of the van as if poleaxed with the metal box landing heavily on top of him as the lid flew open.

The box was there for the taking, but calculating that it was too heavy to run with it, he already had his hands under the lid when he heard the sound of a third man heading frantically towards him.

With not a moment to lose, he quickly found what he was looking for, and grabbing one sample from the rows of copper cylinders packed within it, he sprinted as quickly as he could to the corner of the house, then flat out across the two terraces where he caught one foot on the pile of deck chairs. As he sprawled defenceless onto the broken concrete slabs, two shots rang out driving a furrow through one of them. So shoving the cylinder into his trouser pocket, he picked up a piece of concrete and using it as a shield, dived back into the house through one of the missing windows.

'You took longer than expected. What happened?' Ana asked anxiously as he finally appeared from the direction of the river bank.

'Last things first. It was the receptionist there who saved me. For as I passed through the front door for a second time, she slammed it shut right in the face of the fellow with a gun following me.'

'So if that is the vital evidence you were after poking out of your pocket, let's get out of here, fast! Esmeralda needs no encouragement, Jimbo. Please pop my cell phone back into my top pocket, then hold on for dear life as I stamp on the accelerator, for they are bound to follow us.'

They did.

Esmeralda had the heels on them but only just. The car, unaccustomed to such harsh treatment, was bouncing so hard over the uneven surface of the road that on several occasions, they nearly left the narrow strip of tarmac and plunged into the thorn bushes growing along both of its sharp edges.

'If we are thrown sideways, we are dead meat, Jimbo. How far behind are they?' She shouted, as the dust stopped obliterating everything behind them for a brief moment.

'About a kilometre, Ana, but you're doing fine.'

It had first seemed to him that, apart from the road surface, she was having to pace her precious car far too carefully, but after two hours had passed, she admitted controlling Esmeralda's enthusiasm, saying that due to his blasted detour, they were soon going to run short of fuel.

'I should have thought of that, Ana. How could there ever be a petrol station on this filthy track.'

'If we can make it, which I doubt unless we slow down completely and let the buggers catch up with us, there is a fuel station on the next decent road we come to. It is just before Primavera, where we turn left onto the main highway, and is where I always fill up when returning from staying with Rick and Francisca. After that nothing will pass Esmeralda until we reach Brasilia.'

'Well why don't we let them catch up. They cannot overtake us on this narrow strip of tarmac and if you jam on the lady's brakes suddenly, if we are lucky, they will catapult into the bushes.'

'Don't tempt me to throw you out and save weight, wild man, for I'm not going to have my poor frustrated Esmeralda drilled with bullet holes. We will just have to hope for the best and keep going as we are. If we reach the garage alive, I will get the man on the pump to call the police.'

But when they finally pulled in with the tank showing empty, the pump attendant was not there and, although she drove the car fast around to the back of the building, it was almost too late.

Almost immediately they saw the black pickup joining the road with two men in the cab and another standing in the back holding a rifle. But rather than stop, it sped on towards Primavera.

'Wow, surely they must have spotted us?' She whispered.

'No need to whisper, Ana. I am sure they did, for how could anyone not see your green goddess. It only means that our situation has become twice as dangerous. The odds are now stacked against us, for they will now wait for us in ambush not far ahead this side of Primavera. Yet it is the only route we must take to get you back to your hospital. The answer is for us to wait here until another car passes and then tuck closely in behind it where we cannot be seen until the last moment.'

An anxious twenty minutes passed before they heard a vehicle approaching far away in the distance.

'Quick, Ana, now we have paid that idle man, ask him if I can borrow the knife he has tucked into his belt. While we wait for that car to pass, I'm going to scrape off some of the wax stopper on this copper tube I have in my pocket. This nasty object, which I was hoping to keep as evidence, is one of their highly volatile phosphorus grenades they have been using to set fire to the rainforest. The phosphorus will ignite spontaneously when it hits the air and is our only means of defence.'

When the vehicle, they had heard in the distance, at last passed by the garage, it turned out to be an ancient tractor towing a high sided grain trailer. So, while Ana, who was looking nervous, drove out onto the road and positioned her Porsche as closely as possible directly behind it, the mercenary continued scraping away all but the last of the wax, hoping it would not incinerate them.

'Just the job, Ana. If we are lucky, they will be taking that load of corn right into Primavera, but as it will be moving so slowly, we will have to act very fast if those bastards start shooting at Esmeralda before I fix them with this fire stick. So why don't you search for any likely ambush to the left of the road and I will search to the right. Jeepers, that garage man must be after us for his knife. Look, he is already closing in right behind us on his motorbike! Watch out, Ana! I can already see their truck part hidden behind some bushes on my side of the road barely fifty metres ahead!'

There was no time to dodge around the far side of the trailer, so slicing off the last of the wax with one swipe of the knife, before they had a chance to spot them, the Major opened his door and threw the cylinder far out into the back of their truck as accurately as possible.

There was no explosion, only a blinding white flash as it struck the truck, igniting some fuel and reducing the two men crouching behind it to cinders.

'Hooray!' Ana shouted. But it was too soon.

The sharp crack of a rifle bullet as it punched a hole in the door he was trying to shut and through the dashboard directly in front of him, startled Ana into immediate action. Hardly noticing the second bullet as it smashed through a side window, where his head had just been, and ricocheted off the roof into the back of driver's seat, Ana was already stamping so hard on the accelerator pedal that Esmeralda, with tyres screaming, almost spun out of control.

Then as she passed the corn trailer, wagging her tail, she cannoned off into a field raising such a cloud of dust that they were too late to run over the third man, who had nearly killed them, crouching behind a thorn bush.

'Good girl,' she shouted gleefully, thumping the steering wheel. 'Do you realise, Jim, that Esmeralda can reach one hundred miles per hour in under four seconds!'

'I do now, Ana, but you had better slow down and pull in to the side of the road as soon aa possible for there is blood streaming down your left arm and beginning to stain that pretty dress of yours.'

As they pulled in under the first decent tree they had come across since leaving the rainforest, he ripped off his shirt and asked her to sit down on a broken limb, while he gently unfastened her belt and lifted her blood-soaked dress up over her shoulders.

'Don't worry about the nudie bit, I never wear a bra and sunbathe topless, so what's different?'

What's the difference! He thought while trying to bind up her bleeding shoulder. The difference was that she had the most perfect pair of tits he had ever clapped his eyes on during all his wild life.

'Now jump into the passenger seat as I am going to drive you to your hospital in Brasilia, for although I must now have lost everything, I am not going to lose you, Ana.'

'What do you mean by lost everything, Jim?'

'We should have nailed that third clever bastard who was waiting several metres away from the others to shoot us with his rifle. For even should the garage man, who will have seen it all happen, not bother to report the grisly scene, the next people driving past on the road are certain to have called the police. Ana, I'm afraid that when the police catch that third man, after being told by the garage attendant instead of two charred bodies there should have been three, and that he had witnessed me flinging an incendiary device into the back of their pickup, I will be dead meat.

'Apart from those photographs I took on your phone in Paranatinga, and the metal shard I have in my bag, all I had to pin on the gang was the phosphorus cylinder I threw at the bastards, which must have been destroyed with them. But it could have been worse. If I had not placed your phone into the left-hand pocket of your dress, the bullet would have killed you.'

'As, I'm afraid, it must have killed those crucial photographs you took of them earlier, Jim!'

'Precisely. So how am I going to convince the police about the bastards now, or complete Bob's task without that evidence. Although, we have dealt with two of them, the others must be laughing.'

They were entering Primavera and about to hit route 770, the fast federal highway linking Caceres to Brasilia. 'So, darling Ana, you must not only press hard on Rick's shirt, which I gave you to stop the bleeding, but hold on to your seat like a limpet, while, at last, I give Esmeralda the gun!' With the speedometer reading one hundred and seventy miles per hour, as if their luck had not run out already, he noticed a police motorcycle pull out of a cutting they had just passed with its siren blaring and blue lights flashing.

'Crikey! Ana, is there a speed limit here in Brazil?' But she had slumped into unconsciousness.

As he knew the policeman was able to outpace even Ana's pride and joy, he slowed down and pulled into the next lay-by he could find.

'Do you know how fast you were driving? Do you know what the speed limit is on this highway?' The policeman yelled, lifting the front of his white helmet.

'Forget the speed limit, copper,' Ana said bravely, having lifted herself up from the folded down passenger seat. Then pointing at her shoulder. 'You will see how badly I am hurt. This is a gunshot wound, which my driver will be reporting to your police in Brasilia once he has delivered me to hospital there. Do not delay us any longer but go and find the gunman, who was waiting for us with his rifle by a white building on the right-hand side of the road twenty kilometres this side of Caceres. He has no vehicle and is there for the taking. Go get yourself promoted, big feller!'

The young policeman, lost for words, had never been spoken to in such terms before. Jumping back onto his Honda Transalp before revving it up in a fury, he vanished in a puff of exhaust smoke totally in the wrong direction.

'So tell me the name of your hospital and how to get there, Ana?'

But when he looked over at her, she was back in the land of nod.

The parched Brazilian countryside was already disappearing and as he drove through a small town called Girassol on the outskirts of the capital, he pulled onto the hard shoulder and tried asking her the way many times until, for a fleeting moment she opened her eyes and listened to him.

'Turn left at the lights. Ask for Hospital de Crianca,' she said in a thin voice before fainting again.

The ultra-modern hospital, which he later found out was the best in town, had an impressive entrance set in a red stucco, single storey, building surrounded by colourful flower beds with a fountain playing in the centre. So when Ana was wheeled into a room bordering on a second, scented, rose garden, he knew that she would not take too long to recover.

'We were forced to operate,' announced a surgeon in a purple gown, beckoning him aside two hours later. 'Poor girl, she works here you know. Perhaps you should keep hold of the bullet, which was lodged dangerously close to her brachial artery. We have notified the police and you should hand it over to them when they arrive. Ana is now suffering from trauma and must be watched overnight by us here in the hospital, Senhor.'

'I have already told the police about the incident, doctor. Meanwhile, because I have nowhere to sleep and they may wish to interview me, would it be possible to steal a bed in your hospital?'

'No, that will not be possible, Senhor Major, for we understand that is your name. The police have informed us that, once they have interviewed you, they have a nice bed for you themselves.'

Chapter 9

'Son of a bitch!' Jesse exclaimed, watching the four-foot snake slither back between two of the rocks still rattling its tail end defiantly. 'That was a Mojave, the most venomous rattler of them all!'

Bob, who was wearing shorts and a polo shirt, was looking down at his right shin where the marks of the snake's two fangs were clearly visible.

'Hold still, mate, and keep your arms down, we must not let the poison, which will already be coursing into your bloodstream, drip down into your heart. That would be curtains.'

Then turning to Greg. 'This is mighty serious, pilot, we must get him to hospital in less than twenty minutes, or the bloke's done for.'

'The bloke,' Bob stated, sitting down on a rock, 'has been in serious trouble ever since he arrived in the USA! For I have certainly not found that American Dream all you folks talk about. Instead, Jesse, after just a few days in your country, the Dream has turned into a bloody nightmare!'

'So while I decide where to fly you to,' Greg interrupted, 'Jesse must help you limp across to my aircraft as fast as possible, but with extreme care and without stirring up your circulation.'

The decision was not an easy one. Either he must fly to the hospital Greg knew in Indian Springs, which had a helipad but no landing strip, or to the US Nellis Airforce Base, which was closer. So he chose Nellis, where they had not only an efficient medical centre but Jesse hoped the correct anti-serum, knowing that the Mojave rattlesnake would be also native to their own rugged terrain. 'Hullo, sierra, lima, victor, this is Fieseler Storch November 88, permission to land immediately with a snake bite casualty.'

'Come right in, 88. Runway 21 left, QFE three zero. We will have an ambulance waiting.'

They did, and when they arrived at the medical centre with Bob already beginning to experience blurred vision and difficulty in breathing, there was a guy in US Airforce uniform to greet them.

'Hi, welcome to Nellis. Were you directed here by our 6th Medical Recruiting Battalion in Vegas?'

'No, only by our man Jesse here, who they would never think of recruiting unless they were stark, raving mad! Let's for God's sake get our friend here in front of a doctor before he snuffs it.'

While Bob was being treated, the airman did not let up. 'You understand Nellis is known as the home of ace fighter pilots, famous for TV series like Thunderbirds. In the days it had a bad reputation, it was known as Paradise Ranch, but that's all changed now. Hear this, gents, we are now the top school for training international air combat pilots anywhere you like to name, and it's a privilege to have you with us.'

'Perhaps,' mentioned Greg, 'it helps me to understand what goes on in area 51 as they now call it, for Sam, the pilot of Bob's Gulfstream, who was recently trained by you, has told us that this airforce base is still no paradise, indeed far from it. Apparently, people would once crowd in here to watch the nuclear tests going on in the desert, until there were such a violent outcry against them, that, in total, no less than fifteen thousand demonstrators were arrested.'

'OK, man, you have me there as I was far too small at the time to get excited by mushroom clouds. However, they tell me that there were several hundred detonations at the time, making areas of the Nevada desert dangerously radioactive, just as much as nuclear power stations do today.'

'It would be best, airman, for you to talk to Bob about that, if you get a chance before we leave.'

Luckily, Bob recovered very quickly and when they lifted off from the runway almost vertically, they saw the man saluting them goodbye. Bob, of course, had found him to be an easy convert.

So having dropped off Jesse, who had finally given Greg a couple of snake plants to experiment with, they flew back to land beside Utah Lake just in time to have some more of Rosy's maple syrup muffins which she brought to them on a tray with two cups of strong Californian tea.

'You poor man,' she said to Bob. 'I hope you are not always in the wars. Did you tread on it?'

'No, Rosy, I had just parted the leaves of one of these snake plants we have brought back with us, when the reptile must have decided he had a relation. However, Jesse assured us it is not called a snake plant because it encourages snakes, even as it looks like one. He said it is because it grows from rhizomes, which send shoots snaking fast across the ground like them But I hope that is an exaggeration. If not, maybe you husband can slow them down with his genetic engineering!'

'Thanks for telling me about it, Bob, because Greg is saying that the plant may be just the breakthrough you have been looking for. Once you can think up a method of distributing it, working with my husband and Jeb, who is so clever at inventing things, he says that it could become valuable for fighting climate change. So the best of luck with it!'

Eliot was waiting by the aircraft which had been re-fuelled for the long flight back to Exeter.

'Change of plans, Eliot. Are we also OK for Vienna?' Bob asked him.

'Bob has been in trouble again for he has now been bitten by a rattlesnake,' Sam explained. 'Also being out of touch with his mercenary is not helping. However, he has largely recovered and is now in high spirits due to the visit here at Salt Lake being so successful. Indeed, Macey's parents and her brother have come up trumps for him regarding plant technology. But, although we must admire Bob's determined attempt to get the Yanks on side, The American Dream continues to bug him, for he believes that unless they stop their nuclear nonsense soon, they won't be dreaming any longer.'

**

Vienna unlike the American Dream, is known as the "City of Dreams", largely because Sigmund Freud, of psychoanalysis fame, once lived there. However, it is now better known for its music as Mozart, Hayden, Brahms, Shubert and Beethoven among other famous composers all worked there. Not to forget Vienna's celebrated concerts, or the stirring Strauss waltzes.

But it is also known as a centre for technology, and home to many notable international institutions. But, surprisingly, one of them, the International Atomic Energy Agency, is known only to a few.

The IAEA states that it seeks to promote the peaceful expansion of nuclear energy and to inhibit its use for military purposes, including the production of nuclear weapons. Established in 1957 as the result of a proposal by Dwight D. Eisenhower, it reports to both the United Nations General Assembly and the Security Council. So there was every reason why Bob wished to visit the IAEA as next on his agenda, for not only did it have satellites in many other countries, but it was at the core of everything he was trying to achieve for both his own company and the world in general.

In 2005, the Director General of IAEA, who was later awarded with the Nobel Peace Prize, had stated that just one per cent of the money being spent on developing nuclear weapons would be sufficient to feed the entire planet. But Bob considered the award to have been a mistake, for he thought that the prize should have been awarded to his deputy for suggesting that all the prize money should have been spent on promoting nuclear energy instead.

Certainly, the IAEA headquarters looked impressive, but before Bob was introduced to the director general, who had only recently been appointed to the post, he spent a moment deliberating, for he was determined, by putting his point across with vigour, to be just as impressive himself.

'I have just flown in from the States, Director General,' he started, 'where anything that smells of nuclear is becoming increasingly unpopular. So I am here in Vienna to find out what the IAEA, your esteemed organisation, is doing about it?'

The director general, a tall, good-looking man in his early fifties, wearing a dark blue worsted suit, cream silk shirt and pale blue tie, stood back and replied with a sigh, 'You are right, Mr Buckmaster. We have been too slow on our feet and must do more about pushing nuclear energy.'

'In what way are you suggesting, Sir?'

'Our mission is as straightforward as it has always been. To underpin the safety and security of nuclear energy while encouraging the world to accept new nuclear technology.'

'Director General, surely the word should not be encouraging. The correct word must be ensuring.'

'You mean that now is the moment to promote all the latest technology and see it implemented?'

'Precisely that. You know as well as I do, Sir, that since one of your predecessors was awarded with the Nobel Peace Prize for mere suggestions, unless something more positive is done by the IAEA on countering the increasing amount of CO_2 being released into the atmosphere, which already exceeds thirty-five billion tonnes a year, you, myself and the IAEA will no longer exist.'

Bob, standing by the 25th floor window of the magnificent U-shaped building, was gazing far out over the Danube to where, on the far side, the spires and roofs of the city, touched with the early snows of winter, hid some of the finest buildings in Europe including the Shonbrunn Palace commissioned by Emperor Leopold I as a hunting lodge for his son Emperor Franz Joseph.

'Later, it was passed on to his son, Archduke Franz Ferdinand, who in June 1914, was assassinated with his wife, Sophie, in the streets of Sarajevo, ending the power of the Austro-Hungarian Empire and triggering the outbreak of the First World War.

'So, since the assassination of your heir presumptive in 1914, this is not the first time, Herr Director, that Austria has been at the centre of world events. For we are now threatened with World War Three, not against an adversary armed with nuclear weapons but one armed only with a growing amount of carbon, which will ultimately suffocate the lot of us.'

'So what do you have in mind to solve this frightening situation, Mr Buckmaster?'

'Please call me Bob, as I am always referred to by the employees in my company, Nuklin.'

'Yes, I know all about your company, for it has been more responsible for spreading nuclear weapons around the globe than any other organisation we are aware of. So we are delighted that you have come to see us in order to explain why you and your company have behaved so unscrupulously in the past, Bob. Do I understand, however, that you have at last come to your senses and Nuklin is no longer trading in uranium, and now only concerned with nuclear energy?'

'That's correct, Sir. The situation was, however, akin to that in Africa where those hunting wild animals are endlessly castigated. But if it were not for the hunters paying hefty licence fees, the game wardens would not have been employed, and because of the amount of poaching going on there would be no animals left. The spread of nuclear weapons is no different and has not been the disaster it has been cranked up to be, even concerning the worrying situation in North Korea.

'However, instead of creating war, my avowed intention is now to prevent it, although, in the past, I admit to making a considerable fortune. But that was phase one. Phase two is to use all that money not only to counter deforestation, but also to promote recent advances in nuclear technology as the only realistic alternative to burning fossil fuels.'

'So what may I ask is phase three?'

'That, Sir, will remain a closely guarded secret.'

'And the recent advances you speak of?'

'It is true that tremendous strides have been made in both wind power and solar energy, but because of the world's increasing population, they will never satisfy the demand for electricity. Luckily, however, there are other alternatives joining the market. But apart from hydroelectric power, limited to those countries with mountains, the advances being made in green hydrogen and nuclear fusion, all hoped to generate decent amounts of electricity in due course, will never make it in time.

'No other source of energy will ever compare, ultimately, with nuclear fission, which, although only providing some ten to fifteen per cent of the world's electricity at the moment, based on new technology, will reduce the fifty percent of fossil fuels still being burned to zero.

'It must, therefore, be sensible for the IAEA to concentrate on promoting this far-reaching nuclear revolution to those industrial countries consuming the largest amounts of coal such as China which burns almost four times the astonishing amount the USA, Japan, which is currently building new coal burning plants, and India, are consuming, added together. They are then followed by Australia, Russia, Great Britain and Canada in that order, also burning frightening quantities of coal while forgetting the damage being inflicted by other fossil fuels such as oil and gas.'

'Yes, Bob, but getting them to react to any such crusade will not be easy. However, tell me more about this nuclear revolution of yours.'

'I am sure you know everything about molten, salt cooled, SMRs. For apart from being totally safe, they no longer need to rely on great quantities of water. Also because they will be fuelled by thorium-based u-233 which is barely radioactive and leaves little dangerous waste, there are no expensive decommissioning costs. Small units producing no more than three hundred megawatts with some of less than fifty megawatts, are a far more manageable investment than larger ones, and they will be many times faster to build and install than previously.

'But the beauty of them being modular is that they may not only be factory produced but also be deployed on normal transport in the numbers required to suit the amount of electricity demanded by any one location.'

'That all sounds great, Bob. But how much will they cost and are there enough technicians trained to install them? Presumably your company is then going to profit greatly once again by selling them u-233, which is, essentially, more of your uranium?'

'No, that is why I have come to see you, Herr Director. As I am a very rich man with no wife or children to support, I now wish to give something back to the world before it is too late. Therefore, most of my resources will in future be channelled from war to peace, and my company will not only provide all those countries, who subscribe to my plan, with detailed specifications of the latest SMRs on the market, but also help, if possible, with installing them. Then, once a plant is completed, I will provide them with uranium 233 at cost.'

'But will the price of installing the SMRs not be prohibitive?'

'SMRs are already being earmarked by investors in quite a few countries because, as more of them are produced, the costs will become reasonable. Far too much money in the old type plants had to be set aside for decommissioning. But to repeat, Sir, that will no longer be necessary, and because they will all be factory built there will be, as I have already said, considerable economies of scale. The price, of course, depends on many different circumstances, but may not exceed two billion dollars per unit, or when linked together multiples of that figure.'

'OK, Bob, so where do we go from here?'

'The word we, is why I came to see you, for it would be impossible to pursue my plan without the full co-operation of the IAEA.'

'And your plan, Bob?'

'Well, yesterday evening after we had flown into Vienna, I took the crew of my aircraft, as a treat, to see your famous Spanish Riding School. Afterwards, Sam, my first pilot, asked me how those grey Lipizzaner stallions were trained to such classical perfection. I replied that the magnificent line of horses had been professionally schooled in Vienna for at least four hundred and fifty years, so the alternative method of using carrot and stick had never been contemplated.

'Carrot and stick, it occurred to me last night, must the way forward to get SMRs, which have a much shorter lead time than the old type reactors, being installed in the numbers necessary to knock out coal, oil and gas for ever. It is ridiculous that, largely due to people's terror of another Chernobyl disaster happening, no nuclear power stations have been built in the United States of America since 1990. And now, as in California, they are closing them down prematurely.'

'So, having already told me about the carrot, Bob, what about the stick?'

'Quite simply any government not prepared to finance the SMR's should be fined and exposed as Climate Criminals. And to go about that the IAEA should first contact the presidents of all the industrial nations I have listed but to include Brazil, where there are more than twenty coal burning thermo-energy plants operating already, with more being installed by the Chinese.'

'And if they refuse to take the necessary action?'

'Together we should embark on an aggressive campaign in that country's media, accusing their government of homicide on a global scale. No president like the man currently running Brazil, will last five minutes under the campaign I have in mind. To strive, to seek, to find and not to yield, we have a fight on our hands, Director General, which we must win.'

The meeting was over. Shaking Bob warmly by the hand the director general of an organisation, which he considered had not been doing very much for years, had vowed to come up trumps and hopefully, governments, at last, would be whipped into positive action.

But Bob was not convinced, knowing through years of experience how such organisations worked. Often, they were so set in their own rules and regulations that any new broom would have the utmost difficulty in changing all but the name on their headed note paper. Although seeming to be compliant, when the director general spoke to his board of management, they would find Bob's demands far beyond what they were employed for, and much to their annoyance, their day-to-day routine would be badly interrupted. However, if they refused, Bob reminded himself, he always had phase three up his sleeve.

'Welcome back,' said Sam standing at the foot of the Gulfstream's steps. 'Thanks for last night, it was an inspiration! But there is one thing I must tell you right away for we have just had a call from your butler, Jenkins, to say that you were telephoned once again yesterday evening by the British Ambassador in Brazil, who told him that the Major had, surprisingly, just turned up in Brasilia with a girl suffering from firearms injuries, who he had taken immediately to one of their hospitals.'

'But it does not stop there, I'm afraid.' Macey joined in from the door of his aircraft looking remarkably worried. 'I hate to tell you, Sir, that your mercenary has since been arrested and charged with two first degree murders.'

Chapter 10

The flight to Brasilia had been the longest Bob had ever taken, but chatting to Macey about her home, her parents and her brother had helped pass the time. Also apart from sleeping during the flight from Vienna, he had been writing notes on everything that had transpired over the past few days, and a few more on what he was going to say to Brazil's controversial president and to save his mercenary from being hung.

'Macey, after my meeting with the ambassador, while leaving you and Sam to find your own accommodation, my next difficult job, therefore, is to visit the Major at the police station in Brasilia and find out what the naughty boy has been up to.'

'You may not be aware, Sir, that I have been thinking about the Major ever since you first told me about him. He sounds like another James Bond and I have been looking forward to meeting him. But, sadly now, from what I have heard, I may not even get to see him in prison.'

'That's true I'm afraid, but what worries me more, Macey, is if they discover who sent him to Brazil in the first place. If my hasty telephone call to our ambassador when he first went missing was intercepted by security, there will be police already waiting at the airport to arrest me as an accessory to whatever crime he has committed!'

'Best I talk to Sam then and we dress you up in his captain's uniform to magic you away beforehand.'

'Great plan, Macey, but when they see how young Sam looks wearing my baggy suit, they will haul him in for questioning and then arrest him for being an imposter! So all I can do is surrender to them without a struggle and ask you to bring me a nail file in a bread roll, so that I can saw through the bars of my cell.'

When Bob left his plane, sure enough there were armed policemen waiting for him directly below the steps.

'You are to come with us,' one of the two policemen commanded in broken English.

It was impossible for him to see where he was going as the rear windows of the police car had been fitted with blackened glass. And when he enquired, the policeman, sitting on the back seat beside him, stated that they were only following orders.

Brasilia had always intrigued Bob. Particularly because of the bold decision by a past president in the 1950s to move their capital from over-crowded Rio de Janeiro to a new location over nine hundred kilometres away. There, three men, Oscar Niemeyer, Joaquim Cardozo and Lucio Costa, a student of the modernist Le Corbusier, were all to become famous as architects and town planners. Together, they created a city of such clean lines and open spaces that it was soon to be voted as a UNESCO world heritage site.

Bob was familiar with the city only because of Brazil's substantial deposits of uranium, calculated to be some five per cent of the world's total. Looking down while flying back over Brasilia, the sight appealed again to his creative mind, for the city, in plan form, had been designed in the era of rapidly increasing air travel as a giant aeroplane. During previous visits, he had marvelled at Oscar Niemeyer's twin towers, completed in 1960 as the home of the National Congress.

That was six years before they were eclipsed by the twin towers of the World Trade Centre in New York, briefly being heralded the tallest buildings in the world. He wished he had met the Brazilian genius before he died aged a hundred and four.

But this time he was unable to see the buildings and when the policeman ushered him out onto the road, he was confronted, instead, by a low, unattractive looking edifice, only just visible behind a high metal fence.

'So this is where they are going to pull out my finger nails?' Bob asked, before noticing a smart looking fellow in a grey suit holding the gate open for him.

'Welcome, Mr Buckmaster, the ambassador has been waiting for you.'

The ambassador, who must have been in his early fifties, was wearing a dark grey suit and an open neck white, cotton, shirt. Although, he was trying hard to look relaxed, his hands were never still. Pushing back his shock of ginger hair from his pale face, he had the air of someone not at peace with his situation.

'You may have been expecting the British embassy here to occupy one of Niemeyer's spectacular masterpieces, Mr Buckmaster, but this low-rise building was built by a British architect and due to a tight budget, is not up to ambassadorial expectations. All because of the considerable amount spent previously on our embassy in Rio, which was in operation for less than eight years.

'But, knowing the object of your visit, which is to get your employee, who will only give his name as "the Major", out of jail, I remain conscious, ever since you called me on the telephone, that he was here under your instructions to seek out those setting fire to the rainforest for reasons of blackmail.'

'You are right about the motive, Ambassador, but if I am considered to be an accessory, is that a crime?'

'You will have to argue about that in due course with the police, but meanwhile, knowing about your attempts to curb climate change, which London has told me about, I would like to know what orders you gave your mercenary, who has been accused of killing two foreigners, as I believe he is employed by you.

'Ambassador, my orders were to find out the identity of those arsonists and to prevent them carrying out any further damage to the rainforest, not to kill them.'

'Maybe. But I doubt you realise the amount of stress his arrest is causing us here, although I sympathise with your cause, Mr Buckmaster. I am a mathematician and it is not difficult to calculate how much longer the rainforest will survive if all such irresponsible people including the farmers here, are not brought to justice very soon. It is hard to believe that the British Government will only allow me to employ four environmentalists to quantify the effect those fires being started in the rainforest are having on our climate.

'Strictly between the two of us, the president, who says that he would like to meet you later, may not be helping, for he seems to ignore climate change altogether!'

Having thanked the ambassador for his concern, Bob was then escorted by the police to their North Lake Law Enforcement Agency, as it stated above the entrance of another low, far more sinister looking building.

'Mr Buckmaster?' A middle-aged, overweight man in a senior police officer's uniform enquired. 'Please confirm your name as I am told that you are here to arrange the release of your employee, who is here to stand trial for killing two Indonesians. We understand that it is you who sent him to Brazil. Is that correct?'

'Yes, for you will know already that he was flown to Cuiaba a few weeks ago in my private aeroplane.'

'Absolutely. But why?'

'You already know the answer to that, Coronel, but it was not to kill those two men.'

'So, unless you wish to try out one of our mattresses here with him, how are you going to prove that?'

'First may I see the prisoner, and then I will tell you.'

The man shrugged his shoulders but summoned a guard to lead him down to a what could only be described as a dungeon, where he found his mercenary pacing up and down his tiny cell in a towering rage.

'I had hoped you would turn up before long, Sir, because they are holding me here on two charges of murder. The problem is, as they have been gleefully warning me, that although they banned capital punishment here some years ago, it has been retained for the military. So that nasty looking chap accompanying you, has told me more than once that as I am an army major, I am going to swing for it.'

'Why not, and about time too!' he said, winking. 'No doubt you will have lied to them that you were here under my orders? So to prove my innocence, I am going to ask the colonel to drive us to the scene of the crime immediately. We can then work out precisely what you have been up to.'

It was not yet midday and as they sped out of the city, with the murderer sitting in in the back in handcuffs, Bob, becoming restless, asked the colonel, 'Who then was it that informed the police about all this?'

'It was the pump attendant at a small garage just north of the next town we are coming to. He told us that as your friend here had just stolen his knife he went after him on his motorcycle. He states that he saw something being thrown out of the car's door at two men crouching by a truck, which had passed by earlier. But on reaching the car it sped off while the truck and the two men were immolated in a blinding explosion.'

'Coronel,' interrupted the Major. 'You will shortly see the remains just as the man said on the left side of the road, but the most telling evidence is in Paranatinga, where the gang of arsonists have their hideout. While there is still enough light in the sky, please may we go there first.'

The two black vans were still where they had been parked previously, but just as they reached them, one shot out of the gate.

'That must have been the third man, Coronel, who the garage attendant may not have mentioned, probably because he had been paid good money to take him back to Paranatinga. You already know that the bastard shot my girlfriend through the shoulder.'

'Would you prefer we follow him then, or shall we examine the remaining van first, Mr Buckmaster?'

'The van,' he said, jumping out and approaching carefully as the police unlocked it. Inside were several boxes of copper tubes, and in one of them, luckily, an invoice, which Bob pocketed without being noticed.

'Please note what is in those cases, Coronel,' the prisoner suggested, 'and on returning to the scene of the crime, we may be able to find the pump attendant's knife I threw at them in self-defence. Also you will be able to understand how the explosion was caused by the arsonists themselves when they tried to fling one of their incendiaries at us and it detonated in their hands as the phosphorous hit the air.'

A night was closing in fast, knowing that they were too late to find anything let alone the knife, the Major was relieved when they stopped only for a brief moment to look at the scene again from the roadside.

'Don't worry about what I said to your guard earlier,' Bob whispered. 'I need him to be on my side later.' Then turning to the officer, he said, 'Rather than occupy your cosy cells tonight, Coronel, as you now know that both deaths were accidental, please may your driver take us both to the Royal Tulip hotel.'

'OK, but neither of you are in the clear yet,' replied the colonel. 'Once we have that third man in custody, who the prisoner told our motorcyclist was the man who shot his girlfriend, he will tell us what happened.'

'And admit to attempted murder,' added the Major. 'No doubt he may also be able to lead you to the man who hired me the plane at Cuiaba airport when I arrived in your country. For he arranged for one of those arsonists to shoot me down with a drone and must be charged with complicity to murder.'

They had reached the hotel, which Bob knew from earlier was built in the shape of a horseshoe overlooking a lake. Within the horseshoe were swimming pools and restaurants, plus his favourite massage parlour.

'I am meeting the president tomorrow morning, dear Coronel, so I will tell him what a good fellow you have been in helping us to round up the bastards who have been burning down his rainforest, perhaps faster than he may have realised.'

The police officer, looking straight ahead without commenting, told his driver to take him back to base.

The Major found the hotel breakfast to be outstanding. Before folding his linen napkin, however, he noticed a table laden with forest fruits, all labelled with names such as Pitanga, Caju and Guarana.

'I must have one of those, as provided by my Indian friends,' he told Bob, before continuing with a detailed account of everything that had happened to him since arriving in Brazil.

'So it has been an interesting journey, but come clean with me. Did you kill those two Indonesians?'

'Yes, I did, Sir. But unfortunately, they were the only two, plus the man strangled by the anaconda.'

At that moment, an immaculate looking waiter appeared with an envelope on a silver tray. 'I believe,' he said addressing Bob, 'this is for you, Sir.'

On the back it had the crest of the British ambassador, and when he opened it his expression said everything.

Dear Mt Buckmaster, Since you came to see me, the president must have contacted the police. Realising the reason for your visit, the meeting is cancelled. I am sorry to disappoint you. There was no signature.

'This is the story of our times, Major, for however hard I try to persuade world leaders to take action on climate change, they ignore the Kyoto Agreement altogether. The president here is trying to cling to office by denying that climate change exists, and by opening up the Indian reservations to further exploitation by farmers, and loggers, he believes that he is going to re-generate Brazil's flagging economy by allowing the wanton destruction of the rainforest to continue.

'It seems that the rest of the world can go to hell. Meanwhile, some are saying that only artificial beef will it save the day, while those trying to make their president see sense about the environment are not being listened to.'

'So, apart from my pathetic attempt to deal with the arsonists, what else are you planning for me, Sir?'

'Instead of meeting the president as I was hoping to, and before that policeman comes back with more damning evidence, let's go to the hospital and see how your new girlfriend is progressing.'

'Agreed, Sir. I telephoned Ana last night and she said that she is already out of bed and waiting to see us as soon as we can get there, so I will order a taxi.'

They found her looking wonderful in a dark grey dressing gown printed with forest ferns, swinging monkeys, prowling jaguars and flights of brightly coloured parrots.

'Ana, this is Bob, who you have heard so much about. He has just been prevented from seeing the president about our attempts to save the rainforest, but now you are part of our team, he would like us all to get our heads together over his next step in putting the world to rights. But how is your poor shoulder?'

'The shoulder is fine, Jim, and I am expected to go back to work here shortly, but meanwhile, my father is just about to arrive from Rio to see how I am getting on.'

'So you are really called Jim?' Bob asked. 'Then, at last, I know your proper name!'

'No, it's only because Ana likes to call me Jim as her hero from the jungle. When I was carried out to the farm by the indigenous Indians, if she had not been staying with her uncle there, I would no longer be with you. Only a girl like Ana, would have thought of carrying a bottle of quinine in her medical bag,'

At that moment, a tall, blond haired, aristocratic looking man in a dark blue suit and club tie entered the room looking much like a British guards' officer rather than a businessman from Rio.

'Let me introduce my father, Felipe, who has come to see that his little daughter is still alive and kicking. Dad, this is Bob, who I have told you so much about, and Jim, who was with me when I was shot.'

'It is great to meet you both and gives me an opportunity to apologise for the way you have been treated by my fellow countrymen. I'm afraid that our government is behaving like a headless chicken at the moment. The problem is always money and although, the rest of the world may think that we are a very rich country, it is not the case. Our population, which lives almost exclusively along the coast, has grown from about sixty million back in the 1950s to well over two hundred million at the last count, and soon, unless something is done about it, we will no longer be able to feed ourselves.'

'You will understand,' Ana interrupted, 'that my father is entirely on our side and deplores the fact that the government are allowing the rainforest to be destroyed not only to feed our own people, but also those in other countries, particularly in Asia. He, therefore, intends to persuade the Brazilian government to turn their attention to leading the world in many of the latest technologies instead.'

'You may be surprised to hear,' Felipe explained, 'that despite Brazil's reputation for its dreadful bureaucracy and political corruption, is already leads in technology throughout Latin America. It is hard to believe that despite the overcrowding in its notorious Favellas, Brazilians, in proportion to its population, are the second largest social networkers anywhere and only a few don't own cell phones.'

'You will discover, Bob, that my father runs a company manufacturing agricultural machinery, but at the same time, he is exploring some remarkable ways of distributing the stuff, which he will tell you about.' At that moment, a nurse came in asking the visitors to leave as she needed to renew Ana's dressings.

'So, Major, you stay here with Ana at the hospital, 'Bob suggested, 'while l take Felipe to have lunch at my hotel. Felipe, I see that you are a man after my own heart and just as determined to stop the destruction of your country and the world by uncaring politicians, who, either devoid of common sense, or unconcerned about the dangerous effect deforestation is having on our planet, need to think seriously about the lives of all our children and their offspring in the future.'

Back at the hotel, they chose a fish restaurant, where they ordered, as stated on the menu—Lobster, fresh from Brixham in Devon, England. Felipe, who must have been in his mid-fifties, had taken off his jacket and tie while Bob did the same. Glancing at him, he thought no wonder he has such a glamorous daughter.

'Then tell me all about your business, Felipe, it sounds intriguing.'

'I started by making agricultural machinery for planting soybeans in an old sugar mill some distance north of Rio. But when the business grew, I moved south nearer to the city and have recently completed building a new factory with a 700-foot-long hangar. You will have heard about the Hindenburg disaster during the nineteen thirties. Ever since then, the skies have been largely empty of dirigibles.

'But I saw the opportunity of using them for distributing my machinery and other goods over Brazil as a means of saving the country and its forests from being covered with yet more tarmac. Road building here, you will understand, only encourages a frightening increase in deforestation.'

'So have you managed to construct any of them yet?'

'No, not yet, Bob, but my first project is already on the drawing board. Amazingly, there are supposed to be only twenty-five dirigibles operating across the globe right now, so I believe there will be opportunities outside this country as well, if helium, the only safe gas to fill them with, was not in such short supply.'

'Interesting you should say that, Felipe, because I may be able to help you there. I once studied nuclear physics at the University of British Columbia and know that helium is a not only a by-product of nuclear fission but may be extracted from any ground where there is radioactive decay resulting from the storage of spent uranium. Nothing would give me more pleasure as the owner of a company called Nuklin, through which I have been providing most to the world's supply of uranium, than to provide you with helium.

'It will give us an excuse for getting rid of the Chinese coal powered generating stations your president has ordered, and introduce him to a new form of safe nuclear energy instead. Due to Nuklin's ongoing success, my life's ambition is now not only to reduce carbon emissions, but also to create a means of sequestering the vast amounts of carbon being lost due to deforestation.'

Felipe stood up to shake his hand. 'Ana has told me all about your intentions and how you are now using your immense recourses to save us from disaster. Maybe we could do some of the saving together?'

'Yes, your dirigibles have already given me inspiration, Felipe. Only two weeks ago, I was in Salt Lake City looking at an extraordinary procedure called plant tissue culture for propagating plants in billions. Macey, the competent American girl who looks after me in my aircraft, invited me to meet her father there who had set up an impressive laboratory to sell perfect, disease free, plant clones to local nurseries. But his son, Jeb, a brilliant engineer, took the bull by the horns and since invented a machine he has named a multiplier, which enables them to start selling plants throughout the whole of North America.

'Later Greg, Macey's father, flew me to see a nutter in the Nevada desert, who introduced me to snake plants, which are normally sold as pot plants to old ladies for their bedrooms. However, outdoors they will grow to over two metres in diameter with little or no water, and have the unique ability of absorbing CO_2 at night. Because I intend is to plant them in vast numbers across the world's empty spaces, however difficult the terrain, I am considering drilling them from flying mattresses towed on the ground by tugs, or in the air by drones.'

'So you believe it will be possible to drill your snake plants from the sky, Bob?'

'Yes, Felipe. If you are prepared to build these flying mattresses, and we will need several of them, I will get Jeb down here to help you and also to design the aerial drilling machines I have in mind. Are you on?'

'Sure thing, Bob, that sounds to me like the best idea to land in my lap, ever!'

'Excuse me then while I ring my first pilot, Sam, who is engaged to Macey and knows all about my plans. He will fly to Salt Lake City immediately to collect Jeb and bring him back to meet you as soon as possible.'

'Good work, Bob. Then ask Jeb to ring me when they land back in Rio and if Jim, as Ana calls him, would meanwhile like to stay with us as well, we will get cracking on your ideas as soon as he gets here.'

Bob was intending to remain at the hotel for two more days until he had heard from Sam that Macey had managed to prise Jeb away from her father's laboratory for a time. Once all was in place and his jet had returned to Brasilia, he decided that he would then fly back to England and co-ordinate the plans for tackling the world's major fossil fuel consumers, as agreed with the IAEA in Vienna.

Once back in his room in the Hotel Tulip, after saying goodbye to Felipe, feeling elated, he unfolded the invoice he had stuffed in his pocket at Paranatinga.

It appeared to be printed on rice paper and read: JAMASHI FIREWORKS, 15 Coronado Street, Andayak, Quezon City, Philippines. To Dragon Co. 1000 sticks of white phosphorus. $90,000.

As Bob sat down to dinner that night wondering why he had succeeded where his mercenary had failed, he decided that before researching the Dragon company and trying to find out where their headquarters were situated, he would have to talk seriously to his mercenary again before trying to get a good night's sleep.

But he had hardly started tucking into his favourite Moqueca Baiana, when his mercenary showed up again, hot foot from the hospital.

'Major, I am glad you have returned because I have both good news and bad news for you. Firstly, I have discovered the full address of the firework company printed on the invoice I retrieved from that box of tricks we found at Paranatinga. But the bad news is that because you have not completed the mission I flew you out here for, I will not be honouring the bonus I promised you until you have

117

successfully destroyed the culprit's world HQ, confirmed to be in Indonesia, and have started replacing all the trees destroyed in the Amazon rainforest, including those still being burned by the arsonists you have failed, so far, to eliminate.

'That is a just punishment, Sir, but right now, I have worse news to report!'

'What is that?'

'While worrying about Ana, after I left her at the hospital, I should have been more concerned about her car, although we had left it securely locked in the hospital garage.'

'Yes?'

'For after I went looking for it this evening to examine the bullet hole in the passenger door and its smashed window, to see if I could make the car more secure in some way, it had vanished. When I inquired about its disappearance at the hospital desk, I found that the police, who had meanwhile arrested the man we had seen escape at Panatinga, had not only removed the car, but were holding it in evidence against him.'

'So what? Presumably they are going to return the car after they have taken photographs of it, before charging the man with attempted murder?'

'Sir, that is my point. I had told the police, categorically, that it was the garage man's knife he had seen me throw at the two arsonists, but that was not true. I had certainly used his knife to remove the wax stopper on the phosphorus cylinder I had snatched in Paranatinga, but after I had thrown the cylinder at the two arsonists. I left the blasted knife in the car.'

'And?'

'The problem is, Sir, that when the police search Ana's car, which they may have done already, they will soon find the knife, which I had left under the dashboard. My defence will then be blown wide open and while you may be imprisoned as an accessory, my former guard will be delighted to lead me to the gallows.'

Part Two

Chapter 11

'Thank you for coming to see me in hospital again, Jimbo. It's stupid that I am being kept in bed like a prisoner. But it is you who are likely to be imprisoned again now. Your news is desperate. I should have thought about the knife myself but I did not realise the implications until you rang me and said what you had told the police. God knows what will happen now, when I was hoping to get to know you so much better.'

'At least Bob has got away, Ana. For as I was checking out of the hotel less than fifteen minutes ago, Bob also arrived at the desk. He said that rather than wait to be arrested, he was not going to hang around for Sam to return with his jet, so was leaving immediately for the airport. He had an evening flight booked back to London with Air Portugal.'

'I doubt that will do him any good because the police will be waiting for him at the check-in desk, just as they may be waiting for you right outside my door at this very moment.'

'When I said goodbye to Bob, he told me that he had asked the hotel to deliver a present to the colonel for looking after me so well in his comfortable lodgings, hoping that he would be equally lenient if I was re-arrested. Ana, that was very good of him for I need not tell you what hell it was in those police cells!'

'Just before the police take you to those cells again, Jungle Jim, which I am going to continue to call you rather than stuffy old Major. While assuring you that the colonel will pocket the money and do nothing to help you, please tell me why the military never trained you in jungle warfare?'

'You mean slashing through vines and thorn bushes with machetes to kill people? Of course I was.'

'Then,' she said, shoving one hand under her pillows, 'why the hell did they not teach you to take care of your weapons?'

'Ana, you wonderful girl, if only you had shown it to me when I came to see you before.'

'As my wound was being dressed that would not have been possible, but it shows that girls like myself would make far better mercenaries than you lot, for you are not in any way up to it, Jim!'

'Stop that silly banter, Ana, and tell me how you retrieved the knife while I try to simmer down.'

'Realising its implications, I hid the knife in my overnight bag the moment we parked Esmeralda.'

'How stupid of me not to have suggested it myself.'

'Don't worry, Jimbo, as I know from experience how long it takes to recover from malaria let alone from an aeroplane crash and everything else that has happened to you since. You are by no means a fit man yet, and it is surprising just how much you and I have accomplished together since we drove away from my uncle's farmhouse. What you need is more tender loving care and as you now have nowhere to sleep, I'm getting out of this hospital bed immediately, and once I am dressed, I'm going to take you to my flat, which is only a couple of hundred metres away from here.'

So telling the duty nurse that she was releasing herself, but would be back in the morning, she took him by the hand and led him to her one-bedroomed apartment not far along the road.

'So why don't you have a shower, Jimbo? But first, let's share a small night cap together.'

Having knocked back a glass of Brazil's famous cachaca, and then stepped out of the clothes Rick had given him, he explained from the shower that the only possession he still had left with him was a hotel toothbrush. 'Don't worry about that for heaven's sake, I am seeing naked men all the time in hospital. Just come and join me in bed in your birthday suit, because, as I have left my nighty back in the hospital, I'm going to have to do precisely the same!'

So while Ana was in the shower, he opened the window and shut the curtains before tucking himself between the sheets on one side of her comfortable double bed, suddenly feeling far too well again.

There was still enough light to see her as she crept towards him later. He seemed to have waited for ages with one eye open and as he marvelled at the silhouette of her lithe figure in the pale moonlight, he could not believe what was happening to him. 'You are so beautiful, Ana; more beautiful than any girl I have ever imagined in my dreams.'

'You should have been dreaming already, wild man, and I don't want any nonsense from you either. You know us nurses have ways and means.'

'You mean that you have been trained to deal with naughty men.'

'You bet, and now I no longer have my Esmeralda to look after me, I may behave like a tigress defending her virtue. So be very careful, young man, or you may live to regret it.'

He rolled over. 'Good night, beautiful Ana. I will try to obey but I will not be able to sleep a wink.'

'Oh yes, you will,' she retorted. 'I did not give you that nightcap for nothing!'

She had cuddled up to him immediately, so turning over and putting an arm around her, he started stroking her velvet skin for a moment until he came to her bandaged shoulder.

'You poor girl,' he whispered softly. 'Why the hell did I get you into this?'

'I would not have missed it for the world, jungle man,' she purred, twining a leg around him.

He felt the point of her breast against his chest and her soft mound pressed against his thigh and sighed. 'This is going to be the most wonderful night in my life, darling Ana.' Whereupon, he fell into oblivion.

He was woken after many hours of darkness by a loud shriek.

'What y'er do-in, what y'er do-in?'

I have been doing absolutely nothing, damn it, he thought, as he sat up in bed to find out what was going on. Ana was nowhere to be seen and he surmised that she must have already got dressed and left for the hospital. But she could have warned him last night about her boyfriend, he thought, seeing a large hyacinth macaw looking down at him from its perch with a particularly beady eye.

'Pretty boy,' he said, giving the parrot a handful of sunflower seeds. 'If I'd known you were watching over your mistress last night, I would have kept my eyes shut and my hands to myself.'

He then lay back again, cursing that unfulfilled desire was worse than any torture. But why am still at liberty? He thought, trying to stifle a yawn. How could he ever admit to Ana that, despite her clever move to hide the knife, it would have made no difference. The fact was that the Brazilian police were not as stupid as she might think.

He thought back to the moment he had thrown the tube of phosphorous into the back of the truck for there was little doubt that the garage man had seen him do it. The police would know that to throw a knife at the arsonists would first have been extremely difficult from inside such a cramped vehicle, and why should he have even attempted to kill two armed men with just one knife. Furthermore, they would have carefully searched the wreckage for the knife and when they were unable to find it, but instead, only an empty copper tube lying close to the charred bodies and the burned-out truck, it would have confirmed that the garage man's evidence was true. So although, he was thankful that Bob was now safe, he knew that he was still in mortal danger.

With the first task Bob had set him in tatters and due of his unfailing sense of loyalty, he decided to make a supreme effort to keep out of the chief of police's clutches and make a run for it before they caught up with him again. Perhaps they had already cornered Ana in her office at the hospital, and were grilling her about him.

He was staring out of the window looking for blue flashing lights before opening it to see if there was a police car parked in the street below, when he saw a note stuck to her front door with tape. Tying a towel around his waist, he rushed down to retrieve it.

Jungle Jim, I have gone to work feeling on top of the world. For not only will the drugs, which I mixed in your cachaca last night have saved me from being molested, but will also have speeded up your recovery, however frustrated you may now be feeling. Once you are in your right mind, I feel confident that we will be able to lie together in bed again and please Bob by bringing all those remaining arsonists finally to justice—rather than trying to kill them!

Ana, you beauty, he thought, if only the police had not confiscated Esmeralda, we could have driven back to Paranatinga with them and be able to do that. So he sat by the window for hours wondering at what time she would return and when he would hear from Bob on the new satellite telephone he had left with him. It would not be before the following morning, he reckoned.

He wished he could see some of the great buildings that Bob had told him about, but his view was restricted by the sprawling hospital, where he knew that Ana must be at work with her stethoscope.

It was at the moment he turned away from the window that he heard a car draw up outside and thinking it was the police, searched desperately for somewhere to hide without finding one. Then the parrot started squawking again.

'What y'er do-in, what y'er do-in,' which would have given him away immediately.

So he crept over to peer out of the window again seeing, to his amazement, Ana climbing out of her wounded Esmeralda, which must have been returned to her, holding a letter up towards him.

He rushed down the stairs again and hugged her as she ran into his arms.

'Jim,' she said, barely able to speak. 'I knew as well as you did that hiding the knife was not going to prove anything. Indeed, when I left for work this morning, I was certain that I would never see you again. You were never going to hoodwink the police for a second time once they had returned to the scene of the crime, and it was making me cry to think that despite all your gallant efforts to stop those bastards setting fire to our forests, you were now going to swing for it.'

'So,' he said nervously, 'was that letter you are holding delivered with Esmeralda by the police?'

'No, not delivered, Jim. You may not believe this, but the chief of police drove Esmeralda back to the hospital himself, saying how special she was. He then wrote this letter to you on her bonnet.'

'Crikey, what the hell does it say, Ana, what the hell does it say?'

'Let's first go upstairs and then I will read it out to you as it is written in Portuguese,' she said in a measured voice.

He could feel his heart pounding as he took her hand and pulled her up the stairs as fast as he could before sitting her down in her deep armchair.

'Now, please, read it out to me.'

'Hold on to me while I do so, Jim, as it may surprise you. What the colonel has written is this. You will be aware, Mr Major, that your recent activities have not only been against the law in Brazil but also against those in your own country. First degree murder is regarded as a capital offence irrespective of the reason the crime was committed. As you are a major in the British Armed Forces, it only makes matters far worse.'

'Stop there, Ana. So, for God's sake, what's the punch line?'

'I think it's better for me to read on, Jim. Although, you may not agree with everything the colonel says, he is being very serious. He continues: I am returning the car to your friend as I consider her to be an unwilling accessory. But because you are a foreign national, I have had to consult our lawyers, who say that due to the governments' determination to bring more of the rainforest into agriculture, your intervention has not only been unpopular, but directly in contravention to the president's intentions.

'Indeed, it should have been cleared at the outset according to the rules of international co-operation. As a result, the lawyers wish to treat you as though you were of Brazilian nationality and to bring a case against you at the supreme federal court of justice in Rio de Janeiro.

'Finally he says: But due to the generosity of Mr Buckmaster, who has sworn not to return to this country again, I am going to delay the court proceedings on the one condition that you also leave the country, without the authorities knowing, within a maximum of twenty-four hours.'

'Heavens, what a relief, Ana. I thought I was finished!'

Just at that moment, his sat phone started ringing.

'It's Bob here, talking from Funchal. The Portugoose I was flying in seems to have lost some of its feathers, so I have been waiting here for a connecting flight to take me on to London. I expected to have quite a struggle with that head policeman, but after I had oiled his wheels, I discovered that he was totally on our side. Not only does he recognise the importance of the rainforest, but deplores the president's whole attitude, particularly towards the indigenous Indians.

'Therefore, he has said that he will drop all the charges levelled against both of us as long as you leave Brazil, as I have done, immediately and never return again. So get yourself down to Rio fast, and after Jeb arrives in my aircraft from the States and has met Felipe at the airport, Sam will fly you to Bali.'

'Why Bali, Sir?'

'While waiting for the British Airways plane to arrive, I have bust a gut chasing up that fireworks company. But once I had got hold of them and started enquiring about their clients, they began spelling out all that bullshit on confidentiality. However, from what they said I was able to guess that The Dragons, which are a far larger organisation than we first thought, are operating from an island somewhere in that part of the world.

'If I discover where their base is situated, I will tell you, but you may have to find it for yourself. Meanwhile, get out of Brasilia like a bat out of hell.'

Jumping into Ana's emerald green Porsche again, he knew that chasing up the arsonists remaining in Brazil was never going to happen, but if he could cut the head off the dragon, at least he would have completed the first part of his mission.

'You heard what Bob said, Ana. So we must stop trying to nail the rest of the arsonists here, and I will also have to forget that magical second night I was about to spend with you, for I am now off to Bali. Worse still, all I can give you to remember me by is this spent bullet the surgeon gave me,' he announced, producing it out of a pocket.

'Is that so I may bite it, Jimbo? Of course I am going to bite it because I am coming with you! At only seventy miles per hour, which, before that policeman on his motorbike stopped us, I should have warned you is the rural speed limit here, it would normally take up to twenty-hours to reach the outskirts of Rio, let alone the airport. So I rang the colonel from the hospital not only to thank him for his understanding but also to request a police escort.

'Otherwise, I told him, I would never be able to get you out of the country in the time stipulated. He told me, however, that such an obvious getaway would be noticed immediately. Instead, just you believe this! He has informed all the traffic cops along the route not to stop us, irrespective of the speed I'm driving at.'

So she hit the accelerator again and as the miles flashed past, she placed her hand on his and in a quiet voice that he could barely hear above the noise of the wind screaming through his shattered side window, she said, 'I love you, Jim.'

He tried to lean across to kiss her, but when he found it more difficult than throwing the incendiary stick out of the car, he put his hand gently on her thigh for the remainder of the journey instead.

'Ana, I know that it was not just Bob who won over that chief of police. When you flashed your pretty blue eyes at him, no wonder he drove Esmeralda back to you and wrote you that love letter.'

'That's enough, Jimbo, I see we have been doing better than I expected. Now look at the increasing number of shacks crammed together on both sides of the road, for we are entering the outskirts of Rio and these are the notorious favelas where I started my practical training to become a doctor. Some of the houses have no running water, or electricity, and are divided only by open sewers.

'I worked in the Mare district where the police shoot people solely because they look like criminals. So I spent much of my time patching up firearms victims, many wounded by mistake. I have been wanted to tell you this ever since I met you, soldier, for I too, am not new to violence.'

'Amazing, we have reached the outskirts of Rio in just eight hours. It must be a record.'

At that moment, the Major, tilting her driving mirror, exclaimed, 'Ana, we're being followed!'

No far behind was a sleek black Mercedes, with what appeared to be two swarthy men in it.

'We are not out of the woods yet! But whatever the colonel said, Ana, let's take it easy. We still have sixteen hours before take-off.'

Having passed by many more favelas, which due to the rise in population, Ana pointed out, was the saddest part of Rio she had ever been asked to visit, they drove on until they could see the famous Sugarloaf coming into view out to their left, and the astonishing statue of Christ the Redeemer gazing down on them from the hills high up to their right.

'That car is still on our bumper, Ana. The two guys look vaguely oriental and should they be Indonesians, we need to get rid of them!'

She reacted instantly. For a fleeting moment, the Mercedes had been hemmed in by an impatient courier riding a motor cycle who had squeezed in between them at the traffic lights. So she slammed down her foot again, turned right and fast left, before threading her way through a maze of narrow streets until they hit the main highway again beside the Copacabana beach, renowned throughout the world for its four kilometres of soft golden sand.

Then, driving slowly through the exclusive area of Leblon, home to more billionaires than New York, a row of fine-looking houses, backing onto wooded hills, came into view, which Ana explained was within a national park area.

'That's my home away on the left,' she shouted excitedly.

They drove through some electric gates past newly mown lawns, flower beds and palm trees until the long, well-proportioned house, painted in pale yellow with rows of pale blue shuttered windows, stood proudly in front of them with its front door being flung open by Ana's father.

'Ana told us that you were on your way here. Welcome to Rio, Major.'

Then as a glamorous, dark-haired, lady appeared wearing a red silk dress printed with exotic lilies, he announced, 'And this is Marcia, my wife.'

'Do I understand that you have both very kindly invited me to spend the night here, Marcia? For apart from the lawns and flowers surrounding it and the two swimming pools I see over there, before we go inside I must say what a magnificent house you have. How extraordinary that you are so close to the city, and yet so far, with the whole place nestling hard up against the jungle!'

'Yes, the jungle is part of life here, for I have made friends with so many of the parrots, monkeys and raucous toucan birds that while Felipe is away he no longer has to worry about me.'

'So how long does it take you to get to your factory from here, Felipe, which Ana tells me is on the other side of these hills?'

'Follow me and I will introduce you to my other wife, Sky One.'

His helicopter, the latest Robinson sixty-six, sitting on a circular wooden platform by a small hangar, with steel rails running into it, was painted in the same emerald green as Ana's Porsche. 'That's a great colour, Felipe!'

'It's not the colour that matters, Major, for she sports a British Rolls Royce gas turbine engine.'

After a good night's sleep, followed by an excellent breakfast, Marcia showed him around the garden and then the jungle which was full of orchids, climbing jasmine and magnificent tree ferns directly behind the house, while beyond through the Kapok trees with their fluted roots and twisting lianas, he caught a glimpse of the blue hills standing high above them. After Felipe had shown him some drawings of the dirigibles he had been intending to manufacture, while Ana left Esmeralda to be taken away to be repaired, he asked if he would take them both to the airport.

'If you are determined to go with him, Ana, I hope, before leaving, you gave it more thought and packed some bikinis. Enjoy Bali, but be careful out of my sight. Although, the beaches are almost as good as ours in Rio, I am told that the men looking for an easy catch are even more audacious.'

At that moment, they became stuck in a traffic jam, which, because there must have been a crash ahead, prevented Felipe from driving his gun metal grey Bentley Mulsanne more than a hundred metres down the road for well over half an hour. What was worse when they eventually joined the highway leading past the Sugarloaf to Rio's International Airport, the Major noticed that they were again being followed by the black Mercedes and it worried him that the colonel's deadline was becoming increasingly difficult to achieve.

'Ana,' Felipe warned. 'We must not get you into trouble again. You may have to get out of my car at the next traffic lights and tell those guys in the car following us why it took so long to get here, for they are the police I arranged to escort you until you left. Let's hope you can get away with it!'

Luckily, although Ana had not been convinced about the men, her father was correct and Bob's Gulfstream was there waiting, parked on the apron next to the private aircraft terminal with a man standing by it. Ana, who had only been told briefly about Jeb, recognised him immediately. 'Hi, Jeb, this is my father, Felipe, who tells me that you are going to design something so special that no one will believe it possible. We are being watched, so best of luck with it, Jeb. We must fly!'

Chapter 12

Jeb. Macey's engineer brother

The Gulfstream had already disappeared into the afternoon haze but Felipe waited until he could no longer hear its Rolls Royce engines echoing off the Sugarloaf before turning towards Jeb.

'There goes Ana, the most wonderful daughter anyone could be blessed with. What is going to happen to her now is anyone's guess, I just hope that Bob's mercenary is going to look after her.'

'Well, if he doesn't, my sister Macey will, or at least while she and the Major are on Bob's aircraft. But after that, I agree that anything could happen. To say the least, the guy's quite an adventurer!'

'Precisely, Jeb. That's why we are going to work day and night together to get the planting machine Bob wants us to build for him completed quickly, so you may join the two of them in Bali as soon as possible. If you asked me where the first planting area will be, I suspect that wise old Bob must have chosen the Australian Outback. All I know is that the purpose of the machine we are going to build together is mind blowing!

'Look, we are nearing the most famous beach on the planet. Why don't we stop off for a drink at the Copacabana Palace. That fellow in the white uniform will park my Bentley while I show you the most splendid art deco hotel ever built.'

Jeb was still trying to appreciate that he was in Rio, a city he had only goggled at in videos.

'Jeb, I have heard all about the astonishing multiplier you designed for your father and you must describe it to me in detail, but first, I am going to order two Calpirinhas, Brazil's national cocktail, a fiery liquor derived from cane sugar and then softened with lime juice. You will like it!'

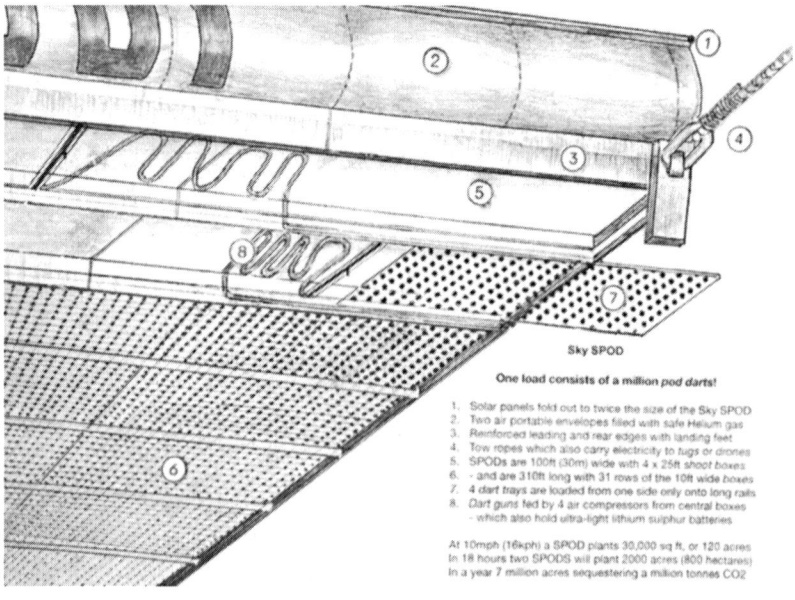

Sky SPOD

One load consists of a million pod darts!

1. Solar panels fold out to twice the size of the Sky SPOD
2. Two air portable envelopes filled with safe Helium gas
3. Reinforced leading and rear edges with landing feet
4. Tow ropes which also carry electricity to tugs or drones
5. SPODs are 100ft (30m) wide with 4 x 25ft shoot boxes
6. · and are 310ft long with 31 rows of the 10ft wide boxes
7. 4 dart trays are loaded from one side only onto long rails
8. Dart guns fed by 4 air compressors from central boxes
   · which also hold ultra-light lithium sulphur batteries

At 10mph (16kph) a SPOD plants 30,000 sq ft, or 120 acres
In 18 hours two SPODS will plant 2000 acres (800 hectares)
In a year 7 million acres sequestering a million tonnes CO_2

'It's fantastic, Felipe, but it is the last drink I am having in Rio until we celebrate the first planting machine we have built together. Until then, I'm going to have to keep a very clear head indeed.'

'Touché. So you are both intelligent and also have common sense. Tell me about yourself, Jeb.'

'It all started soon after I graduated from engineering college, for I could see the potential in going a step further than the advances in tissue culture my father had achieved. It was not just being able to divide the plants into yet more plants, but coming up with a way for packing and transporting them in large quantities. So I started by measuring up lorries and then working backwards. It was not rocket science but the multi-pocketed megatrays I had made then are the future of our business.'

'Bob has assured me that they are an essential component for the extraordinary drilling machine he and the Major has in mind, which they named a SPOD, or Seed Pod Overhead Distributor. Their idea, apparently, grew on him after he had spent two days with your family in Utah, and then again later when I told him about my blimps over lunch in Brasilia. He has an extraordinary fertile brain and does not miss a trick, which is why he sent his jet back up north to fetch you in such a hurry.'

'I was uncertain about his ideas at first, Felipe, as he was not around to answer my questions. It was my sister who made my mind up for me. She said that when looking after Bob on his jet he told her how he preferred flying at night. It never stopped annoying him looking down on the empty spaces of the world, she said, for he wanted to plant them up to combat climate change, but had no idea how to accomplish it.

'It was simple for a billion Chinese to plant as many trees in their backyard, but trees did not grow fast enough. So it was only when my father flew Bob to see those snake plants being grown by a long-haired hippy in the Nevada desert, that his eyes lit up.'

'Jeb, I know nothing about plants, however Bob impressed on me that the snakes not only grow with little water, but they also absorb CO_2 at night, one of the very few plants to do so. He also believes that your father may be able to manipulate their genes to make them grow faster and be virtually drought proof.

'As I told him over lunch in Brasilia, there is too much tarmac covering the ground here already, so in order to get my machines into some of the most difficult places on earth, particularly when it comes to establishing crops of soya

133

in remote parts of the rainforest, I have designed a new type of load carrying blimp, although I have not yet built one.'

'We all know how roads encourage increased destruction of the rainforest, Felipe, but surely Bob must have been unhappy about that idea, for they will also make the forest more accessible?'

'You are right, Jeb. Although, it was only to be the start of the wider operations I was planning, facilitating farmers in this way has always been a worry. But now Bob's visionary ideas have launched me, or rather us, into a new and exciting direction. Rather than corrupt the planet, his SPODs may provide one of the major solutions to climate change the world has been waiting for.'

'So give us the nuts, said the squirrel, and together we'll crack 'em, Felipe!'

'Yes, you are right on the button, Jeb, but before I show you the nuts tomorrow, it may be best for us to start by discussing the project right now. I hope you will not mind waiting for a moment while I ring Marcia, my clever wife, for I am going to ask her not to cook dinner for us tonight, but instead, to join us here at a table, which I am going to book in the hotel's Cipriani restaurant.'

When Marcia arrived at the table, she was accompanied by the suave, dark suited, hotel manager.

'This is Jeb, darling, who has come to stay with us and take me away from you for longer than ever. But Mr Santorito, who has so kindly escorted you here, will soon be seeing much more of us. Due to my increasing truancy, in future we will dine in his restaurant every Monday evening.'

Dressed in green silk, which suited her thick auburn hair admirably, she looked stunning. 'Jeb, please don't worry about my husband, who is one of this country's greatest workaholics. However, what he has achieved over our 23 years together has been breath-taking.'

The dinner was also special. Starting with sesame crusted cheese buried in puff pastry and garnished with truffles, it was followed by a prime Brazilian filet au poivre with roasted faijaoda, before finishing with apple and butterscotch crumble plus marshmallow ice cream. Washed down with Espirito Santo, one of Brazil's favourite wines, Jeb said he would never forget such a feast.

'But, Jeb,' remarked Marcia, 'although you think our meat is delicious, it is only because so many other people in the world think the same that we are losing our rainforest. The one consolation is that because of the growing demand for clean meat, or meat that has never been near an animal, tastes may change. But that will take years and I don't think I will ever want to eat it.'

'You are right, Marcia,' Felipe agreed. 'We should also be mindful that if cows blow off up to twenty per cent of the world's greenhouse gas, our increasing number of beef cattle plus the crops grown to feed them, may, someone warned, be damaging the atmosphere more than that caused by the population of Italy. The loss of so many trees is already creating serious water shortages.'

'We must first think about water when deciding how best to plant the rhizomes,' chipped in Jeb.

'It is not going to be easy but must head the list of the requirements we must draw up, just as I did by working back from the size of the lorries I needed in Salt Lake City.'

'Not a bad idea, Felipe,' enthused Marcia. 'Let's list them so that Jeb may suggest some answers.'

'Starting with water then,' Felipe kicked off. 'We must ensure that your father has made the plants as drought resistant as possible. But after planting, they are bound to need a little water?'

'Agreed, some water is essential,' Jeb replied, 'and as my father explained to Bob, he will now manipulate the genes of the snake plants they brought back from the desert accordingly, although they are known to grow without very much of it. However, getting them started with a drop of water is essential. You will understand,' he continued. 'That during the flight to Rio my mind was in top gear. So as I have already thought how to encapsulate tiny fragments of the snakes into seed pods. It will then not be too difficult to make them into what I have named pod darts.

POD DARTS

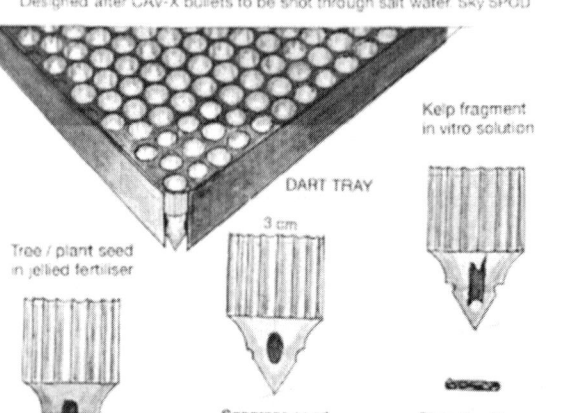

Made in transparent, sunlight enhancing, bio-degradable plant fibre.
Designed after CAV-X bullets to be shot through salt water. Sky SPOD

Kelp fragment
in vitro solution

DART TRAY

3 cm

Tree / plant seed
in jellied fertiliser

Seagrass seed
in vitro solution

Glue ring fits
on nose groove

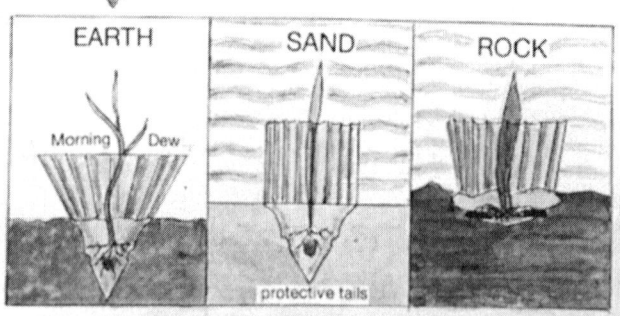

EARTH

Morning Dew

SAND

protective tails

ROCK

'The pods, like my example here, will be manufactured from biodegradable plant fibre. If I design them as darts five centimetres long by three centimetres wide, large numbers of them may be packed at five-centimetre intervals in my pod trays. Their sharp points will carry the plant fragments packed in jellied fertiliser, but best of all, when the darts hit the ground, their pleated rear ends will open up into eight-centimetre-wide funnels for collecting the early morning dew.'

'That sounds extraordinarily ingenious, Jeb. So presumably,' Marcia continued, 'your idea is then to load your trays into racks underneath Bob's remarkable SPODs, which Felipe has already told me about, without too much difficulty?'

'Precisely,' replied Jeb. 'As each tray is eight feet wide by twenty-five feet long, built to fit onto lorries, I have calculated that one SPOD will carry thirty-five of them along its length multiplied by four across its width making a total of one hundred and forty trays per load—all adding up to quite a weight. So talking about weight, Felipe, were you intending to fill your blimps with helium?'

'We will decide on the most suitable gas shortly. But by using compressed air as a propellant for firing the darts into the ground, we will not be using it for that. When the SPODs are loaded with a hundred and forty trays, each of seven thousand two hundred darts, totalling over a million shots, the amount of helium needed to shoot them would be prohibitive!'

'Wow, Jeb, we see why Bob flew you down to join us here. Now that you have Felipe also fired up, there will be no stopping him!'

'So, as I believe they are to be towed, what size of blimp are we talking about?' Felipe asked.

'To carry the number of trays I mentioned, each SPOD will have to be a hundred metres, or three hundred feet long by 33 metres, or a hundred feet wide, equalling about half the size of a football pitch. Meanwhile, the hundred and forty shoot boxes plus trays, each weighing about twelve kilos, have to be considered, for the thin array of solar panels that the SPODs will carry on top, will add almost the same weight again.

'That will mean that we need an envelope of at least fifteen cubic metres. But, Felipe, you must decide on the SPODs' final dimensions according to the amount of factory space, believing they will resemble large, square sided, flying sandwiches.'

'Your ideas are impressive, Jeb, and towing them will save the considerable weight of aero-engines.'

'As much as four thousand kilograms, Marcia. I will be describing how they will be towed later.'

'Then shall we turn to considering the materials,' suggested Felipe. 'Marcia warned me earlier that our whole project will come to nothing if there is even the faintest sniff of fossil fuels in them.'

'You are right, Felipe, and that is why we must turn now to your own side of the business.'

'To keep your shoot boxes within the weight limit, Jeb, aluminium, rather than plastic, comes to mind. But, as Marcia says, we must beware of such materials because, during aluminium's smelting process, CO_2 is released. All, apart from the envelopes, should be made from the new generation of biomaterials including carbon fibre made from lignin, a polymer found in wood.'

'I totally agree, for it is also found in snake plants. So what about the blimps themselves, Felipe?'

'The envelopes must be made at present of Tedla, the only material currently on the market, which is produced by DuPont in the USA. Indeed, should we construct the SPODs with double skins, they will be considerably safer than any commercial airliner.'

'Does that not depend on the gas you are inflating them with, Felipe?'

'Yes, Marcia, but choosing between the two types of gas currently used for inflating balloons is not easy. Although, I was hoping to fill our SPODs with the safe gas helium, it is becoming increasingly scarce and expensive. Indeed, stocks of helium are running out, and because we are hoping to build several SPODs, it would cause an uproar if we were to interrupt the supply of helium to hospitals, for instance, where the gas is used in their MRI scanners.

'However, as Bob said earlier, because it is a by-product of depleted uranium, he may well be able to help us. Before coming to a decision we must first remind ourselves of the loss of the Hindenburg, the massive German airship, which, in 1937, was believed to have been caused by some leaking hydrogen being ignited by a spark of static electricity. Today, as a result, all airships are filled with helium.

'The advantages of using hydrogen for our SPODs are certainly appealing, for not only does it provide more lift, but is also cheaper and may be produced using renewables. But although, we will be following every safety measure in the book, when hydrogen is mixed with air, it becomes highly flammable and may still be far too dangerous for us however well we seal the envelopes.'

'We will only be inflating the SPODs,' continued Jeb, 'to fly at a maximum of ten metres above the ground, which, apart from doubling the planting area, will use less gas and enable them to be flown anywhere. So helium may do the trick, Felipe. Also rather than bleed off any of the valuable gas to bring them down to the ground again, we will use internal compressors powered by the solar panels to do so. These will reduce the volume of gas with the same result. Should compressed air cylinders be needed and mounted on the SPODs, they will be replaced from unmanned, pre-programmed, electric tugs, which I also had time to design on the flight down here.'

'Then do tell us more about them as well, Jeb?' Marcia requested.

'Two of the tugs, powered by the vast array of solar panels mounted on top of each SPOD, will be secured to their front corners by self-adjusting ropes, while two heavy steel cables, attached to the rear two corners, will be dragged behind the balloons to stop them wandering in the wind.'

'Amazing, Jeb, you seem to have thought of everything!'

'No, Marcia, there is plenty more to think about, particularly concerning the firing mechanisms.'

'So how do you propose those are going to work?'

'Why don't we break off here and have some coffee by the pool?' Felipe interrupted. 'How Jeb has managed to create such an extraordinary aerial drilling machine in such a short space of time, defies the imagination. But before we go any further, we must also consider how we are going to transport the SPODs to Australia, if that is Bob's idea, and all those other empty areas across the world, which he may be researching. That must be one of the most important factors of all.'

'Agreed, Felipe, and it may be no surprise to you that I have cracked that one as well. Meanwhile Bob, who at the moment is back concentrating on his nuclear solution of factory built, small modular reactors, which may be combined to produce all the electricity needed anywhere in the world, will give us more detail about the massive area he's chosen for us to start planting. I have talked enough and before explaining any of my ideas in more detail, I can think of nothing better than to sit down with you both and enjoy some of your special Brazilian coffee.'

The manager had arranged a table for them on a private balcony overlooking the sea and from it, peering through the palm trees, Jeb could see countless games of beach ball being played by girls the colour of walnuts, all wearing tiny bikinis. What fun, he thought, itching to join them. The whole city was vibrant with life and colour, while the shimmering sea beyond the crowded beach seemed to beckon him to dive in to it as soon as possible.

'So, is this where the famous Carnival takes place, Marcia?'

'Correct, Jeb. The Carnival, which sets Rio alight in February, starts as a samba competition between the various dance schools around the city, when the men strut their stuff in unbelievable outfits representing everything from God to the devil, and the girls wear scanty clothes that would excite men who normally are as dull as ditch water. Often, they travel on floats, which even you, Jeb, with your extraordinary powers of imagination, would find hard to dream up.

'It all started back in the 17th century and because of its heady mix of Catholicism and European paganism, has become the greatest event of its kind anywhere. But to answer your question, the Carnival takes place throughout many parts of the city over five days, ending up right here in this hotel, where the Magic Ball is held as the final ceremony.'

'I have always been intrigued by the Rio Carnival, so having looked at my father's videos before I flew down here, it sure got me revved up and ready to take part in it, if I should ever be so lucky!'

'Our conversation this evening has been enlightening enough already,' stated Felipe, standing up. 'So before you start joining all those pretty girls wearing only flamingo feathers, Jeb, why don't we wait until tomorrow morning for you to concentrate your mind more on the many other important details you are proposing for the SPODs. After breakfast, I will show you the models of the blimps I was going to build until Bob changed my mind, before flying to see my factory and getting down to some serious design drawings.'

He then rang the concierge and asked for his car to be brought to the door, saying, somewhat flippantly, that he hoped nobody had planted a bomb in it.

'Don't scare the poor fellow, Felipe,' exclaimed Marcia. 'We only know of one bomb incident ever happening in our peaceful city and that turned out to be a firework!'

'They all seem to be mime artists here,' Jeb commented. 'For watching that video back home, it was the corpse left behind by the coffin bearers that caught my eye. They staggered off carrying a heavy weight but when the camera panned back, the corpse was still visible, but now lying on a bed of roses raising a glass of champagne. That started me thinking about the design of the shoot boxes for our SPOD, as the coffin, obviously, must have had no bottom to it.'

When they arrived back at the house, the hills behind were outlined by a flaming orange sunset.

Overwhelmed by its beauty, Jeb watched as the parrots flew up to roost and the forest went to bed.

'How the other half live, Marcia!'

'True, Jeb,' she replied, standing beside him. 'But however hard we try to make things better for those poor people living in the favelas, which our daughter, Ana, who was training to be a doctor will tell you, they breed more and more children, making their lives increasingly intolerable. I hate to tell you, that during the 1980s grupos de exterminio, or death squads, are known to have murdered hundreds of street children in the poorest suburbs of our city.

'In truth, the population of Brazil has grown from about thirty million to over two hundred million in less than a hundred years and the country can hardly support itself any longer. So, we are not relaxing in the sun as many people think we do much of our time in Rio. Far from it; together with friends, we are part of a drive to help the people survive by finding new ways to boost the country's economy.

'Now, speaking as the city's chief medical officer, my personal aim is to provide better treatment for everybody, and Felipe is just as determined to increase the efficiency of our agricultural industry. But that's enough of our "do gooding". Let me now show you to your bedroom.'

The following morning, Jeb was woken by a cacophony of sound as the forest behind the house burst back into its colourful life again. He lay for a time ruminating about what Marcia had told him, and about the people surviving in the favelas, wondering why the natural world was so much better at controlling its numbers.

For apart from the fact that birds have only a short nesting period, and long migrations to breeding grounds, elsewhere in the animal kingdom, following their individual cycles, reproduction has many constraints including similarly brief breeding seasons, and often, long periods of winter hibernation. So why are humans so hopeless at controlling their population unless forced to do so, as Bob, he had been told, also had on his mind.

Annoyed that he was unable to find any answers, he jumped into some bathing pants, and although, nobody was awake yet, threw himself into one of their Olympic sized swimming pools.

Felipe welcomed him back into the house saying, 'Good morning, Jeb. I hope you had a reasonable night's sleep and a refreshing swim. Extraordinary enough, the sea here is far better to look at than to swim in. Too often it is rough and not particularly warm. It also has some dangerous currents. Once Marcia has given you breakfast, she will show you to my office where we can have a look at the designs of some of the dirigibles I was working on before I throw them in the bin.'

Felipe's office was a revelation and totally different to the small room he had been allowed at Salt Lake City. It was, he reckoned, almost as large as the whole of his father's laboratory, and was equally full of tables and shelves stacked with models of agricultural machinery on one side, and of every type of airship and blimp on the other. Felipe then led him to a cabinet at the end of the room and started pulling out some drawers.

'You will see that I have done a considerable amount of research on those flying machines, Jeb, some of which have rigid frames, others semi-rigid ones, and those we know as blimps, having no skeletons in them at all. But you will notice from my models over there, and the drawings in front of you, unlike the barrage balloons tethered over cities throughout both world wars, blimps always move under their own power.

'Your concept of towing them at low level with tugs powered by solar panels, which will fold out, if required, to twice the area of the SPOD, is a far better one and, as Marcia pointed out, it saves a considerable amount of weight and other complications.'

'Yes, of course, but it will become more difficult when the ground is no longer flat and featureless. So instead, when planting in more demanding areas where there are trees and hills to cope with, the SPODs will be towed by two powerful drones in the same manner as the tugs, connected to the solar panels by lines carrying electricity, with heavy steel cables being dragged behind as before.'

'Directional control and speed are, presumably, critical, Jeb?'

'Yes, everything will be controlled by GPS, including the speed, which will be at sixteen kilometres per hour, or ten miles per hour, until all the pod darts have been fired. I will describe how I intend to shoot them into the ground shortly.'

'Jeb, you are already increasing my confidence on this extraordinary venture, which must be the one and only method for replacing the world's vanishing forests. I agree that to achieve the same result by using machinery on the ground would not only take a countless number of years but also be entirely dependent on fossil fuels. However, we must decide how you to ship the SPODs.'

'I started working on that before I went to bed last night. Take a look at this, for as you will see from my drawings, each SPOD must be split down the middle and built in two halves. Not only will two separate envelopes make them safer to operate, and easier to construct in Felipe's hangar, but each side may then be packed on a small, air-portable, pallet.

'The two envelopes will then be assembled on site by part inflating them before using built in straps to attach the solar panels above and shoot boxes below. Both the solar panels and the shoot boxes will then all be bolted together on the ground to make them into one semi-rigid flying sandwich, as I described earlier.'

'Brilliant, Jeb. I was thinking about the problem on much the same lines. But because the shoot boxes plus firing mechanisms will have to be manufactured elsewhere, it may be best to wait for others to specify their design, plus the material they intend to use, before proceeding any further.'

'No. As I have already suggested, they must be made from a strong, hemp based, composite material, which is both rigid and not too heavy. The trays, which will have the darts inserted in close fitting tubes, will slide into, open bottomed, shoot boxes set in grooves across the width of each SPOD. The darts will then be blown downwards by two powerful jets of compressed air, moving laterally on rails above the shoot boxes.

'This will be controlled by GPS, so that all twenty lines of trays across its width are activated sequentially. On reaching the end of a planting run, the direction of the firing mechanism is reversed so that after a SPOD has been replenished, it is ready to drill the next strip in the opposite direction. This reduces the distance support vehicles will have to travel.'

'That all sounds very sensible, Jeb. So tell me, are these outline specs I have written down, correct?'

Envelopes
They are to be a hundred metres long by thirty-three metres wide, but packed in two halves.

Their height will depend on the amount of gas needed to lift the total weight of the SPOD.

They will be double skinned and filled with helium for safety, which may then be compressed.

Planting
Fragments of snake plants are to be encapsulated in jellied fertiliser within self-watering darts.

One hundred and forty trays, carrying a total of a million darts are mounted under each SPOD.

The design of shoot boxes and dart guns to be agreed with the fabricators as soon as possible.

'That's spot on, Felipe. But the choice of plants must also not be agreed without help from horticultural specialists. So now is the magic moment when we calculate the size of the planting areas.

'Although, the plants will grow to more than three metres in width, perhaps more if Dad has manipulated their rhizomes, to get maximum coverage they must be planted three metres apart. Fifty darts will, therefore, be fired every three metres. Flying at a height of ten metres, they will cover one 180-metre-wide strips with the SPODs needing to move forward many times. All somewhat of a mouthful, I'm afraid.

'So to answer your question, Felipe, the total distance covered by a SPOD in one run is best calculated by dividing each load of a million darts by fifty of them fired at three metre intervals, which comes to the surprising figure of sixty kilometres, or some 37 miles. Then, because the SPODs will be towed at sixteen kilometres per hour, to plant one load to will take, including an estimated turnaround time of about half an hour, not much more than four hours.

'You asked me to calculate the area planted in one run, Felipe. Drilled in a 180-metre-wide strip, sixty kilometres long, all I can say is that just one SPOD should be able to plant an astonishing amount of ground per day.

Felipe, Ana's father, in Rio.

'Agreed, Jeb, and because it is said that the total area of trees lost to the Amazon rainforest since the 1970s is about seven hundred thousand square kilometres, by operating several SPODs at a time, it must be possible to plant the same amount of ground with snake plants, or similar carbon eating vegetation, within a very few years.'

'Precisely. Then consider what one SPOD will accomplish compared a countless number of tractors—all being constantly filled with diesel, petrol or gas. Or think how many people would be needed to plant them individually at only a tiny fraction of that speed. Unless they are scattered from aircraft, or helicopters, which would never be successful, there are no alternatives.'

'It is remarkable, Felipe, that in just twenty-four hours we may be on our way to creating a method of carbon sequestration never before thought possible. Meanwhile, Bob is working on methods of preventing all that carbon reaching the atmosphere in the first place. Both projects are game changers!'

'Perhaps, Jeb, but we must not be too confident. First Bob has to get permission to drill the trees, or plants, finally chosen, unless the Major pushes on regardless without such permissions, which he is more than capable of doing. But God help him and all of us if he stirs up a hornet's nest, for then all Bob's planning plus all the SPODs we are hoping to build, will go up in smoke.

'Meanwhile, we must banish all such foolish thoughts from our minds, Jeb, for, in a moment I will be able to show you the hangar where it should be possible to fabricate the two envelopes for each SPOD in less than a week. Once I have the material, I will then be able to provide Bob, or his mercenary, with twelve completed SPODs per year, the first being available in under two months' time.

'So why don't we now jump into my chopper, and we'll fly over to the other side of the hill and have a look at my business, which I have named Mana Engineering after my wife, Marcia, and our daughter, Ana.'

It was a beautiful day and looking down on the tight, seemingly, impenetrable, mass of trees that rose skywards from the back of Felipe's house, he wondered how much carbon was being absorbed by them alone. He had listened to a professor explaining about sequestration while he was at university, remembering that, depending on the variety and intensity of the greenery, the amount of carbon came to the astonishing figure of seven to eight hundred tonnes per hectare.'

His thoughts were interrupted by Felipe, who speaking through his mike, as they started losing height towards a plain of endless soya fields, encouraged him to search for his engineering works, which having been constructed just within the edge of the forest, were almost hidden from view. It was only when the word MANA suddenly appeared, painted in dark green lettering on the roof of its long brown hangar, that, realising how environmentally conscious his host was, he could not help enthusing over the intercom, 'Manna from heaven, Felipe!'

But that was wishful thinking.

Chapter 13

'Dear Macey, now we are off to the land of Kama Sutra, how was your flight to Salt Lake City?'

'Not a problem, Major, for it was such a treat collecting my brother. Now you must introduce Ana, and once I have brought you both something to eat and we have reached our cruising altitude of thirty-eight thousand feet, Sam and I are itching to hear what the two of you have been up to?'

'That would be best left to Ana, Macey, for we have just been through hell and high-water together. But the poor girl needs to get some shut eye first. Trying to keep alive over the past three weeks has been such an ordeal, I wonder how she has managed to retain her sanity!'

'Nonsense, Macey,' Ana interrupted. 'It's this guy who needs to be put to sleep, permanently. Why I have become so attached to him in less than two weeks is a total mystery, For not only is he a born killer, a liar and a thief, but watch out he can charm the leaves off the trees, even when being looked after by pretty Indian girls in the Amazon rainforest. But I hate to admit it, Macey, although he may be a danger to have on your aircraft, I am beginning to fall in love with him.'

She had brought them some waffles soaked in her parent's maple syrup plus two steaming mugs of coffee, which they had hardly finished drinking when Sam, wearing his smart, dark blue, pilot's uniform, appeared from the cockpit.

'Hi, Major, good to have you on board again as we thought you were a goner. And greetings, Ana. One day, you may realise what a mistake you have made joining this desperado on our flight to Bali. I hope you know you are not allowed to share a room there without a marriage certificate!'

'Maybe, Sam, but this is not a holiday we are taking together, rather it is the most dangerous mission either of us has ever undertaken in our lives. I was nearly killed recently training to be a doctor in Rio's notorious favelas, but this man who I have named Jim, has not only just survived an air crash while looking for the arsonists burning our rainforest, but has since recovered from malaria after being rescued by an indigenous Indian from the jaws of a jaguar. I met the man only when they carried him out of the forest to my uncle's house, where, very foolishly, I saved him.

'Jim told us that he had found the arsonists were a gang of Indonesians named the Dragons. So we went after them in my Porsche and found they were directing operations from a boarding house overlooking a dried up river bed just south of the Xingu National Park, where Jim discovered they had a hoard of fire sticks. While trying to, I was shot in an ambush and taken by Jim to hospital in Brasilia, where, having saved me, he was locked up, charged with double homicide.'

'Good grief, Ana, what happened next?'

'He lied to the police that he had thrown a knife at the bastards from the door of my car in self-defence just as they blew themselves up with one of their own incendiary bombs. But the knife was still in my car! Jim was about to swing for it when Bob, who had flown from England, stopped the hangman with a load of dollars. We were then told to get out of Brazil and never return.

'So I released myself from the hospital, where I had been recovering from my gunshot wound, and just managed to drive Jim to Rio's airport, which we have just left in the nick of time before the police, who were following us, arrested him again. Why I am still with the guy is sheer lunacy!'

Throughout her tale, she noticed her friend relaxing in Bob's armchair pretending not to listen. 'Then tell me what you are up to now with this poor girl, Major?'

'I have absolutely no idea, Sam.'

'It is certainly not to go building sand castles together,' Macey interrupted. 'Bob told me on the flight out to Rio that because his mercenary had failed to eliminate the arsonists operating in Brazil, his next task would be to assassinate the chief dragon, once he managed to find him.'

'But why Bali, which is best known for tourism?' Sam asked.

Before Ana was able to respond, the radio suddenly crackled into life. 'Major,' Sam said passing him the headset. 'I have Bob on the line and he needs to speak to you.'

'Major, I am at last back at the ranch, but only to find out that someone was trying to break in here overnight. Jenkins says that when he woke up this morning, he discovered that every line into the place had been cut, our internet

148

jammed and all our security devices professionally disabled. Have you any idea why this should have happened?'

'Is the front gate secure, Sir?'

'Yes, and I have sent Jenkins down to the police station to tell them about the vandalism and ask for their immediate protection.'

'Bob, keep out of sight until the police arrives. Someone is definitely after you. Do you think it was because of that call you made to Brazil which you were so worried about?'

There was no answer. Only the sound of a shot being fired and after that, nothing.

'Sam, there's a problem. I think Bob may have copped it.'

'Oh my God, that is the last thing we need. Here we are flying ten thousand miles around the world to Bali, and yet we have no idea what Bob expected us to do when we get there. We will just have to pray that he is OK, for he has made it clear to me that I must never try to contact him back, except on his satellite phone, which is now as dead as a dodo. It means that he is either lying on the floor with a bullet through his head, or has been abducted by some very nasty people again.'

'You are right, Sam. It was due to an unguarded moment when he rang the British ambassador in Rio on an insecure line that everything started to go wrong for him. Ever since I left England, his life seems to have gone pear shaped. However, knowing that Bob is a man who is never defeated, I wouldn't be surprised if it was he who fired that shot!'

'Agreed. In a few hours' time, we are going to have to re-fuel the aircraft in Muscat. So while Eliot flies the plane, why don't I come back and join the three of you so we may put our heads together and work out what to do next?'

Macey returned from the galley that moment with some wafer-thin biscuits topped with beluga caviar, so they sat round a table on four revolving chairs, while the Major attempted to make sense of the situation they now found themselves in.

'We must remember that the affairs of mankind are pitifully small in such a vast setting. But Bob is, or was, an extraordinary fellow. For his age, no-one else I know has such energy and charisma.'

'Also unbelievable powers of intuition and initiative,' added Sam. 'In the short time I have known him, thinking of our discussions on this aircraft, his knowledge of what is going wrong with our world and his determination to put it right has been extraordinary. Meanwhile, as the nuclear industry declines, he has never stopped thinking about his employees and their uncertain futures.

'Bob knew that nuclear was never going to be a dying duck. Rather he believed that the protests his company is facing could be turned to their advantage if they changed from mining uranium to mining the alternative isotope thorium, which they are already busy researching. It had been claimed that thorium-based fuel, or u-233, which is only barely radioactive, is both safe and superior to u-235—the nuclear fuel used at the moment by all power stations.

'Also, it will produce cheaper energy than coal, a fact which will apply to wind and solar in due course. But he said he did not push it too hard in Washington, or in Vienna, believing they would not listen to him yet.'

'But how does Bob, who we must not talk about in the past tense, expect to market this new type of nuclear fuel, which has no track record?' Macey asked. 'He will be fighting like King Canute against an overwhelming tide of complacency.'

'It is only due to climate change that the element thorium is now being considered as the basis for a nuclear fuel again, although there has not yet been much of an attempt made to mine the stuff, which Bob is planning to do. But you are right, Macey. Nuclear energy now carries such a stigma, that as renewables become increasingly popular, he is facing an uphill struggle.'

'So while you, Major, accompanied by Ana, have been sent on an equally important mission, Bob's intention of replacing old nuclear power plants with new ones to provide the world with permanent clean energy, means that he must be on to something astonishing!'

'Is that not the reason why someone is out to kill, or abduct him, Macey?' Ana enquired.

'We don't know at this stage what has happened in North Devon,' chipped in the Major. 'However, what I do know is that although some crooks may have just been after his money, as you have suggested, Ana, it is more likely to be a matter of either those trying to prevent him developing his ideas, or much more likely, those trying to steal them, who will stop at nothing.'

'While I was serving in Afghanistan,' Macey continued, 'I saw what the human race is capable of doing to each other, including the worst type of torture. Defending their land and their valuable crops of poppies was excusable, and we had to remember we were rich westerners aiming to take away their world. They are such determined fighters that I doubt anyone will ever defeat them.

'Since meeting Bob, I have regarded his combative spirit in much the same way, although his motives are quite different. His greatest difficulty is to put at ease all those people who believe there is about to be another Chernoble. He implores them to open their eyes and start thinking straight, for clean nuclear energy is the only possible solution to global warming. Meanwhile, Jeb, on Bob's instructions, is already busy creating such an innovative method for sequestering the CO2 falling from the atmosphere that it too must be a winner.'

'But, even if Jeb and Felipe between them come up with something special, if anything bad has happened to Bob, without his money behind the project, surely they will get nowhere?'

'You are right, Ana. The moment we land in Muscat, rather than telephone the Devon & Cornwall police ourselves, we will have to ask someone in the British embassy to try and find out what has happened to Bob, for without him we are scuppered.'

'But, my brilliant fiancée,' asked Sam, 'are not the costs of changing to a different kind of nuclear fuel and introducing such an extreme method of carbon capture far beyond the pockets of any mortal being?'

'Yes, of course, you are right. However, you may remember me listening in to your conversation with Bob on that long flight across the Atlantic. For, afterwards, I had the cheek to ask him that.'

'So what did he say, Macey?'

'His reply was inspirational. He told me that because punters are now deserting fossil fuels in droves, every oil business in the world, like Exxon, Dutch Shell and BP, is now looking for other means of providing the world with energy. So he has been sending them, plus other possible open market investors, a company leaflet, inviting them to join his The Thunder Club.

'Rather than spend too much of his own money at the sharp end, he has told all of them if they join his club, he will provide them with all the necessary technology for commissioning the small modular reactors, or SMRs, he will be encouraging the IAEA to promote from Vienna. We have talked about those already, but just imagine them being manufactured in vast numbers and then deployed wherever there is a demand for electricity, not necessarily financed by governments, but by the private sector according to normal market forces.

'Any investor must be encouraged by the fact SMRs leave little nuclear waste, thus saving the mind-blowing decommissioning costs.'

'Bob has also said,' interrupted the Major, 'that now his company, Nuklin, has turned from mining uranium to mining thorium, he will provide them with as much of the stuff as they need at cost, or depending on their situation, at a substantial discount.'

'What an intelligent way of tackling the problem,' added Ana. 'Not just getting the top international players to take part in this new form of energy, but saving his company Nuklin at the same time. Hoping that he has limited the invitations, how many oil companies have joined his club to date?'

'Bob told me, from his four replies so far, Chevron and Total already seemed to be interested.'

'So what about the other two, Macey?'

'Exxon, another of the world's largest oil companies, have said they would like more information. The other enquiry was from a Russian outfit called Voztok. I tried looking them up on the internet, but they must be a minnow among the Chevrons, Totals and Exxons of this world, and I got nowhere. But you are right, Ana, maybe the invites should have been fewer in the first place.'

'That's my point,' replied Ana. 'We know about corporate jealousy and surely Voztok must be the prime suspect now for trying to grab Bob's ideas and his plans for mining thorium. I know from my father's business how difficult it is to keep one's intentions under wraps once you start developing a new product, and although, you say that Bob is one of the most careful men on earth, his company should never have distributed those leaflets so widely, for any criminal determined enough to get hold of Bob, would have discovered where he lived without much difficulty.'

'You are right, Ana,' said Sam. 'Give me a couple of minutes and I will find out everything possible about Voztok, so when we land in Muscat, we are able to point a finger at them and warn the British police about our very realistic concerns.'

While Macey started making some more coffee, Sam disappeared back into the cockpit.

He was only gone for a minute. 'Folks, hear this. Some joker is trying to divert us to Riyadh saying that new orders from Bob are waiting for us there, which is nonsense. I don't like the smell of it, and once we have landed in Muscat, we may find the story is very different. The buggers who abducted Bob must have discovered our destination when we flew out of Rio. Should we have

152

followed their instructions, after arriving in Riyadh, we would have been carted off to a Saudi jail.'

'Are you able to trace that message, Sam, for they are trying to stop me coming to Bob's rescue?'

'No, sadly not, Major. I have asked the Omani's that question, who say they are not able to do so. They have tried to get hold of the caller twice, but without any response whatsoever.'

'Of course, we could always alert the British police about the attempt to divert us to Riyadh,' Macey piped up from the galley. 'Except that any transmissions from this aircraft would only cause us further problems. As they told us in Afghanistan, radio silence always matters, Sam.'

'Correct.' Then reaching for his second mug of coffee, he added, 'The news is not good for any of us. In fact, its bloody awful! Bob's initiatives have been so exceptional that once his ambitions hit the press, the whole world will be trying to poach his ideas. But at least it may help solve the climate crisis.

'The good news is that the British media have been saying that due to the aggressive campaign of the Extinction Rebellion, and the young Swedish environmental activist, Greta Thunberg, BP are also now looking for ways of going carbon neutral. Apparently, they are not only losing credibility with the world in general, but also with their staff, while their oil and gas has created another problem, for a considerable quantity of their oil is used for manufacturing plastics.'

Ana agreed with him, and as a shaft of moonlight shone through one of the plane's windows, lighting up her golden hair, her dangerous companion said she looked ravishing.

'I am so excited arriving at dawn in Oman, Jim,' she said, ignoring his compliment. 'It is somewhere I have always longed to visit. A beautiful country of endless sunshine, mountains, fine buildings and friendly people. So, apart from trying to find out about what has happened to Bob, which is our top priority, I must then take you shopping in the souk so I can buy you some clothes.

'Since leaving my uncle's farm on the edge of the Amazon rainforest, apart from one night at my home, you have not had a moment to wash, for while you were incarcerated in that Brazilian prison, you told me that they only gave you one glass of dirty water.'

'True, Ana. But let's listen to what Sam has discovered about Voztok before I attempt to become human again by taking another shower in Bob's bathroom and get rid of this flea ridden beard.'

'Although, Bob has been trying to solve the greatest crisis our world has ever known,' Sam started. 'It is unbelievable that he should have been threatened, not only by those dangerous Indonesian arsonists, who blackmail governments to stop them setting the world's forests on fire, but now by that bloody Russian oil company, which, from what I have just read, seem capable of carrying out every crime in the book!'

'What crimes, Sam?' Ana asked looking at him with her wide, astonishingly beautiful, blue eyes.

'Just listen to what I have found out about Voztok on the internet, particularly about the man who owns it, and you will understand what I mean.'

Voztok, a minor Russian oil drilling company, was founded after Perestroika in 1988 at the time the Soviet Union fell apart. Due to the policy of privatisation then introduced by Mikhail Gorbachev, most of the Russian oil industry fell into the private hands of speculators, many of them now known as oligarchs. One, Grigor Vilovitch, a recognised gangster, soon started hiving off all the oil fields around Nolabrsk, a town in north western Siberia noted for its oil potential although all of its black gold lay under the permafrost.

Calling his company Voztok, he soon set about stealing every other drill site he could get his hands on. However, when his oil started running out and there was talk of a carbon tax, he became notorious, even amongst his fellow crooks, for extortion, abduction, bribery, money laundering, smuggling, gun-trafficking, drug running and contract killing.

'Wow, is he the man that Bob, through no fault of his own, may have found himself up against?'

'Almost certainly, Ana, but it was always guaranteed that as a result of privatisation, Russia will experience more corruption including theft, than it has ever known in its history. Just as the Russian president, who, having acknowledged climate change, is trying to increase drilling for the very hydrocarbons that are warming our planet, while, in the same breath, stating he will stop the permafrost from melting, which is outrageous.

'Meanwhile, because they know that such efforts are in vain and the Russian oil business is unlikely to survive, vicious characters like Grigor Vilovitch will take desperate measures, even murder, to look for alternative sources of revenue.'

'So, as Bob's paid mercenary, Sam, I am now torn between two difficult decisions. Either to travel south with you and fulfil the mission Bob has set me, which is first to locate and then kill the head Dragon, or alternatively, to travel north and save us all by eliminating this Russian thug and his hit men, who, if they gain possession of Bob's secrets, will ruin everything.'

'Fully understood, Major. But we also have a dilemma. Do we fly on south to the fleshpots of Bali with no idea of what Bob had in mind for us, or do we wait here for further instructions. But let's not worry about all that right now. Before we touch down in Muscat, why don't we all have a siesta while Eliot flies the plane.'

They did, only to be woken, as they entered Oman airspace, by a violent thunderstorm.

'Perhaps it is a good omen,' remarked Macey, as she prepared their breakfast of eggs and bacon. 'This is all you're getting, for Bob has always insisted on me buying fresh food every time we land, but I did not get a chance in Rio to buy a loaf of bread so we may have a proper fry-up. Meanwhile, I hope to persuade Oman, which was once rich in oil, to join Bob's Thunder Club.'

Airport security at Muscat was a doddle until they found the garage attendant's knife tucked into one of his socks. 'I am a British secret agent on an important mission,' he said. 'Take the knife if you wish, but please help me to telephone the British ambassador immediately.'

'Ambassador,' he asked having got through. 'I am employed as a security agent by a British businessman named Bill Buckmaster, who may have been murdered. He has been living in North Devon and was hoping to put forward some ground-breaking solutions to climate change. But I am worried that the Russians may have either killed him, or be trying to abduct him. Having just flown in from Rio, please may I use your embassy telephone to alert Special Branch in England.'

'Go ahead, but may we have a few moments together afterwards.'

The embassy in Muscat, a low rise building full of arches and Arab architecture, surrounded by mown lawns and healthy-looking palm trees, was far removed from the British embassy in Brasilia, which had so disappointed him earlier. However, before he had time to talk to the ambassador, Special Branch rang back from England to tell him that they had been contacted the previous afternoon by a Mr Jenkins, who said he was frightened his boss, Mr Buckmaster, had not only been abducted, but despite continuing efforts by the local police, he had still not been found.

'Realising the situation was serious, we placed a stop on all ports and airports, particularly on those in the local area. Unless he has already been flown out of the country, we hope, in time, to be able to locate Mr Buckmaster, who we are told carries a bleeper, and arrest those responsible.'

But when he rang Special Branch again the following morning, the police admitted that they had made no progress whatsoever.

'Sam,' he said on returning from the embassy. 'I must go and search for Bob before he is smuggled out of the country, most probably to Russia. So please fly Ana on to Bali where she is to await my return at a hotel of her choice. But tell her that she must not contact me from there. Rather she must telephone her father in Rio to say where she is. Once I have sorted out the problems in Blighty, I will ring Felipe straight away.

'Meanwhile, I will take the next commercial flight to London, expecting you to collect me from Exeter airport in one week's time. But don't tell Ana any of this until I am already airborne. Since the ordeal which happened to us in Brazil, she doesn't believe I am capable of looking after myself for a minute and would be determined to come with me.

'On this occasion, it will be far more dangerous than ever. Should I have a problem with the Russians, the Devon & Cornwall police will know all about it. But don't contact them either. Once I know what's happened to Bob, I will ring on my satphone.'

Chapter 14

England was looking decidedly bleak when the British Airways airbus touched down at Heathrow. Below the steps, he could see the two officers from Special Branch, one looking more senior, waiting to drive him to Devon. He climbed in stiffly, praying he was not on a wild goose chase.

'Good morning, Superintendent. Tell me, is there any news of Mr Buckmaster yet?'

'You will be pleased to hear, Sir, that the Devon & Cornwall Constabulary have managed to locate him, plus two Russians, in a barn near a village called Ashcombe, where there is a moorland airstrip. He had initially been drugged, before being bound and gagged while they waited for a light aircraft which flew in just as we arrived. One of the Russians ran out to warn the pilot about us and was killed by the propellor, while the other, I'm afraid, escaped in a red post office van.'

'So where did they take Mr Buckmaster afterwards?'

'They took him home immediately, where his butler already had technicians working on the security devices, which they said would take only a short time to restore.'

'So has he meanwhile been provided with police protection?'

There was an ominous silence before he replied, 'No, Sir, he said he and his butler did not need it.'

'I should not have been out of contact. It is a frightening error on your part, Superintendent, for there is one Russian still free. After what happened at Ashcombe, which they will regard only as a minor inconvenience, Vilovitch, who owns the oil company Voztok, and is a Kremlin butcher, will be even more determined to magic Mr Buckmaster away. He is in serious danger, so please ask your friend to put his foot down, for we must get to his house in Devon before we are too late.'

'It looks as if we are already too late.' the superintendent exclaimed as they approached the drive.

One electric gate was swinging wide open with the red post office van sitting on the road outside, while not far beyond a pool of even brighter red blood trickled into an iron grating set in the tarmac. Just below, lodged against the branch of a tree, was the twitching body of Jenkins with a bullet hole through his forehead, still gripping the envelope he had been about to give the postman.

'Are you armed, Sir?'

'No, I seldom carry a weapon. Guns are far too dangerous,' he replied.

As they moved swiftly towards the house, they suddenly froze. 'Did you hear that shot above the noise of the waves just now, Sir? It came from that far lawn overlooking the sea. You know this place so you had better go forward and have a careful look while we cover you.'

Running towards the lawn, while keeping low behind a wall so he could not be seen, when he saw the second corpse, he could not help himself, shouting back, 'Oh my God, it's Mr Buckmaster!'

As the body was lying half over the cliff, it was only partly visible, but it was the brown shoes that had sent shivers down his spine. Then, as he hid behind some bushes to search the cliffs beyond, it dawned on him that the Russian would surely never shoot Bob. His orders must have been to seize him and deliver him to that son-of-a-bitch Vilovitch in Moscow, or face the consequences.

Meanwhile, the local police had arrived with one of their more stalwart officers shouting, 'Stay right where you are, Sir, while we approach the body.' But as two of them turned the corpse over to see its face, it slipped from their grasp almost taking them with it, and dropped out over the cliff.

He could hear the crunch of bones breaking as it bounced over the rocks and plummeted into the sea. Raising his arms in despair, and seeing a couple of garden chairs nearby, he asked the superintendent, who was following him, to sit down and decide what to do next.

'As I told you in the car, Bob ran a company called Nuklin, which used to provide the world with uranium for making nuclear bombs. So, having changed to supplying it exclusively to fuel nuclear generating plants, the great man should have been rewarded with a medal, not murdered. But now, sadly, it's too bloody late.'

'Too late?' A quiet voice over his shoulder enquired.

He whipped round, as the police officer, while reaching for his pistol, fell heavily off his chair.

'I hired you as a professional, Major, but you have disappointed me again,' started Bob. 'If you had explored beyond where I shot that bastard with my Smith and Wesson just now, you would have discovered why I chose this to be my home. Not far below are a series of caves running back into the cliff face and from them a secret passage leading up to my house, cut through the rock a long time ago by men involved in the noble trade of smuggling brandy. So welcome to the scene of the crime, and please ask Jenkins to bring us three glasses and two bottles of my favourite Krug.'

'Bob,' he said, trying to recover his composure. 'I hate to tell you, Sir, but before you dealt with that Russian, he had already shot your butler dead when he opened your gates to post a letter.'

'Ignoring that unfortunate occurrence, Mr Buckmaster,' continued the superintendent, 'please now tell us precisely what those Russians have been up to?'

'Briefly a Russian oligarch has been out to abduct me and steal my ideas. Yesterday morning, just when I sent Jenkins off to alert your police, two of his gangsters, who had already disarmed the security devices, must have remained here watching the place. While I was out in the garden talking on my secure telephone, I heard them shoot their way through my gates, luckily giving me time to throw the telephone into a flower bed.

'After drugging me, they took me to a small airstrip where they gagged and bound me. When your police arrived, they were on the point of flying me out of the country. But having brought me back here, all I remember, after hearing a bullet being fired, was running towards my hideout from where I shot that brute who was brandishing a Soviet era Stechkin, from a weapon slit my company had recently cut for me through the solid granite.'

'To fill you in, Sir, one of the two Russians we discovered at the airstrip was killed by a propellor blade. The other, who had helped drug you before taking you there in a stolen postal van, then drove it back here and rang your bell posing as a postman. But as you must be in a state of shock right now, we will come back later to go through the reasons behind all this, which are baffling us.'

Once the police had gone, Bob fetched the champagne himself and they both sat down in the library.

'Pity about Jenkins, he was a good man. And thanks, Major, for returning so smartly from Muscat on your way to Bali. When you sensed that something was wrong, am I right in saying it was you who asked an official from the British embassy in Muscat to call the police?'

At that moment, his house telephone rang. 'This is the chief constable. Who am I speaking to?'

'I am Mr Buckmaster's personal assistant.'

'This is to tell you that since your arrival at Heathrow, when you impressed my superintendent on how important Mr Buckmaster is to us all, we have decided to send him an efficient young police lady to look after his every need until he finds a new butler. At the same time, please tell him that he will have 24-hour police protection for the time being, irrespective of the upgrade being carried out to his security devices, which should have been linked through to us in the first place.'

'Thank you, Chief Constable, I will give him the good news immediately.'

'Perhaps,' Bob replied. 'I should not have leafleted my Thunder Club after all. The last thing I wanted was the police getting involved. Before you advise me on what to do next, Major, my immediate intention is to ask the CEO of my company Nuklin to scrap the leaflets and to telephone the top companies about my club instead. That must continue to include the largest Russian oil outfits like Lukoil and Rosneft. But first, they must see that Voztok is either taken over, or their son of a bitch owner, Vilovitch, is put to the sword. I must not make mistakes like that again.

'But let us now turn to sequestration. Before all this happened, I was talking to Felipe in Rio, who told me that my choice of a young partner for his SPOD venture was admirable. He said that Jeb had come up with some great ideas and he was confident that they would have the gas envelopes under construction very shortly. He told me that the SPODs will drill a vast acreage. But we both agreed that the drilling mechanism Jeb has designed, plus his tugs, should be fabricated in Japan.

'I have not yet told you about my choice of planting areas, as I have no doubt that we should start off in the Australian Outback. There are several advantages in going to that flat and largely unobstructed terrain first, which does get a spot of rain from time to time. Also Australia is one of the country's most responsible for climate change due to the increasing quantities of coal they are mining and then exporting, particularly to China. At the same time. it is where Nuklin will be able to start mining the largest deposits of thorium in the world. It's a win, win, situation!'

'So what would you like me to do next, Sir?'

'Your mission has already been decided. First, you must locate the international headquarters of those monstrous Indonesian arsonists who are continuing to destroy the climate faster than we are able to repair it. After you have dispatched the leader of their wretched organisation, you must decide where to assemble the first SPOD and plan a cunning means of smuggling it into Australia without being seen.

'Once you have tested it on site and won over their government, you must arrange for more to be delivered to a suitable airfield close to your chosen planting area. You will operate them there as long as it takes to replace all the sequestration lost to the Amazon rainforest.'

'So, have you yet managed to discover where the Indonesian arsonists are operating from, Sir?'

'No, because of the latest shenanigans, I did not get the chance, so I am leaving that to you, Major. You will be remunerated as I was going to pay you in Brazil, but this time, your bonus will not depend on how many of those vermin you can dispose of, but solely on eliminating their leader. In order for you to do so, I will make life easier by lending you my fast motor yacht Atlantis, which I named after my wife, Atlanta, before she left me.

'It has been chartered ever since through a friend of mine in Thailand. Meanwhile, having binned the Thunder Club leaflets, I am out to interest every investor I can find in the SMRs and the thorium-based fuel I hope to have in production very soon. Good luck, Major. Here is your new sat phone, while I go and retrieve my own from the flowerbed!'

**

'Good to see you again, Major,' enthused Macey in the cosy departure lounge at Exeter airport. 'Thank goodness, you managed to find Bob. Is he OK?'

'We should not have thought any differently, Macey. However, he will now be better protected by the police, although he is going to miss his butler, Jenkins, who one of the Russians shot dead.'

'I never met the poor fellow but it all sounds pretty desperate. You must tell us all exactly what happened when we are up in the air again. And by the way,

Ana has written this love letter for me to give to you. She also asked me to give you a white dish-dash she bought in the souk after you left for England. She said you must wear it the moment we arrive back in Muscat again to refuel.'

'How touching, Macey, let me open the letter then.'

Dear Jungle Jim,

What a naughty boy you are leaving me behind like that without telling me. You must have got yourself into terrible trouble on your own, and I pray that you are still in one piece.

On arrival in Bali, I looked up all the best hotels and was collected by a limo from the Banyan Tree, which has some private, one-bedroomed, villas with swimming pools overlooking the Indian Ocean. I'm sure you will not mind breaking the law and sharing it with me as Mr and Mrs Smith? During our brief stop in Muscat, which I never had time to explore, I took a taxi to the souk where I met a charming Sumatran called Anwar, who said it would take less than eight hours to make you a suit.

While I was buying you some tropical clothes for wearing in Bali, he told me about his friend, Ari, who lives in Brunei. He said that Ari knows all about the arsonists, and until he gave up his boat, he fished off every island between Bali and West Irian. He believes the Dragons must have their base on one of them, but he says if you wish to see him, you must be disguised in the dishdash, I have given to Macey, from the moment you arrive.

Apparently, the damage the Dragons have caused to the forests here, particularly in Borneo, is as bad as that in the Amazon rainforest, and Ari's life is in danger for trying to stop them. So Anwar says you too are on a very dangerous mission and must take every precaution. He needs to give you Ari's latest position which, meanwhile, he is going to find out, but he is frightened that the Dragons will come after him immediately, if he is seen talking to another westerner again.
Love, Ana

After re-joining the aircraft, he said, 'We are diverting to Brunei, Sam, I hope Ana waits for me!'

'You'll be bloody lucky, Major, Not only are she and Macey the prettiest pair of birds I have ever clapped eyes on, but they are both far too intelligent. If

I was her, as you have already left her alone once to fight off the sharks in Bali, I would refuse to see such a callous man ever again!'

'Sam, some girls may call me a loose cannon, not callous. But most think of me as a cannon ball!'

The flight was to take them over Syria and Macey pointed out that far below lay the city of Aleppo where the civil war had started eight years earlier, ending only after four miserable years when the Syrian army captured the city with much bloodshed. She deplored the fact that many of their best people had fled to other parts of the world, such as Germany, only creating a longer-term problem.

'Agreed, Macey, but nothing like the disaster we are facing with climate change, for although there may be no war, it will be impossible to escape from the heat, even to the North Pole!'

'Not with Bob back in charge. For both Sam and I are confident that you are going to sort the climate out together. However, in your case, it will only be possible if Ana holds your hand.'

After they landed an hour later and he was able to don his dishdash and hire a taxi, thinking of Ana and the part she was playing, he became focussed on the dangerous task she had set for him. Finding the Dragon's lair was going to be difficult enough, but at least she may have helped him head in the right direction. But was it?

He had managed to find Anwar's stall in the souk without having to ask where it was as it appeared to have better quality material than any of its rivals, although half hidden between those selling carpets, jars of frankincense, camel saddles, jade necklaces and other eastern paraphernalia.

'Anwar,' he enquired in a soft voice, not wishing to give himself away. But despite trying again above the hubbub of the crowd milling around him, there was no answer.

There seemed to be a back entrance to his stall, almost obscured by bolts of multi-coloured cloth. So he peered in, hoping to find Anwar talking on the telephone. He was there alright, but lying on the floor with a dagger in his throat, surrounded by a dark, gory mess of congealing blood.

There was not a moment to lose before someone else found the Sumatran, so he quietly withdrew while cursing under his breath that he no longer would be able to find the man living in Brunei.

'I was hoping to visit the Grand Mosque while I was in these glad rags,' he said to Sam and Macey, on returning, 'but I found the Sumatran, who may have helped us, dead with a dagger in his throat. Ana said he knew a fisherman in Brunei who may know where the Dragon HQ is. It was certainly the Dragons who have killed him, even more reason to divert to Brunei immediately.'

Should Anwar have given away Ari's location before his throat was cut, Bob's mercenary knew that the retired fisherman would soon be their next victim. So finding him before the Dragons did, seemed to be the best and, perhaps, his only opportunity of completing Bob's second assignment, while avoiding any further cuts in his remuneration. So, despite the task becoming increasingly hazardous, he had no alternative but to go looking for him.

The Sultan of Brunei had once been hailed as the world's richest man, largely due to the fact that he ruled one of the smallest countries with proportionately the largest oil and gas reserves anywhere. But tucked away on the western coast of Borneo, Brunei, with no need to plant oil palms, while deploring the relentless deforestation in Borneo. had retained its dense cover of trees.

The Major did not know the Sultan, only one of his staff, a British officer, who had been a cadet with him at the Royal Military Academy Sandhurst. His friend had then joined the Gurkhas and later been seconded to Brunei, where he had remained on the Sultan's staff for many years. So going to see him at his office in the Istana Nural Iman, the largest residential palace on Earth, was at least a start.

Driving his hired Mercedes along a road running beside the Brunei river, it was not long before he was confronted by the golden dome of the Great Mosque rising above the trees. After arriving at some gold painted gates, he was ushered into a guardroom, and while one soldier parked his car, another led him to the brigadier's office.

'Where have you come from, old friend?' he said, jumping up to shake his hand. 'How very good to see you again. I understand that you have just arrived in Brunei to look for a missing person.'

'Yes, that is what I told them at the airport, Tom, but it will be like looking for a straw in the wind. All I can tell you is that he is called Ari and is a retired Brunei fisherman, who has since become passionate about preventing the fires being lit next door in what remains of Borneo's forests by a gang of arsonists, just as they are doing where I have come from in Brazil. So because he may be always on the move, I was hoping that you may be able to arrange for me to meet a forestry official in your Darussalam, who will know how to find him.

'Unless I am able to warn him about the arsonists, who have just cut the throat of his friend in Bali, he will quickly suffer the same fate.'

'Understood, but I am unable to suggest such a person, not being responsible for the forests. Why not talk to the warden of the Ulu Temuong National Park, which is only thirty miles south west of here near the coast. If the man was formerly a fisherman, he may still be somewhere in that area.'

'That, I know, is the best lead I am going to get here. Thanks, Tom.'

The warden's hut was where Tom had said it would be. Maybe he had been fishing there, for after parking the car and following a fast-flowing river for about a kilometre, there it was standing in a clearing close to a waterfall with below a wooden bridge crossing over it. But no-one was there.

Awestruck by the sight of the lofty trees surrounding it, which were at least seventy metres high, he had failed to notice a man hiding among them watching him though a pair of binoculars. He jumped to his feet as the Major moved forward, and in a voice which was hard to hear above the roar of the waterfall, shouted, 'Alan trees, some of the tallest in the world!'

Seeing the lean, deeply tanned man, wearing just a pair of khaki shorts and a friendly smile, he relaxed immediately.

'What a stunning place you have here. I am looking for a man named Ari, who I believe is living somewhere in this area of the forest. Later on, I'm bringing my wife here trekking, and have been told that Ari is the right man to show us the best part of it. Do you happen to know him?'

'I did some years ago before fish stocks started declining so badly in the South China Sea that many of us were forced to sell our boats as scrap. The last I heard of him was that he had become very political and was trying to get those maniacs next door to stop destroying their forests in order to sell more palm oil. Although, they may make millions by providing barrels of it for cooking, or for making biodiesel, it is said they no longer absorb the carbon as the forests used to do.

'By lighting all those fires, they are also decimating the habitat of many of our native species like the clouded leopard, the sun bears and the poor orangutans, which may soon be wiped out here altogether.'

Wondering why the man was so well informed, and thinking back to what Tom, whose job was always on the line, had told him, he realised in a flash that it was Ari himself he was talking to. Obviously, Tom had not dared say his name due to the man's reputation of being an activist.

165

'Today,' he continued, 'your population in Great Britain is approaching sixty-eight million people but ours in Brunei is just under four hundred and fifty thousand, so disappearing acts don't happen here. Yes, I am the man you are looking for. Tell me, why have you come so far to find me?'

'Because you may know where the arsonists, who call themselves the Dragons, have their base?'

'Risky business, for I am a prime target of theirs. But I may be able to help you. I know of one island south of here, whose inshore waters are never fished as there are live dragons living there.' At that moment, a bell tinkled.

'It's one of my trip wires,' he whispered 'The arsonists are here. But they will never make it across my wooden bridge, for it will collapse and impale them on some sharply pointed bamboos I have hidden underwater. Now let's both get out of here fast!'

Running downstream, they heard men screaming, as the river turned crimson with their blood.

Chapter 15

Ud. Mad terrorist and firebrand.

'Sam, although I fear for poor Ari, luckily, I have returned intact with the information I was after. I hope you don't mind flying such distances in the Gulfstream while Bob and myself stick our necks out trying to fix the climate. Of course, if the do gooders knew what mileage we are clocking up and how much fuel we are burning, they would say we are the problem! So, Sam, unless we complete our mission before Bob buys you a new aeroplane powered by electricity, hydrogen, or rubber bands, as far as they are concerned, we might as well go and put our feet up.

'I have been talking to Bob on the replacement sat phone he gave me, who says that Jeb has just completed all he is able to achieve working with Felipe on the SPOD envelopes. So once we arrive in Bali, sorry guys, but you and Macey will not be stretching out on those glorious beaches again. For Bob says you must fly immediately to Rio, pick up Jeb and then take him on to Tokyo, where he is arranging for the shoot boxes, tugs and tray trucks to be manufactured.'

Sam let out a deep sigh, although acknowledging his job was to pilot Bob's plane wherever he was detailed, this was getting crazy. He had now flown to Cuiaba and back, then to the States and back to Rio, on to Salt Lake City and then back to Rio again. From Rio to Muscat, then on to Bali and back to London. From London to Exeter and back to Muscat. From Muscat to Brunei and on to Bali again. Now it had to be on to Rio and then Tokyo, before flying back to Bali once more.

'Do you realise, Major, that over the past weeks, Eliot and I have flown a total distance of nearly a hundred thousand miles, or a hundred and sixty thousand kilometres, which is four times around the planet. Apart from that stop in Salt Lake City, we have not had time to walk off the tarmac!'

'And that may only be the start of it, Sam. So, therefore, I am going to ask Bob to award you both with at least a month's holiday in Bali once you have returned from flying Jeb to Tokyo. After that, we shall not be with you for a time as we attempt to find and then eliminate the head Dragon behind those bloody arsonists. I sense we are about to land at Bali, so good luck with the next leg. I hope to see you back here soon.'

'Do take care, you devil, and see that Ana looks after you as well as she must have done in Brazil,' said Macey, as they began to lose height and Sam moved back into the cockpit. 'You will never survive without her!'

Apart from her drive and enthusiasm, he admired Macey's vibrant personality as she sat down at the front of the cabin wearing a figure-hugging tropical dress based on the uniform Bob had previously designed for her. Looking at her smiling lips, twinkling blue eyes and thick chestnut hair tied behind in a chignon, plus her slim waist and perfect legs, made him begin to feel like his old self again.

Although, he could not wait to see Ana, not for the first time in his life he began to feel a little uneasy, for he could not take his eyes off Bob's stewardess.

But that had to be forgotten as he picked up his small bag and climbed out into the steaming heat of the Indian Ocean.

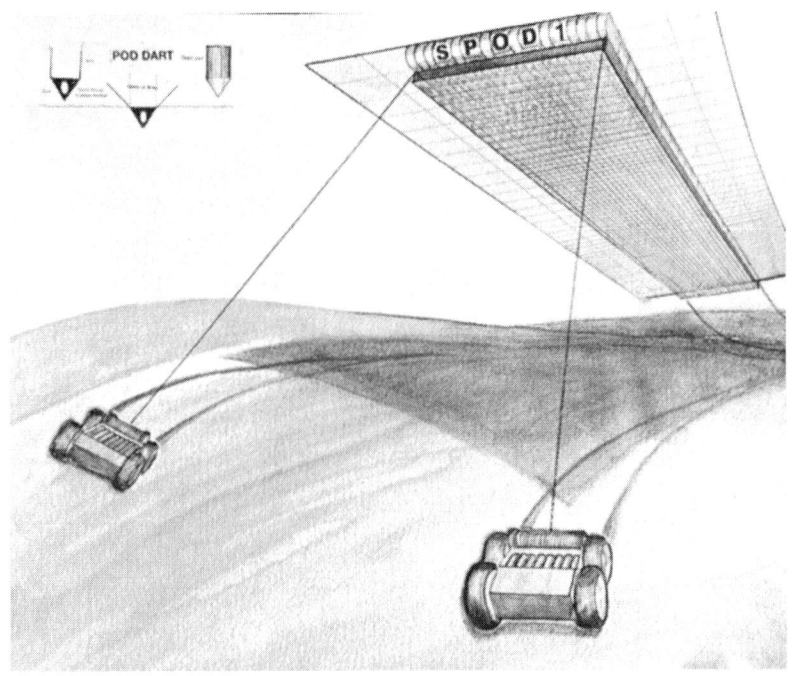

Jeb's illustration of a Sky SPOD drilling darts.

When Sam lifted the jet into the sky and headed into the setting sun, Macey realised just how smitten she had also been with the mercenary, who, since he had boarded the jet in Rio only two days before, had struck her as just the handsome gung-ho type she had imagined him to be, someone whom she had dreamed about all her life. Before she left medical school in Los Angeles, she had pinned photographs of Clint Eastwood, Steve McQueen, Harrison Ford and many other famous swashbucklers around the wall of her bedroom and he reminded her of all of them.

Flying back from Brunei, she had felt a tingling sensation creeping through her body, which she had found impossible to suppress. As he sat there, the sight of his firm jaw, high cheek bones and swept back dark hair had made her feel weak at the knees, for she had been imagining his rock-hard body against hers…no she was on duty.

So, hoping he had not noticed, she turned her mind back to Sam, whom she loved dearly, if not for his looks, for his enthusiasm, grip on life and dedicated professionalism. So, she went to the cockpit with two glasses of fresh lime juice.

Sam was a very different character to the Major, but just as determined to succeed, she thought later. But, apart from that, he would look after her far better than the mercenary, who she would not be able to trust for more than five minutes. Previously, while serving in Afghanistan, she had met a handsome young British officer in the Special Air Service, who was spending most of his time behind enemy lines trying to coax the Taliban to return to their villages.

He, like the Major, was braver than the brave, but although she admired the fact that both of them had been trained for every eventuality, she was put off by their unpredictability and utter ruthlessness.

Bob, as a result, she concluded, had the perfect team working for him. Two men who believed in getting things done against all the odds stacked against them irrespective of the consequences, which for the mercenary meant death. And two ladies, who not only had no fear of any blood being spilt, but were mentally tougher than both of their boyfriends put together. Then there was Jeb, her brother, who they were about to pick up in Rio.

She was immensely proud of him for no one she had ever met was so innovative and determined to succeed. And finally, there was Felipe, Ana's father, who, although owning one of the most beautiful houses in Rio, unlike most of his neighbours, was a man of action prepared to employ his engineering firm not only to help the local farmers in Brazil, but the rest of the world in general.

When he boarded the jet in Rio, Jeb was thinking much the same. 'I have had a very productive time with Felipe in Rio being looked after by one of the nicest ladies I have ever met, who seems anxious that Ana, her daughter, does not get into any more trouble with that naughty mercenary, although she is powerless to prevent it! I must show you what Felipe and I have been up to.'

On reaching cruising height, he laid out some drawings on a small table as Sam came to join him.

'First, I should point out that every component of the SPOD, Bob's name for what you may think of as a "flying sandwich", may be transported by air, or sea, to anywhere in the world. Although, it is thirty-tree metres wide by a hundred metres long, it is fabricated in two separate, double skinned envelopes designed to fit standard pallets. Once inflated with helium, these will be secured by straps to an array of solar panels, which will unfold to twice it's width, mounted on top, before being joined below to a large number of shoot boxes, which when bolted together create an impressively strong planting machine.

'You may think that a SPOD, by being half the size of a football field, will be hopelessly unstable. But because it will be towed on the ground by two tugs, on land, and in the air by two drones, with two heavy steel cables being dragged behind, it should be able to fly successfully in wind speeds not exceeding twenty knots. When the wind speed increases, it may be lowered by compressing the gas in the two envelopes and then anchored down.

'Needless to say, there is plenty to go wrong, but what I find stimulating is that although the suggested speed for the tugs, or the drones when the ground becomes difficult, is set at sixteen kph, or ten mph, by operating several SPODs we believe that we should be able to replace all the sequestration lost to the Amazon rainforest and elsewhere in only a very few years.'

'That sounds remarkable, Jeb, but when we start planting so many plants, or trees, how do we deal with the environmentalists who complain about the damaging effect it will have on wildlife?'

'That has also been taken into account, Sam. After replenishment, SPODs will drill the next strip of plants in the opposite direction, leaving a 50-metre gap between plantings for wildlife.'

'How then do you replenish the trays at the end of each run?'

'We do that with two electric tray trucks carrying two hundred trays on two trailers behind each of them, plus a third to start collecting the empty trays. Because the strips are planted in parallel, at no time will the trucks travel out of range to their base and its separate solar farm.'

'So where are you going to establish your snake plants, or their alternative, Jeb?' Macey asked. 'And does our father really believe that plants are better than trees for sinking the carbon?'

'Absolutely. But to answer your first question, Bob has chosen the Australian Outback because of its size, its flatness and the fact that it is largely devoid of obstacles. The Great Sandy Desert, which benefits from dew at night, also gets over thirty centimetres of rain per year, which will, it said, continually increase after planting. So it certainly appears to be the right place for us to start.

'As for trees, although the world must continue planting as many as possible in the right places, they not only grow too slowly to catch up with climate change but may not be so easily engineered to make them drought tolerant and capable of trapping the maximum amount of carbon.'

**

Surprisingly, he found Ana already waiting for him at Bali airport in the private aircraft arrival lounge.

'You lovely girl, how the hell did you know I was flying in right now, I meant it to be a surprise.'

'The world does not work like that, Jimbo, if a girl finds it impossible to do without her man for a moment longer. You have no idea how hard it's been to fight off the opposition here. Although, their eyes are always hidden behind dark glasses, I feel that every man here wants to undress me.'

He had followed her out into the car park towards her hired fiat cinque cento. 'No wonder, Ana, for wearing only that open necked silk shirt and those pink hot pants which show a chink of flesh where your lovely derriere joins the softness of your brown, suntanned legs, there is not much left for them to take off!'

'Stop it, wild man. If you knew how stifling the weather has been here, no wonder. In fact, apart from the air conditioning in our posh chalet, the only place where I have felt cool was when I came back here yesterday to find out if there was any news of you. They kindly allowed me up into the control tower where I asked the guy to call me the moment Sam checked in on the radio. It seems I just got here in time. But again, I was being followed by men in dark glasses, which frightens me.'

'Why you, Ana, you were the coolest cat around when we confronted the arsonists in Brazil, but next time around, I don't want you to go anywhere near them!'

'You have got that wrong, Jimbo.'

'Maybe, but let's forget all that for a moment. If that is your nook coming up, it looks delightful.'

'Not half as delightful as our own private pool. Once we get out of this tin can, I'm going to dive in as nature intended and while you do the same, I will look the other way.'

He felt as though he had been wrapped within the tentacles of an octopus, for so violent was her passion, it seemed he had been consumed in one mouthful and gone straight to heaven.

'Am I still really alive, Ana, or have you drowned me in a sea of stars. Give me time to recover for a moment, so I may return to this miserable world and start to think straight again.'

'Yes, we will both have to start thinking very straight soon, for I was approached by a much more sensible looking guy on the beach yesterday, who said he had come here looking for you.'

'Did he have a dragon tattooed on his right arm?'

'No. Much to my relief, he was a very nice black man who introduced himself as Barney. When I told him who I was, he said that he is the captain of a yacht which Bob has sent down here for our exclusive use over the next few months. So I have invited him to come and tell us all about her.'

'I never knew Bob owned a yacht until I saw him back in England, luckily alive and kicking, after two men had tried to abduct him to Russia with all his secrets. It is time I told you what happened. The reason we heard that shot before his telephone went dead, was that one of them fired a bullet through the lock on his gates. But before they both grabbed hold of him, he was able to throw the sat phone he was talking to us on into a flower bed.

'They drugged him first and then drove him to a lonely airstrip where they gagged and bound him before one of the Russians, who had rushed out to meet the light aircraft destined to fly him to an airport, was killed by walking into its propeller. The police, who had been alerted by Jenkins, took Bob back to his house only to find one of the gates were hanging wide open with his butler lying dead in a pool of blood.

'So he dashed through and grabbed his Smith and Wesson, before running to his bolt hole in a cave at the end of his garden from where he shot the Russian dead. Since then, a policewoman has been sent to look after him, and until things return to normal, he will, thank heavens, continue to be given police protection.'

'What a drama; someone should make a film about it!'

'Although, Bob has still no idea where the Dragon's den is situated, he told me he was lending us his yacht to facilitate the difficult task we would now be faced with. The yacht is named Atlantis after his wife, Atlanta, who later left him because of his dealings with North Korea, when they were on holiday in Thailand, where she's been on charter ever since. He said that we may also need

173

to use her later when taking the SPOD across from wherever we decide to assemble it, to Australia.'

Ana, now wrapped in a bath robe printed with pink flamingos her mother had given her in Rio, was looking so gorgeous, he lifted her up and carried her to where they could become one together.

'Let us forget room service, Ana, my guardian angel. Now I have told you all about my time back looking for Bob, before we go anywhere, let's enjoy life, for it will never get any better!'

It was at that moment they heard someone banging on the door.

'Ana, who the hell is it? After Sam's remark, I must disappear before anyone sees me here.'

'While we are on our honeymoon, Jim?'

It was only after he had rushed into the bathroom and slipped into a white towelled gown that he heard Ana opening the door to welcome Barney, who, as she invited him in, sounded very worked up about something.

'Hullo, it's a pleasure to meet you, Major, for Bob has told me all about you. I believe you are his special operations manager. The mission he has sent you on must be a dangerous one for when I returned to the yacht after meeting Ana on the beach earlier, I saw a black drone with a livid red insignia on it fly over her, obviously taking photographs.'

'Did the insignia look like a dragon, Barney?'

'Precisely. But what that hell does that signify? It looked so bloody sinister, I downed it with my radio jammer.'

'You are right to have done so, Barney, for it means that the bastards, who are a band of arsonists named the Dragons, are already on to us. To put you immediately in the picture, Bob has given me two difficult tasks to complete. His first is to locate the Dragon's HQ, which may be on an island between here and the coast of West Irian, and then to eliminate their leader.

'The Dragons are a particularly unpleasant lot, who have been burning down many of the world's forests with phosphorus sticks dropped from drones, while blackmailing governments to stop them doing so.

'Bob's second task is no less demanding, for it is to find a suitable place in Indonesia to assemble a planting device he has named a SPOD, which I will describe later. We must then tow it, without being seen, across the Timor Sea to the northern shores of Australia to help combat climate change. But how those Dragons already recognised Bob's yacht defeats me. Tell me about her?'

'She is a 90-metre state of the art rocket ship, man, powered by two gas turbines driving twin water jets, which Bob had built in Holland eight years ago. This not only gives her a top speed of 45 knots, but means she can manoeuvre in shallow water without fear of damaging her props. Painted in dark blue with a thin orange stripe along her waterline, indicating that she belongs to Nuklin, Bob's company, her streamlined hull is instantly recognisable.

'I'm afraid it is possible that the head Dragon may have chartered her recently. But as they leave false names in her log book, I never know their true identity, or am able to tell one rich Indonesian from another.'

'Well, most drones only have a range of five miles with about thirty minutes flight time, Barney, so I believe it was either flown from here on Bali, or from a boat not far offshore.'

'When I arrived here, Sir, I read up some of the history of Bali for it has not always been the paradise it is now supposed to be. In 2002, bombs were detonated in three nightclubs by Islamist fundamentalists, or so it was believed, which killed over two hundred people. Although, three of the supposed perpetrators were executed, a fourth known as The Prince, escaped and either he, or his brother called Ud, whom I have been reading about, could well be the man you are looking for. If so, they will have spies in Bali watching every move. Both are known to be violent criminals and are extremely dangerous.'

'As you cruised down the gulf of Thailand and the South China Sea, were you followed, Barney?'

'No, because it is the most dangerous area in the world for piracy, I had a man on watch throughout our passage south, and apart from container ships and fishing boats, we saw no other vessels.'

'In that case, I suggest that we must sail tomorrow night. But first directly north, hoping that if the drone was flown from somewhere onshore here, the Dragons will not work out our true heading.'

'So where exactly is your objective likely to be, as you have not let me into the secret yet, Major?'

'It is only a hunch, Barney, but after visiting Brunei recently, where I was given some clues by a retired fisherman, I believe that the Dragons are named after that vicious breed, some as large as leopards, which live on the island of Komodo, about six hundred kilometres due east from here.'

They cast off at midnight from the quay adjacent to Bali Yacht Services in the port of Benoa. Then, as Atlantis headed first north and then east at 35 knots, making nothing of the short sea being kicked up by a strong headwind, Ana endlessly scanned the ocean with powerful binoculars.

Meanwhile, beside her on the bridge, the Major suggested Barney should find calmer waters to reduce the bow wave, or "bone" as known by ancient mariners, which could easily give them away.

'I calculate, Major, that to reach Komodo, it will take us ten hours passing either to the north or south of the island. However, as it gets light, if we approach from the south we will be visible for miles. So before we reach Tenggara island, we must alter course and head north again.'

Barney had just gone below to fetch Ana a jacket, when she shouted down to him that she had seen a boat following about three kilometres astern in their phosphorescent wake. So returning fast to the helm, he threw the throttles forward, saying, 'You are right, Ana, and she's gaining on us!'

Hardly had he said so, when, above the howl of the twin turbines, Ana distinctly heard the whine of a drone. Searching the night sky, lit only by a slither of moon, she soon managed to locate the evil machine, but only because of the shiny metal object dangling beneath it.

'Barney,' she yelled in his ear. 'There is a drone about to fly over the yacht and it is going to drop one of those nasty phosphorus bombs on us!'

'No, it ain't!' Barney yelled back, while pressing the button on his multi-frequency jamming device just done so successfully in Bali.

She failed to see the drone hit the waves for grabbing hold off to the rails while the yacht rapidly altered course, she was mesmerised by the craft behind, which continued to gain on them.

'It is a ten metre "cigarette" hulled powerboat with one guy at the helm and, I hate to tell you, another manning a heavy machine gun mounted on the bow!' She shouted.

'So how do we get rid of those bastards, for they must be from Komodo, Barney?' The Major asked. 'Apart from a flare pistol, do you have any other weapons on board? If not, from past experience, the only alternative is to ram them, which could end up by us going down with them.'

'Agreed, but beyond Mojo, the next island after Tenggars, I see that there is a smaller one shown on the chart with a rock to one side, so leave it to Atlantis, for only she knows bast how to kill.'

They were travelling at forty-five knots but when they reached the tiny island, instead of throttling back, Barney threw Atlantis hard to port, pretending to circle the island. Then, as they rounded a high cliff with a rock just showing above the surface some fifty metres out from the shore, he slammed back the controls into hard astern, stopping her almost dead in the water. Masked by the bluff of cliff, the helmsman following behind did not stand a chance. Failing to see Atlantis until too late, in trying to avoid her, his boat smashed into the half-submerged rock at full speed.

There was a blinding flash, a shower of broken fibreglass and a body flying through the air to be quickly lost in a cloud of spray. Then, as it subsided, there was nothing left to be seen apart from a struggling swimmer, probably the machine gunner, crying for help in the violently disturbed sea.

Launching a small dinghy, Atlantis's crew hauled the man out of the water before shoving him up the companionway to confront a gleeful Barney, who found him to be, largely, still in one piece.

'You are correct, Major, the dragon tattooed on this scoundrel's arm certainly proves that they dislike our presence here, but if he refuses to tell us where the arsonists have their base, I will show you a trick, which in the days of life before the mast was known by sailors as keel hauling.'

As they approached the northern tip of Komodo Island with the engines now barely ticking over, Barney, true to his word, had the gunman brought back on deck. Then getting his crew to tie the man's legs together before passing the rope under the yacht's keel, he had him talking immediately.

'He says that there is a wooden landing stage close to a horseshoe cove half way down the eastern side of the island called Pink Beach. Some eight hundred metres north of it, hidden in a deeply wooded ravine, is an entrance to a tunnel leading to the bastard's HQ. But he warns us that it is surrounded by Komodo dragons lying up in the shade until it gets dark when they go foraging. There is a lookout on one of the steep hillocks overlooking their camp, so best to wait until it gets dark, approaching stealthily in the dinghy, while leaving the yacht hidden behind a point there.'

'He sounds cosha, Barney, but do you, seriously, believe him?'

'Yes, surprisingly, I do. He now knows that I am looking for a second crew member and he will do nicely when my Browning machine gun is delivered, which I am having mounted on the foredeck due to the growing number of pirates threatening us in the South China Sea. He also knows that Bob pays excellent wages. So because of what he has told us, I am now going to anchor Atlantis in that bay over there, where we may shelter unseen until the light starts going.'

'Does he suggest how you shoo away the Komodo dragons before entering the tunnel?' Ana asked.

'Sadly not! The guy simply told me that no one goes out of the entrance during the day, for the largest of them are over two and a half metres long and their bite is so poisonous that all but one of the few people known to have been attacked by them died within a few hours.'

'Ana, I am tackling this one on my own. It seems that their camp must be just beyond the hillocks the man mentioned, and once there, because the place is likely to be surrounded by razor wire, it may be difficult to escape without your help from outside the wire, if you hear shots being fired.'

Having dropped anchor where the man suggested, all went according to plan until after creeping past two of the largest dragons sleeping near the tunnel entrance, the Major was challenged and then arrested by an armed guard. Then, having been frisked and relieved of the knife, previously returned by the Omani customs, he was poked in the ribs with a Kalashnikov and shoved into a corner of the rock face while the guard phoned through to someone about their unwelcome visitor.

Two hours passed before two men in black baseball caps appeared and tied a rope around his neck as if they were about to hang him. They then proceeded to pull him so violently into the mouth of the tunnel that, although he tried to shout he was being throttled, they paid no attention. Neither did the fourth man waiting at the far end, who, having almost blinded him with a powerful torch, pressed a revolver to his head and searched his body again so roughly that he wanted to hit him.

After being dragged further along a stoney path to a dimly lit hut with blacked out windows, his tortured eyes just made out a row of the most powerful looking drones lined up beside it he had ever thought existed.

'Hi,' a tall sinewy fellow in a black track suit with rolled up sleeves welcomed him, as he was shoved through the door. 'I don't think you should be here,' he said, sliding forward like a cobra about to strike.

His right arm was tattooed with a red dragon matching the bandana tied around his head, which partly hid a livid scar running down from above his left ear to the corner of his cruel looking mouth, making his sneering face look all the more terrifying. His eyes were part hidden in the shadows but he could sense they were projecting a scorching beam of hate.

'So, Major, you have killed two of my key operators in Brazil, four more in Borneo I have been informed, and now two more of them manning one of my fast boats, have gone missing.' His voice was quiet, high pitched and menacing.

'If you have been reading the Rio press about me killing two of your operatives, and since then have lost four more of them, who were trying to kill my friend in Brunei, before we dispatched those two bastards in your boat, you are correct,' he replied in as strong a voice as he could muster. 'Indeed, I wish I was detailed to kill the lot of you, but my latest orders are just to kill you.'

The man had pulled a long, cruel looking, knife from his waist band, and as he took a step forward to stroke it across his throat, he cursed, for no one had ever filled him with so much fear.

'Your whereabouts are now known to the CIA, who are fully aware of your appalling reputation, Ud, from the time your father was murdered beside you in Cambodia working for Pol Pot in the killing fields, to your life stealing food in the ghettos of Manilla, before trying to sell doctored heroine to anyone who would buy it.

'When you eventually found a job working in the docks there, which you helped make into one of the most dangerous places on earth, your reputation for brutality was such, I have discovered, that several of the dockers tried to drown you with an anchor tied to your feet. So what made you change to setting the world's forests on fire, Ud?'

There was a long pause before standing up to his full miserable height, he replied, 'Money!'

'So before the CIA have you in front of a firing squad, if I not have killed you with my bare hands already, did it fill you with joy that your Dragons, ultimately, were going to destroy all of us?'

'You've got your facts wrong, Major, even if it was the CIA who found me here, which I doubt, you know as well as I do that the Central Intelligence Agency has no powers of arrest. So before I slit your throat, you had better think again.'

'Tell me then, Ud, before you do so, what is the purpose of those new-fangled drones I noticed before I entered your den of iniquity?'

'Assembled outside my hut are the first of my super, long range, drones that have just been delivered, Englishman. Why you have the brazen impertinence to poke your nose into my affairs when you should have been hung for double homicide in that Brazilian prison not a month ago, defeats me. But the answer is simple. The drones have been developed at huge expense for precisely the same reason that you were sent to Brazil. For now, at last, I am able to rid myself of all those useless operatives there, you, so pathetically, failed to kill.'

'And, presumably, be able to fly them over longer distances with a greater payload of phosphorus sticks to wherever you choose. No wonder the name Ud in Indonesian means firebrand.'

'Correct.'

'I also noticed that you have two Indian HAL helicopters sitting beside that shed near the far end of your compound, which presumably, is stacked to the roof with your elicit incendiaries. And, by the way, it was not the CIA who were going to arrest you but my friends, the SAS, who are respected throughout the world for the way they deal with terrorists like you.

'I can assure you that, should you fail to come to the agreement I am about to put to you, which is why I have been escorted here to see you, Ud, before you attempt to get away in those two choppers, there is an assault group of SAS tough guys waiting nearby on Raja Island, ready to tear all of you to pieces!'

'That sounds a little over dramatic, Englishman, for if you wish to interfere with my future plans how do you propose to compensate me for all my new equipment here plus the considerable amount of income I will be losing?'

'Better to say all that un-earned filthy lucre, Ud, but perhaps, you are beginning to see sense. Apart from being a British agent, I am employed by a very rich man, who, unlike most governments, and totally against my principles, will pay you a large sum in compensation should you stop your devilry. But only if you are willing to turn your attentions to saving the world rather than setting out to destroy it. For then you will be backed by more money than you have dreamed about.'

'So what other alternative do you have in mind, agent 007? You had better tell me fast for my lookout spotted your yacht when you first arrived off Komodo and I can assure you that my own alternative, before I cut your throat, is for you to join him and watch us blow both your yacht and its crew out of the water!'

'The task of last resort I'm offering you, Ud, before you get over dramatic yourself, will be given to you once I have your contact details and those of all your operatives, who must be stood down immediately. But, before passing you the five million dollars my boss has for you when Barney, my black skipper, returns here later with a naval escort, you must provide him with the full stock of your latest drones, apart from six, which you will retain for the special operation I have detailed for you in this envelope, not to be opened until I, personally, send you the codeword.'

'That does not sound like much of a bargain to me, Englishman.'

'No, but if your chances of staying alive don't look bleak enough already, Ud, I can assure you that without your help when I call for it, the planet will warm up so rapidly that neither of us will live to enjoy life much longer.'

'For you no longer!' Ud shouted in a sudden fury, flying at him with his knife and only stopped from cutting his throat when the camp radio started blaring. He listened to an agitated voice, then throwing the radio on the floor, he spat out, 'We have another problem, you wretched numbskull. One of my guards has reported seeing a woman near the entrance to my tunnel, who, when challenged, shouted back she was looking for you. At dawn, all my dragons return from foraging for food to sleep there and one of them, an aggressive three-metre-long male I named Gizzard, has grabbed and bitten her.

'So take these details you wanted and get the hell out of here before I kill both of you, and don't try pleading for the use of one of my choppers to take the bitch to hospital.'

The man with the torch reappeared and having roughly pushed him past the razor wire and down the tunnel again, the Major watched as the guard moved the dragons away from its entrance with an evil looking electric prodding stick, before he rushed past him to pick up Ana where she was sitting bleeding under a giant Ulin tree. Taking her from him, he kissed her on her forehead and lifting her gently over his shoulder, carried her back to where the man with the dinghy was waiting.

Before reaching Atlantis, he took one last look backwards to see Ud standing there on the shore watching them through a pair of binoculars while on the hillock above, he noticed two men aiming another heavy machine gun in their direction, as bullets started whipping the water into a frothing mass all around them.

Barney was waiting to receive them, and as they rounded the cliff to where he had dropped anchor, he breathed a sigh of relief.

'We must take Ana back to hospital in Bali flat out, Barney, for she has been bitten by one of those nasty dragons. I was far too long in that den of thieves, arguing the toss with their leader, a nasty piece of work, who is indeed called Ud. But Ana should not have started worrying about me. I have told her a million times that I am capable of looking after myself.'

'Am I expected to believe that, Major, after she told me what had happened in Brazil? But if you look at this chart here, it shows there is a decent hospital in Bali, very near to where we dock, called Siloam. I was told by a doctor, when I rang them that they have only once succeeded in saving a person from an injury caused by a Komodo dragon, although they have no idea if the victim, who released himself from their hospital, eventually survived.

'As the dragon's bite is considered to be life threatening, they will have a leading surgeon waiting for her when we arrive. The doctor said that as long as we return to Bali faster than the short amount of time, I told him it had taken us to reach the island last night against a head wind, they may, if she remains strong and her heart does not give up, be able to save her.'

'Hell's teeth, Barney. Then let's go for it!'

Chapter 16

Macey.

The Gulfstream was still sitting on the tarmac at Narita International Airport just outside Tokyo when Sam received an urgent message from Bob's mercenary.

'Please contact Felipe in Rio, Sam, and tell him that his daughter, Ana, has been bitten by a Komodo dragon. We are speeding back to Bali from the island of Komodo on Atlantis, Bob's incredibly fast boat, to see a leading surgeon at

Siloam hospital, who has already been alerted. So once you have returned from Tokyo with Jeb, your holiday there may have to be delayed yet again while you fetch Felipe from Rio to join Ana in the hope she survives. However, it will be quicker for him to book a flight with Varig, or another Brazilian airline if Varig no longer exists.'

'Wilco. But what desperate news. Wait a minute while I ask Macey if she knows anything about bites from those primeval lizards.'

'Macey here. Luckily, I have been reading a book about Indonesia, so straight to the point. Dragon bites are known to cause anticoagulation, when the patient's blood will not stop flowing. So first make certain that the wound is tightly bandaged, and if that does not work, apply a tourniquet if necessary. Secondly, Ana is likely to suffer from extreme hypotension, or low blood pressure, so you must give her plenty of water and mugs of coffee, as caffeine will help. But have a look for Melodrine in Barney's first aid cabinet, as it is often part of their emergency kit on boats.

'I am afraid that my book states the dragons are carnivorous and due to their like for rotten meat, they carry poisonous microbes in their saliva, which may be fatal if not treated quickly with a strong course of antibiotics. An alternative view is that the dragons inject venom into their victims like many other species of reptiles. But we must hope that is only an old wives tale. Because the attacks on humans are so rare, unlike most snake bites, sadly no antidote has ever been developed.'

'Oh my God, I was beginning to fall in love with Ana, and now, if she survives, she will consider me to be even more dangerous than she thought I was in Brazil, and she will never want to be anywhere near me again. Meanwhile, Macey, all we can do is try everything you have told us to do and pray that we are not going to arrive back in Bali too late.'

'Jeb has not arrived back here yet from the Japanese factory he has been visiting. But when he returns, having heard the bad news about Ana, he wants to contact you immediately.'

'Major, Jeb here, there is no one in the world who will know how to deal with such a situation better than my sister after her experiences in Afghanistan. So when you arrive at the hospital, why not ask the doctor to ring her on your sat phone?'

'Good idea, Jeb, but how have you been getting on in Tokyo?'

'It is all fixed. Sanaka Tec are building us not only six tray lorries and six tugs but also an initial forty shoot boxes plus firing mechanisms from an exceptionally light composite material. They will all be flown to wherever we decide to assemble the prototype SPOD within four weeks.'

**

They were making good progress towards Bali at 46 knots with the wind now behind them.

So, much to their relief, they managed to tie up at Benoa in Bali not long after mid-afternoon, where there was an ambulance already waiting for them at the dock.

'Thanks, Barney, great ride. I may be away with Sam over the next couple of days, which will hopefully give Ana more time to recuperate. There is not much point in me holding her hand, for without me around, I expect she is far more likely to pull through. So please wait here for further orders. Meanwhile, refuel the ship for the next leg of our journey, which you may find interesting!'

He then accompanied Ana, who was by now only semi-conscious, to the hospital, where they were met at the entrance by Professor Fry of Queensland University in Australia, who had been trying his best to create an antidote for dragon bites for several years, as yet, without success.

Ana was immediately wheeled into an emergency ward, where after a thorough investigation of her wound, the professor, who admitted that his antidote was still a long way off, re-appeared looking a little more positive than he had first expected.

'Major, if I may address you as that after your urgent telephone call. Your friend Ana has, so far, been luckier than the few Komodo victims I have had to deal with in the past, who all, apart from one, died within a few hours.'

'You mean she is somehow managing to hold on?'

'No, it is more that the dragon failed to hold on. If one of its filthy teeth had pierced an artery or even a large vein, because it took you over six hours to get here, she would no longer be with us.'

'It would have been sooner if only the bastard I was visiting on Komodo had lent us his helicopter!'

'I have always known about the dangers of visiting that island. This injury should not have been allowed to happen and it was wrong for you to have taken her there. It is still touch and go, but we will give her a blood transfusion and a cocktail of antibiotics, which may help if nothing else does.'

Back at their lodge, he immediately rang Felipe's wife in Rio.

'You will know most of the frightening story already, I expect, Marcia. Ana is desperately ill, but we are all willing her to pull through. Has Felipe now left, or is he waiting for Bob's plane?'

'Knowing what you get up to, Major, I was frightened for Ana from the moment she decided to join you. Felipe left directly for the airport and should be at the hospital by tomorrow evening.'

'Then I will take a taxi and meet him at the airport if you can text me his time of arrival. I am so sorry, I should never have got your lovely daughter involved in this.'

Marcia had been more understanding than many mothers, he thought, although he held back on telling her the rest of the story and how important their journey to Komodo had turned out to be.

He then put a quick call though to Bob, anxious to tell him what had happened.

'Major, you have disobeyed me again, I told you to kill that Indonesian imbecile, but you failed.'

'Yes, but situations change, Sir. I realised, not just because I had a knife to my throat, how much more important it was to come to an agreement, which Marcia will relay to you later. If he does not follow that to the letter, I have made it clear that the CIA will ask the SAS to deal with him and his gang accordingly. They have assured me that his every move will be monitored by satellite.'

'Wrong decision, Major, that man should not be trusted for a moment, for however much he is watched in future, he will be able to cause mayhem. I sometimes wonder about you and your training at Sentinals, for you were, obviously, told to be nice to those who were about to kill you, instead of being told how to turn the tables and slaughter them instead? If I had been in that situation with a knife against my throat, and was a fit whipper snapper like yourself, I would have executed a quick backward somersault and grabbed the man's knife as I did so.'

'Rather than come to a sensible agreement, Sir?'

'What bloody agreement? You will have told Marcia a load of hogwash as far as I'm concerned, and what you have done by going against my direct orders is mind blowing. Just consider the situation where that man Ud, instead of reducing his operations, now extends them, and with new found energy, having invested more of his fortune in all the latest technology, such as the long-range drones currently being developed in Turkey. For he will then start threatening countries such as Australia, where I have just tasked you to carry out the most intensive campaign of carbon sequestration ever undertaken.

'His use of phosphorus, large quantities of which he is said to have bought previously from Muammar Gaddafi in Libya, should be our greatest worry. White phosphorus, apart from being used to create smoke screens, is sob notorious for burning human flesh and causing other dreadful injuries, that it is banned as an incendiary device by every self-respecting nation on Earth. So who's to say that your friend Ud will not go further, Major, beyond setting light to the forests?'

'You are right to be so critical of my raid on the Dragon HQ, Sir, but resulting from my drone deal with Ud, we are now able to extended our operations by being able to tow our SPODs with them.'

Knowing that Bob would eventually find out about his orders of last resort, and hoping that Ud, who he had given the codeword, would never be asked to implement them, he tried to forget the conversation, instead ringing the hospital to be told not to visit Ana, who was in an induced coma.

'She is not yet out of what is known on Mount Everest as the death zone,' the professor said, when he came to the telephone. 'She has to climb that mountain right now and let's hope she makes it to the top. Sad to say the previous person I managed to save from a Komodo dragon's bite never gave me a single word of thanks and refused to leave us his address.'

He thought of reassuring the professor about Ana, her training to be a doctor, and how he had implored her not to follow him onto the island, but he decided it would be pointless.

When Felipe arrived on the flight from Rio, after he had enquired briefly about the latest situation with his daughter, they drove straight to the Mulia, one of the top hotels in Indonesia.

'Once we are able to go and see her, poor darling,' Felipe suggested, 'I must also meet the professor, for he has an international reputation and after what you have just told me, there is no doubt that his patient who survived the dragon's bite was Ud, the gangster, who tried to kill you on Komodo. Since you left Rio in such a hurry, I must also tell you that after a session with the thumb screws, the arsonist who shot my daughter gave the police such a detailed description of how you killed his two mates with a fire bomb, you are fortunate, Major, to be still above ground.

'Ana, I know, is like a cat on a hot tin roof, and it is no fault of yours that she followed you when you failed to return on time from seeing that criminal. It is unbelievable that he would not fly her to the hospital in his chopper after his life was saved in a similar situation. What a mean bastard!'

'Agreed, Felipe. if only the professor had let the bugger die, for now I am in big trouble with my boss for not getting rid of him myself, as I was ordered to do. Bob's instructions were, as usual, quite straightforward. I was first to find and then kill the head dragon, and secondly, now that you have developed the SPOD so successfully, discover a perfect site for planting the snake darts which Macey's father will be sending down to us from his laboratory in Utah. They will eventually total many billions!

'The deal I came to with Ud, who told me that he has already managed to get rid of most of his operatives, is as follows. In exchange for his freedom, he will not only agree to cease his operations for ever but will also hand over all his new drones, apart from six of them, to Barney, the outstanding black skipper of Bob's yacht, when he returns to Komodo Island with an escort later. Once he has done so, we will use them to tow the SPODs over difficult terrain.

'As I am about to join Macey and Sam in searching for a suitable island to assemble the first SPOD before smuggling it into Australia without being seen, would you very kindly ask Marcia to relay all that to Bob in order to keep him quiet for the moment.' He then heard Felipe's cell phone ringing.

'It was the hospital who say I may go and see her now. If all goes well, I am certain that she will be at the point of our troops once we get cracking. So while I am with her, why don't I order a bottle of champagne for us so we may spend a few moments looking at the SPOD drawings I have brought with me. If Jeb has been successful in Japan, once you have decided from where you are going to launch the prototype, we will be on our way to accomplishing the task Bob set for us.'

Ana was sitting up and wondering what all the fuss was about, when Felipe arrived at her hospital bed. Her right arm was still heavily bandaged and so the bite marks were not visible, but she had brushed her hair and put on some makeup the hospital had given her. As a result, she was not only looking gorgeous, but rearing to get out of bed and rejoin her naughty Jungle Jim, she said.

'Tell me, Ana, before you go on any crazier adventures with that desperado again, how did you manage to fight the dragon off, I'm told it's never been done before?'

'I didn't even try, Papa. I was just very nice to him!'

**

Three weeks had passed, as expected, before Ana was allowed to leave hospital, giving Felipe and Jeb more time to finalise their ideas. Meanwhile, the Major, Sam and Macey had flown to Papua New Guinea, having made certain that the North Australian customs authorities at Kununarra, the airfield they had chosen for assembling the remaining SPODs, would be, as they thought, totally against anyone trying to import any such material without getting government authority.

Later, when flying over an airstrip partly hidden by trees near the mouth of the Fly River, the Major standing beside the pilot remarked, 'Did you know, Sam, that during World War Two, the natives here cut out clearings in the jungle hoping to entice American aircraft to come down from the sky and shower them with goodies. Known as the Cargo Cult, it must have caused aviators endless problems and I would not be surprised if that airstrip you can see below us, is one of them.'

'What we are actually looking for, Major, surely it is not a ruddy little airstrip but an aerodrome as close to Australia as possible, near a beach from which to launch your SPOD without difficulty.'

'Yes, Sam, and there must also be to a flat assembly area away from prying eyes, particularly from the headhunters, for they are still said to be living in some of the forests here. No wonder it is difficult to search for such a place when flying in a private jet at a speed of mach point eight!'

So they flew back towards Agats on the coast of West Papua, notorious, during 1961, for the murder of Michael Rockefeller, son of America's former president, who, after being shipwrecked was captured, killed, and eaten by cannibals. But it was too far from Wyndham, their chosen destination in northern Australia with the result that they banked steeply away south, passing the island of Trangan, which appeared to consist solely of scrub forest and mangrove swamps, until the larger island of Timor-Leste came into view, which looked far more promising.

'I notice that there is an airport positioned half way down the coast of the island directly facing Australia across the Timor Sea, which must be as close as we are ever going to get to it. It may be just the ticket, Sam, so why don't we land and take a look at what goes on there?'

Sitting in the co-pilots seat, he could see a ribbon of road leading from the single runway only a short way down to the shore, so, feeling more confident, he passed Sam a stick of chewing gum.

'They worshipped the GIs down here during the war, so let's pretend the three of us are Yanks. However, when we touch down at Xanana Gusman International Airport, which I note has recently been upgraded, we must first explore the beach before coming to a final decision.'

Leaving the Gulfstream parked in front of the brand-new terminal building, they walked out of the gate and down a wide, tree lined lane, which ran in a straight line directly towards the sparkling ocean and a long strand of soft white sand. It appeared to have everything they were looking for, even an area behind previously levelled out for parking all the plant and machinery, plus all the stores and accommodation needed while the airport was being re-built.

'When it is fully inflated the SPOD will eventually cover half a football pitch, you said, Major, so after the solar panels and shoot boxes that Jeb is organising, are flown in from Japan, we will need all that space and more of the beach as well.'

'Sam, you are right. But don't forget the tugs and tray trucks, which must arrive not long after we reach Wyndham. When all those plus the gas cylinders are added, there is a serious load to be shipped over to Australia behind us.'

'So having found your site and are established in the Outback how does it all work?' Macey asked.

'I believe Jeb told you on the flight back to Bali, that all the dart trays and other items flown in to Kununarra will then be forwarded to us by C130. At the end of every planting run, SPODs will be dropped to the ground and loaded by the first of two tray trucks while the third, having delivered replacement gas, starts loading the empty trays from its far side. It speeds up turnaround to no more than an hour after which the tow ropes and drag ropes are reversed and the SPOD is moved across the 50-metre environmental strip to travel back in the opposite direction.'

With their task now complete, having visited the control tower and paid their landing fees, Sam filed a flight plan back to Bali and they climbed swiftly back into a cloudless sky.

'Do you know,' enthused Sam, when the Major came forward to the cockpit again. 'Your remarkable idea of seeding the Outback using SPODs is really beginning to grab me. But although, the concept is incredibly imaginative, I have been kept awake at night knowing that there is still something missing, even after my beautiful Macey has snuggled up to me in bed.

'The one problem that does not make sense to me is your method for towing them. What if the ground is uneven and dotted with scrub, trees, rocks or deep fissures. Has Jeb also designed the tugs themselves to fly?'

'You are correct to raise that, Sam, but I have not mentioned the drones yet, for they will enable us to take the SPODs anywhere in the world. But it will make harvesting the plants more difficult.'

'What do you mean?'

'To let you into a secret, Sam, before poor Ana was bitten by the Komodo dragon, I had managed to come to a deal with Ud, the terrifying Indonesian brigand who has his set up his Dragon headquarters there. In exchange for allowing him to live, he would hand over to Barney on his return to Komodo, most of the powerful new drones he has recently acquired, which will then be used to take over towing the SPODs from the tugs when the going gets difficult.

'However, because I am also hoping to harvest the mature plants for their valuable fibre afterwards, which one day, will take over from plastic, it may cause problems. But that is for the future, once we have tested our first SPOD in the Outback. What is more important right now, is to decide how we are going to enter the Northern Territories with an object half the size of a football pitch without being seen, and then creep past the customs at Kununarra without being challenged!'

'But, Major, all our endeavours will be of no consequence if Bob does not get the world on side thinking nuclear again, like Rolls Royce, with their experience of building reactors for nuclear submarines. Despite Greta Thunberg and David Attenborough warning us all that if we don't reduce burning fossil fuels immediately, unless we get stuck in now, there will be no turning back.'

'I agree with you, Sam, for while most of the population are living in cloud cuckoo land, believing that climate change is a passing cloud, which in due course, will drift away, there are others who think that renewables, hydrogen power, and nuclear fusion will save us in the end.

'Meanwhile, nuclear fusion is a long way from certification and requires such complex engineering, that it will be impossible to install elsewhere. Hydrogen, although simple to extract in quantity from the air, is not so simple to store, transport, or to create as a fuel. Also, it is more aimed at powering vehicles than generating electricity. As for renewables, although adding a valuable contribution, they are not suited to all parts of the world, are too dependent on weather, and will never be able to provide half the electricity needed by the growing number of consumers.'

'If what you say is correct, Major, unless everyone starts thinking, as Bob is thinking, in the same direction, apart from the Chinese who I am told are already testing small, salt cooled, thorium fuelled, nuclear reactors with the intention of getting rid of all of their coal fired power stations, is any dramatic action likely to be taken by the free world to do exactly the same before it is too late?'

'I hope so, Sam, but as for the trees that have been wantonly destroyed over the last two decades, it is also hard to believe that although, some eight years ago, the world agreed to replace the loss of sequestration with a trillion trees, less than two per cent of that number have yet been planted!

'While you consider that, and the difference it will make if we can get our SPODs to the other side, why don't you hand over the bird to George and come back to join us for some brain storming?'

'When lying on the beach in Bali earlier thinking too much of me was hidden by my old bikini, you may be surprised, boys, but I, Macey, your humble stewardess, managed to solve that problem.'

'So what devious plan have you thought up for us, Macey?'

'It is certainly deceptive, if not devious, but also practical. First, however, am I right in saying that Felipe has designed the SPOD to be assembled in two halves?'

It was at that moment, they entered such a violent thunderstorm, they were forced to break off their conversation while Sam returned to his cockpit and they both sat down to fasten their seat belts.

Then, as the aircraft seemed fall out of the sky, there was a sudden call on the radio.

'Bob here. Thanks for your views on western complacency while the Chinese exploit climate change. I have been talking to Marcia, but I need to hear more about Ud from the horse's mouth?'

'First, Sir, I'm not a riderless horse. If I had eliminated the bastard, it would have jeopardised our whole operation. Not only is he known to be highly intelligent and useful by the surgeon who operated on Ana, but if I had not got hold of his long-range drones, we would not only have lost the opportunity of pushing on faster with the SPODs in Australia, but also in other countries later.'

'You should have killed the swine all the same, Major, you never cease to worry me!'

'Those long-range drones are the one device that Jeb would never be able to reproduce in a hurry for its secrets are known only to Ud, the firebrand, himself. Everyone is aware of the various uses for drones, such as taking photographs and delivering shopping, but most of them are controlled by humans with keypads, whereas Ud's, which may be the most powerful of their type ever built, are operated by computers guided by GPS.

'Because they are pre-programmed and are large enough to carry more incendiary bombs than previously, he told me on Komodo that he would shortly be able to dispense with all his arsonists, meaning, I'm afraid, that the fires may become more widespread than ever. But as I had a steel blade pressed against my jugular, and my own knife, or rather that Brazilian garage man's knife, removed when I arrived there, I decided, knowing about his gruesome past, that it was best to bargain with him, discovering that his real name is Akmal, who five years ago passed out top at the Massachusetts Institute of Technology.

'I told him that the CIA would now track him by satellite wherever he was hiding. Also, if he preferred not to face a firing squad, he would have to hand over all but six of his new-fangled drones to Barney, when he picked them up later. Once he had done so, even should he not have completed my special mission, I assured him that you would reward him with a million dollars.'

'But why leave him with six of the drones?'

'Because his new drones have such a long range, he will be able to programme them to help us achieve our goals with a dramatic last-ditch stand, but only, I repeat, on receiving your codeword.

'Also, I have promised Ud five times that sum should he be asked to do so, and told him that we will never divulge the last-ditch plan should his fellow countrymen come to the conclusion that he is helping us. For if he is found out, Ud says, he will be hunted down, tortured and killed without mercy.'

'That all sounds sensible, Major, but as you are not prepared to tell me any more about your plan, I would prefer not be implicated. But whose goals are you talking about, mine—to prevent the stuff going up, or yours—to catch it coming down?'

'Both, Sir. But to tell you about my more immediate plans. After we have landed on the beach we have chosen near Wyndham, the SPOD, which we hope to have smuggled over there partly by night, will have its tow ropes removed from Atlantis and secured to the two motor caravans you have hired for us there. Meanwhile, the rest of the equipment plus Ud's drones, which, attached to the solar panels, will give the SPODs unlimited range, will catch up with us at Kununarra later.'

They were approaching Bali and as they started losing height, and he said goodbye on the mic to Bob, Sam lent across to the co-pilot's seat, where he was sitting, and shook his hand.

'Bob may cut back on your pay again, but surely he must approve of the end result!' At that moment, talk of the devil, Bob came on air again.

'Major, because they logged the number of my aircraft when you landed in Timor-Leste, I will now tell you the bad news. I have just been notified by a member of the East Timor government that you have been viewed pacing out the beach near their International Airport without asking their permission, or more seriously, without passing through their customs. Why so, when customs must be so much on your mind at the moment?'

'Crikey, Sir, why the hell should this happen to us when we have just found the ideal spot to assemble and launch our first SPOD!'

'This may mean finding somewhere else to launch the SPOD. So what shall I tell them, Major?'

'Difficult, Sir! Why not say that we were looking for sea shells, or tell them the truth and we will take the consequences. But we would much rather you came clean and admitted that we were carrying out a recce on your orders. Needless to say, we paid them the landing fees before we left, but as we were only looking at the beach for an assembling our SPOD later, we considered it unnecessary to walk to the main terminal building and go through all that customs rigmarole before we actually returned with it.'

'Not much of an excuse, Major.'

'One other idea, Sir, before I am locked up in prison again, why not say that although we were not entirely innocent on this occasion, our whole intention is to enter Australia unnoticed and to avoid their customs in precisely the same manner when we get to the other side. We are now about to land at Bali, so I will give you my reasons for suggesting this approach, which I know will please them, when we speak again. Over and out.'

Chapter 17

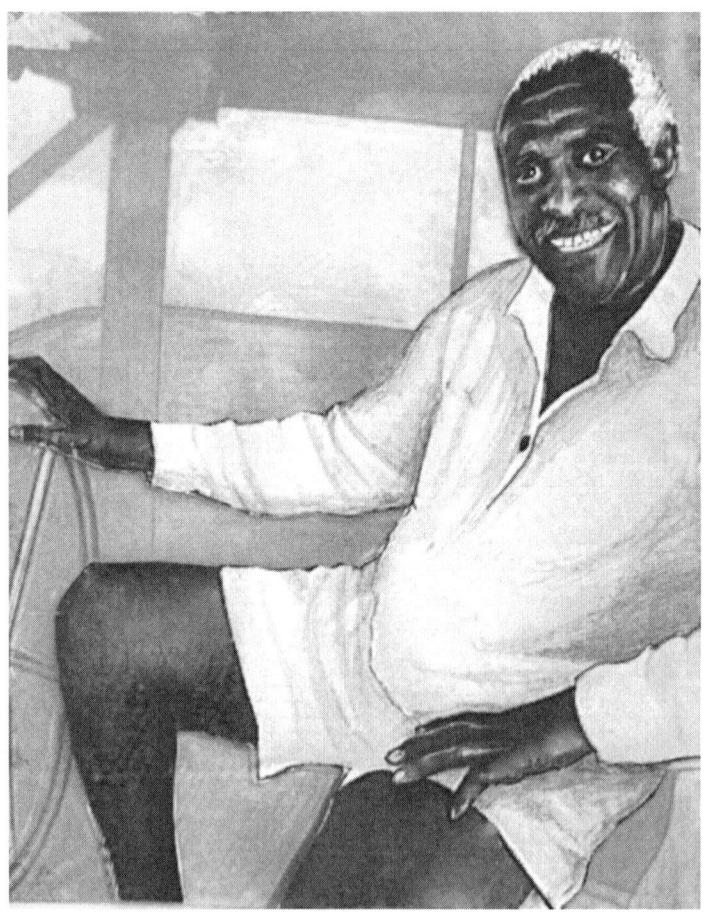

Barney. Bob's motor yacht skipper

After they had parked the aircraft and the mercenary had returned to greet Ana back at his lodge, thankful that he had not told his boss most things, Bob was back on the line again. 'Since we spoke, having contacted the East Timor government once more, I found it hard to explain what you are up to at their airfield. So when you inflate the SPOD, I'm having nothing more to do with it.'

'Leave it to me, Sir, but since we have had to abandon plan A, which was to fly everything to the airport at Kununarra and assemble the SPOD on the wide expanse of grass there, everything has changed and the airfield in East Timor is now our only alternative.

'As I wanted to tell you earlier, my clever girlfriend, Ana, who is recovering fast from her ordeal with the Komodo dragon, has got hold of some useful information. Worrying how to encourage the Timorese to aid, rather than obstruct what she now refers to as our Carboneering expedition, she has found that they thoroughly dislike the Aussies and may be won over quite easily.'

'Why is that?'

'Apparently, since East Timor gained their independence in 1975, when over a thousand Timorese were killed in horrific scenes of violence, partly engineered by Indonesia, Australian soldiers had to be brought in to calm the situation. However, since then, when some of their own soldiers became violent, relations between the two countries have been undermined by long and contentious negotiations over their maritime border, in particular that concerning the Greater Sunrise oil and gas field, which straddles it.

'Matters came to a head when there were allegations in 2013 that an Australian had spied on Timorese officials during the previous negotiations, when they argued that the bulk of the oil and gas fields lay on their side of the median line.

'You may know,' the Major continued, 'that East Timor is one of the poorest nations on the planet with more than forty per cent of its population living below the poverty line. So, because the Australians, who have not yet ratified the treaty granted them ten per cent of the oil field's annual proceeds, are still sitting on the sixty million dollars owed to the East Timor government, the Timorese have every right to be angry.

'For heaven's sake, Sir, the Great Sunrise oil and gas field is said to be worth no less than sixty-five billion dollars at the moment! So both Ana and I agree that they have been most reasonable when dealing with the Australians, which you should mention to their prime minister, when explaining our future plans.'

'In that case, due to Ana's research, crack on and I will continue to deal with the East Timor government accordingly. So, this time, Major, listen more carefully to my instructions.

'Return to Timor-Leste in Atlantis with Felipe, Jeb and Ana as soon as you hear from the Timorese authorities that the SPOD envelopes are on their way from Rio in one of NASA's old Boeing Super Guppy's, which I have chartered. After, subsequently, flying in the solar panels and shoot boxes from Japan, the aircraft will then be based in Tokyo throughout your time in Australia.

'Other than the tugs and tray trucks, which will be shipped to you later, all further SPODs will be flown to Kununarra to be assembled there by Jeb, once you are established in the desert and have the Australian prime minister on side. Meanwhile, please ask Sam and Macey to relax in Bali for three weeks, before they return to Exeter and fly me back to California so I may conclude my own work there.'

'So how do you suggest we get the tray trucks and the tugs across the Timor Sea to Wyndham, where there is no dock to land them on, Sir, for I'm sure you have worked that one out already?'

'You were not old enough, Major, nor was I, when the Japs invaded Timor-Leste in February 1942 and landed at Dili on the other side of the island from your airport. They were resisted by a tiny number of under-equipped Allied military personnel known as Sparrow Force. But although, a more stubborn resistance was continued for some time by the Timorese themselves up in the mountains, it only resulted in thousands more of them being killed unnecessarily.

'They did not know, poor people, that General MacArthur, who was commanding the US forces, rather than relieve Timor-Leste as was his original plan, decided instead, to concentrate on defeating the Japanese in Papua New Guinea and the Solomon Islands.

'Apart from a few bullets being fired when the Japs arrived, it resulted in a number of Toku-Class landing craft being left undamaged in Dili throughout the war, to be employed later by the Timorese for inshore trading. I have, therefore, arranged for three of the surviving craft to be sailed to the port of Tokyo to collect the new vehicles when they are completed. They will subsequently carry them across the Timor Sea to the beach near Wyndham, where you will have previously landed and checked out yourselves.

'In future, however, we will be using a nuclear-powered vessel rather than ones propelled by fossil fuels to do the job.'

'Thanks. The landing craft will be ideal for the task as long as the Australian authorities have accepted our rude invasion by then. Ultimately, I agree, we must be totally carbon neutral.'

On hearing the first SPOD had been loaded at Rio airport, while leaving Sam and Macey behind to enjoy their holiday, Barney immediately set course for

Timor-Leste, or East Timor as marked on his chart, passing close to Komodo again. As they stormed past the island travelling at their cruising speed of thirty-eight knots, Ana shook her fist at it with Barney telling them that because the Xanana airfield still lay six hundred nautical miles away, it would take two days to get there. So not to waste a moment, the Major asked them all to gather round on the bridge for a briefing.

'Since talking to Bob, and believing that he will have tamed the East-Timor authorities by now, we have three more problems to resolve. Firstly, having assembled the first SPOD, we must decide how to tow it across the Timor Sea without being spotted. Secondly, we must think how to then move it to the Great Sandy Desert without being stopped by the Australian customs in Kununarra, who are known to be aggressive. And thirdly, having tested the SPOD, we must then decide how to move the others, plus their support vehicles, from Kununarra to the Outback?'

'Jimbo,' Ana intervened. 'Macey was saying how she arrived at her brilliant solution to the first problem while she was lying on a beach in Bali, worrying about too much of her lovely figure being concealed by an old-style bikini. She was about to explain her idea on Bob's aircraft when you were hit by that thunderstorm on the flight back from Timor-Leste. So, because Macey is back taking in the sun there again, would you like me to explain how she suggested we should disguise the SPOD before attempting to cross over to Australia?'

'Go ahead, dear Ana.'

'Felipe, may I once again confirm that you have built the SPOD in two halves divided along its 300-foot length, each half being fifty foot wide?' Felipe nodded.

'Then the task is reasonably straightforward. Barney has already told us that crossing the Timor Sea, a distance of about two hundred and fifty nautical miles at a speed of no more than sixteen knots, will take us from eighteen to twenty hours depending on sea conditions. He also says that after we land, because it must still be dark when we tow the SPOD past the customs at the other end, we will be forced to undertake much of the crossing during daylight. So, we must use the same tactics often employed during World War Two, by pretending that the SPOD is not a SPOD.'

'That's a great idea, Ana,' remarked Barney, 'but won't hiding them from the air be impossible?'

'No, Barney, because you will tow the two halves of the blimp in line astern, flying just above the surface of the water, pretending that they are empty coal barges you are towing back to Australia.'

'But how the hell do we make the SPOD look like a couple of empty coal barges for God's sake?'

'Much depends on all those guys who are finishing decorating the new airport. When we finally inflate the two sides, they will paint impressive looking hatches on each of their folded set of solar panels. But the secret lies in them providing us with some heavy material to hang along their flanks. They will then paint RIO TINTO COAL in large letters on one side of the material, with paintings of lorry trailers on the reverse side ready to be flipped over when we land in Australia.'

'Ana, when I was a kid living in New Orleans,' suggested Barney, 'we used to tie a stick between two ropes and then, hanging on for dear life, try and surf behind my father's lobster boat. So, before we leave, why don't we grab two branches ripped off by the wind and do the same by lashing them between the two stabilising ropes dragged behind each barge to simulate their wakes?'

'That's clever, Barney. Yes, let's go for that idea as well.'

'Once we have accomplished this incredible conjuring act,' added the Major, 'I would like you to return with Atlantis to Komodo Island to collect our first consignment of drones before Ud, who, on my orders, will keep six of them, delivers the balance of those promised to Kununarra later. But until we have tamed the Australian government and they have, hopefully, provided you with an armed naval escort, it may be too dangerous to consider doing so.

'There remains one other topic before we reach Timor-Leste and that is the friendly relationship we will have to establish with the Aboriginals who will become our work force in the Outback. Firstly, and of great importance, we must never refer to them as Aborigines, or Abbos as some like to call them, for they are very conscious of any racial connection to Australia's colonial past. They, therefore, prefer to be known as Aboriginals.

'Also, they do not like the word tribe. So, when you are talking about a group of Aboriginals, please refer to them as a mob. They are proud people who have occupied the Outback continuously, indeed longer, except in a few parts of Africa, than any other human population on Earth. It is believed that the modern Australian Aboriginal is a direct descendant of a number of people who emigrated from Africa some seventy-five thousand years ago, being among the first to successfully cross the oceans.

'After that, they may have remained isolated from the outside world until, apparently, they were contacted by some Dutch fishermen. But that was five hundred years ago. It is extraordinary how the Aboriginals, who have much in common with the indigenous people of New Guinea, have always resisted any serious integration.'

'So why should they like us any more now?' Ana asked.

'That is the problem for not only do they continue to face racist abuse, but, until recently, the compulsory acquisition of some of the land where they have lived for ever, needless to say, has also made them dangerously resentful. Since 1788, when the British fleet landed in Australia, many years after Captain Cook first sighted the country, right through until 1992, when stealing land from the Aboriginals was declared a crime, they have suffered from a social stigma that gives us reason to tread very carefully.'

After an uneventful passage, when they landed on the beach near the airfield, Felipe marvelled at their choice of assembly area with the lane leading only a few hundred metres directly up to the runway. 'Well chosen, Major, so is there a decent bed somewhere near here where I may sleep?'

'Yes, Felipe, in your comfortable cabin here on Bob's yacht, but if you would prefer somewhere less comfortable on shore, it may be arranged,' he joked, not knowing it was about to happen.

They heard the Super Guppy coming from a long distance away and when it flew over them its brute like appearance caused such a stir on the beach that the three tourists walking there ran up to the airfield to watch it touch down and find out what it was carrying, only to be disappointed when just two very large packages emerged, plus a smaller one, but not a herd of elephants.

The envelopes, flat packed on pallets as the Major expected them to be, had subsequently been carried down to the beach on airport baggage trucks but when Felipe, reaching up to untie some straps put his foot on what he thought was a waterlogged branch of fallen palm tree, it wasn't! Salt water crocodiles are not only known to be particularly vicious, but with males stretching to six metres in length, are the largest of all reptiles.

Apart from their bite, their massive tails are so powerful that they are able to lift themselves bodily out of the water. But, fortunately, it was only the croc's tail that had hit him, Felipe's left leg had been broken in two places.

Without uttering a word, except to curse roundly for treading on the beast, Felipe's only option was to agree to being loaded onto one of the trucks which had brought the envelopes down to the beach, before being driven through the shallow, croc infested, mouth of a river, which meandered over the sand, to a medical unit in a small town about five kilometres away.

'I'm afraid that it probably needs more specialist treatment, Dad,' announced Ana soon after he arrived. 'As the nurse here says she has seen bone poking through. So, now they have straightened and splinted your leg, we are getting hold of Sam again who will fly you back to the same hospital in Bali where I was incarcerated. Then,' she continued, as he was put to bed in a small room with white walls and bamboo printed curtains.

'Once you are back on your feet again, it would be best for you to take a return flight back to Rio, so you may look after my mother, who is worrying herself stupid about me while trying to keep Bob informed of our progress. Then, of course, you will need to press on with manufacturing the envelopes for more SPODs, while Jeb helps us join both of the prototype's two halves together, once we make it to Australia.'

Sam arrived at the airport within a few hours, and berating the crocodile for interrupting his well-earned holiday, he collected Felipe by taxi and after a fond farewell from Ana, who asked him to encourage Rick to continue fighting the fires in the Amazon rainforest, they took to the air again.

After one of the two envelopes had been finally unwrapped, it was then part inflated from the bottles of helium that had been packed separately.

'Jeb, on reaching Wyndham,' the Major said, 'we will have to hitch both sides up to Bob's camper vans fast, for with dawn approaching we will have only one hour of darkness left to get motoring?' But that was wishful thinking.

As they lay in their comfortable bunks on Atlantis trying to get some sleep, they were aware of the rising wind and the waves slapping increasingly hard against her hull. So, when they awoke in the morning, it was not surprising that the semi-inflated part of the balloon was no longer to be seen. In panic, the Major and Barney jumped into the dingy to search the fringe of palm trees growing along the shore in both directions, before realising that the envelope must have been blown over them towards the airfield. It was then that they heard the distant roar of approaching jet engines.

'Oh my God! Quick, Barney. While I sprint to the control tower and warn them what has happened, row back and tell them on Atlantis there is about to be an international air disaster!'

But as fast as he ran, he thought that he would never be able to make it in time when he saw the aircraft already starting its final approach with its undercarriage being lowered. As hard as he tried, he still could not see the rogue envelope, but noticing how the fronds had been ripped off the tops of the palm trees in line with the runway, there was nothing he could do but sprint even faster.

A red flare then shot into the sky accompanied by the howl of the aircraft's twin turbofans as the pilots desperately hurled the throttles forward. He could only see the first part of the runway because of the trees lining the lane, but praying he had seen the Boeing's nose starting to lift, he yelled, 'Go, go, go, please, go,' as he ran on, desperately gasping for breath.

At last, he had reached the control tower and as he leapt up the stairs, the runway remained blotted from view for another anxious moment as he finally reached, a door flung open above him.

'If that's your monstrous bird cavorting over there,' the duty controller bellowed at him in airfield English, 'you're dead meat. Trying to inflate that thing on our beach was crazy, man. You'd better go retrieve it and get out of here fast. Our beach is reserved only for birds in bikinis.'

'So, do those crocs of yours also wear bikinis, air trafficator?' He retorted on regaining his breath. 'It's not my choice of holiday destination! But tell me, do you not receive an evening weather report? And were you not warned about those thirty knot winds blowing up last night? Perhaps you should not be in charge of landing aircraft here if you fail to take action in such circumstances, which have resulted in your runway being blocked by broken palm fronds. So, what happens next?'

'It seems you were in luck, mate, for I have been informed by the crew of our fire engine that they managed to grab the wretched thing and tow it from where it had been caught up in the runway lights, just in the nick of time. If, son of a bitch, you look towards that large grey hangar on the far side of the runway, it's not a hangar but that bloody balloon of yours!'

'Jeepers, you are right, Inspector Cluso, I would never have suspected it, although it is larger than any hangar I have seen in my life, except the one in Brazil where it was born.'

'So, what are you going to do about the situation now that we have swept the runway and our first aircraft is still waiting to land, dumbo? You had better apologise to the pilots before you piss off.'

'No, we will pay for one of your trucks to tow the balloon back over the palm trees, having first topped it up with more of our precious gas, unless you wish to be stuck with us here for ever.'

'You ruddy dill! I know your game! Wait here, imbecile, while I talk down that plane from the Philippines for it's their second attempt to land, poor devils, entirely due to your incompetence.'

Cluso had just returned from glancing at his computer screen when a solemn faced official entered the control tower with gold braid half way up his sleeves. 'Because of the near miss just reported at this airport, concerning your balloon, there must now be an official investigation of this totally irresponsible and near fatal incident. Do you wish to ask any questions, Englishman?'

'Yes, Inspector, how long is your official enquiry likely to take?'

'Possibly five to six weeks, but that's if you are lucky.'

'Ridiculous! As long as your crocs leave us alone, it will take us only a maximum of days to assemble the SPOD, as our dirigible is called, and be out of here. We then intend to fly it across the oggin to upset your Aussie friends with many more headaches than we have caused you here.'

The inspector stood back for a moment and waving his spectacles in a gesture of hopelessness replied, 'Major, you limey bastard. Because our government approves of your intentions, you may be surprised to hear that I have only been sent here to put the fear of God into you for treating our new airport with such disrespect. This lunatic, who finds it difficult to land more than two aircraft in any one day, will tell you that after one brief telephone call, the East Timor government has decided to help you avoid the authorities in Australia, just as you have attempted to do here.

'Trying to assemble your balloon on a sloping beach surrounded by our toothy friends down there, however, will drive all of us bananas,' Cluso concluded. 'So, before you unpack the rest of the damn thing, bring it back up here and put it together beside that other sagging monstrosity.'

'Thanks, Cluso, for your remarkable generosity, I must remember you in my will! And thanks also to you, Inspector. When we have both parts inflated and the Super Guppy has flown back from Japan with the solar panels to mount on top and the shoot boxes to attach underneath, all we ask is that your decorators, we see working on your buildings over there, give our monstrosity, as you call it, a lick of paint before we finally get out of your hair.

'We are bound for Wyndham on the north coast of Australia, and lucky for you, all our remaining equipment will either be flown there in the Guppy, which will be stationed from now on in Tokyo, or carried by sea. So, unless we find we are unable to do without you, dear Cluso, there will be no reason for us to return.'

After the second half of the SPOD had been inflated down on the beach as the crocodiles were kept at bay, it was towed carefully over the fringe of palm trees by a baggage wagon to join its partner on the airfield just as the decorators were assembled by the major to start work.

The result was remarkable, but unless seen from a distance the barges were unlikely to fool anyone. 'However, crew, don't let's start counting our chickens,' Barney remarked. 'For just imagine what would happen to them should it blow as it did two nights ago. Then those bloody barges of yours would lift my beautiful Atlantis clean out of the water. So, nobody will be happier than the captain of this ship to see the back of them when we reach the other side.'

'Fair Dinkum, as they say in that wretched country somewhere down under,' enthused Cluso, who seemed, at long last, to understand what they were up to. 'I can see you have done everything possible to fox those gum suckers, but when they get hold of you, they will flay you with stock whips and bury you alive. So, once the two balloons, or barges you hope they resemble, are go, I guess you will then want us to tow them down to your ship, so they may be dragged behind it?'

'Correct, you budding genius, for should we have tried to enter the country officially, we would have been sent back to you immediately. Therefore, as we intend to get past their customs before they fall out of bed, please accept this money from our boss while hoping there is not a next time.'

Having settled the Guppy's landing fees, two of the airport trucks towed the now fully inflated "coal barges" over the top of the palm trees and then down the beach for Barney to secure them, line astern, behind Bob's motor yacht. 'Lift off!' He shouted after attaching his two wake-makers behind them, while Cluso, who had come down to watch the proceedings from the shoreline, shrugged and then walked slowly back up the lane to the airfield, shaking his head in disbelief.

'I have been learning more about the Australian Border Force,' announced Barney, once they had settled down on the heading for Wyndham with the two barges being towed four metres above the waves behind them, 'and it does not make pleasant reading.

'Apparently, their maritime law enforcement arm employs several Dash 8 surveillance aircraft equipped with Sea Vue multi role radar systems, enabling them to detect the smallest targets at night and in any weather conditions. They are supported by helicopters equipped with other sophisticated surveillance and camera equipment, plus rope rappelling systems, which means they may try and search the two barges we are towing, God bless them, while we are still underway.

'Their success rate in countering illegal activity off the Australian coast is impressive, on one occasion, a year ago, seizing the entire crew of a vessel trying to enter the Northern Territories illegally. The article, written recently, states that the crew are still fighting their case from gaol.'

Despite what Barney had said, the crossing, which at a speed of only sixteen knots seemed to be taking an eternity, was remarkably uneventful, apart from seeing one aircraft flying at high altitude in the opposite direction. But as they crept towards the Australian coastline, just becoming visible a long way to the south, they began to feel increasingly uneasy as they attempted, over the noise of the engines, to listen to Barney recounting his yarns about piracy in the South China Sea.

'Barney,' Ana interrupted eventually, jumping up from the life raft on which she had been sitting, 'ever since I mentioned Macey's brilliant idea of disguising the SPOD as two coal barges, I have been worried by a couple of facts we have overlooked. First, is there a coal mine near Wyndham, and second, how would the police ever expect us to load our barges there, as it has no docks?'

She had been meaning to bring them a smoked salmon sandwich and a glass of champagne, but before Barney was able to reply, Jeb had also jumped to his feet. 'What the hell is that light shining out there on the surface of the ocean far away to the east of us? Quick, pass me the binos, Barney.'

'No need to, Jeb,' he answered, with a broad smile. 'I can clearly see that it is a police helicopter, which unfortunately, is coming fast in our direction. Because I know far too much about the trade, you can bet your bottom dollar that they are looking for drug smugglers, which are often caught trying to enter Australia from the Pacific islands lying on their doorstep. Apart from New Guinea, Timor-Leste is said to be the worst of them. But they may not suspect us of carrying drugs, when they see, for some reason, we are only towing empty coal barges towards the coast.

'However, if they suspect us of drug running, apart from praying, I always have a trick up my sleeve. When they reach us and shine their lights down, the barges will cast such a shadow on the water, they will guess immediately that they are fakes. So to fox them, as Cluso said, I will flood the whole scene with so much light from that powerful lamp mounted on our stern, it will not only kill all the shadows but indicate that we are indeed pukka coal merchants, happy to be recognised!'

'Pukka, my foot!' The mercenary commented as the chopper banked sharply away to the west. 'Pretending that we are carrying two empty coal barges may have worked out in mid-channel, but now we have been seen heading for Wyndham, Ana is right, it may not do us any good at all!'

The beach was deserted apart from the two electric camper vans Bob had ordered. Their Aboriginal drivers, whom they found asleep, were soon put to work helping to haul the "barges" over the sand where the helium was condensed with their internal compression pumps to drop them to the ground.

Jeb, who had been standing operating his remote control then climbed quickly up a ladder and, while he secured four electrified tow ropes to the front corners of the two arrays of solar panels, and four heavy steel drag cables to the rear of each of the SPOD's two halves, the Major flipped over the painted sheets hung along their sides, turning them, miraculously, into two lorry trailers.

'Before we say goodbye to Barney, who has done such a great job getting us here,' announced the Major, 'let's now have those sandwiches, Ana, then toast our landing here with that champagne. And here's to our brave skipper,' he said as Barney jumped back into his dinghy.

'I was hoping to arrange for the Australian navy to escort you back to Komodo Island, but having been spotted by that chopper, it will now be too dangerous for you to hang about here until I get the Aussie prime minister to agree to it. But mind out for that scumbag when you land on Komodo again, for not only is Ud the most unpleasant character I have ever come across, but without question, is likely to be the least trustworthy. When you collect the balance of his new-fangled drones, Barney, how will you make certain that he is left with just six of them and has not done us in the eye?'

'I was talking about all the tricks I keep up my sleeve for such dodgy occasions, and this is one of them. You told me about the drones being stacked against the wall of his office, well some of us have drones in our lockers as well. On board Atlantis, I have one "state of the art" drone, which is not only minute and hard to spot, but because it flies not with propellors but on four jets of compressed air, is totally silent.

'I will, therefore, be able to take photographs of the drones he has left behind in his compound, and before leaving Komodo threaten him again just as you did, not with a knife at my throat, but from the safety of Atlantis until he brings them out to me.'

'OK, Barney, good plan, but keep Atlantis well beyond machine gun range, and once you have stowed away every one of them, tell the scumbag to get the remaining drones, once they are delivered to him, over to Kununarra as quickly as possible. Only then will Bob be prepared to pay him for them.

'Once you have completed your mission, please return to this beach at night to meet up with the landing craft when they finally arrive here. The drones may then be loaded onto one of the tray trucks and delivered to Jeb at the airport. Meanwhile, the task I have given Ud for those six remaining drones, which I did not dare tell Bob about, is making my hair turn grey!'

Chapter 18

'It may sound corny,' Bob remarked, joining Sam, the pilot of his Gulfstream, as they winged their way back towards America at six hundred miles per hour 'but the reason I named my house in North Devon Fish On was not because it overlooks the Atlantic Ocean, but because of my crusade against the reluctance of most Americans to combat climate change with clean nuclear fission.'

'Sir, please will you fill me in on that again.'

'The world's burgeoning population has such a growing and insatiable appetite for electricity that although, most people believe that driving electric cars will help, turning to hydrogen as a fuel or covering our precious land with solar panels and the sea with wind turbines is not the final answer. Indeed, as I am once again attempting to persuade the Yanks, nothing is further from the truth.

'Today, fossil fuels provide over fifty per cent of world's energy needs, renewables twenty per cent, nuclear about eighteen per cent, biofuels some six per cent, while hydro provides only about four per cent, although countries such as Iceland and Paraguay, because of their unique situations, use it as their sole method for generating electricity. Meanwhile, those who believe renewables in thirty years' time will produce most of the world's energy need their heads examining.

'A more realistic figure is forty to fifty per cent, meaning that due to the world population increasing from say eight billion to ten billion by then, coal and gas will continue to make up most of the deficit. That is why getting rid of the coal and gas element is so vital if fossil fuels are not to create the greatest catastrophe the world has ever known.'

'I agree with you totally, Sir,' joined in Macey, his lovely flight attendant, while bringing them two steaming mugs of Brazilian coffee. 'Perhaps that's why men are setting out to colonise Mars. But although, you believe that my countrymen have thrown nuclear energy out of the window it is no more correct than the former president of the United States does not believe in climate change. Do you think he believed that the wrestlers he used to watch such as Hunk Hogan and Randy Savage, were playing fair?

'No, he followed them because they played dirty, the same reason that countless people continued watching them in the States. The president was learning how to play as lose a game as they did, knowing that by being controversial he would attract headlines in the world's press every day of the week.'

'Macey, you are so right and I greatly appreciate having you as the stewardess of my aircraft. But I do not agree with you about Trump and climate change and, like Sam, I believe you are in two minds about my mission, which has concerned him right from the start.'

'That's also not true, Sir. Both Sam and I admire you're brave, if not pugilistic, approach to tackling climate change. However, knowing the attitude of my countrymen and remembering the appalling reception you received on the last occasion you visited California, we are concerned that you are presenting your argument on nuclear energy to the same people again far too soon.'

'Macey, yes, it's true that I'm in a hurry, but there is a difference between foolhardiness and bravery. The first is when you approach your enemy with no idea of his strengths and weaknesses. The second is when you tackle him knowing precisely what you are up against. My approach, which I assure you will be vindicated, lies somewhere between the two.'

They already knew that Bob's intentions, as always, were set in concrete. Bob had impressed on them how important it was to prevent carbon from entering the atmosphere in the first place, but as large quantities would always continue to do so, he had explained why he had contracted the Major to tackle deforestation and then create a realistic method for sequestering carbon on a massive scale.

'Speaking only as your pilot, Sir, but seeing you being carried on a tide of passion that even King Canute would not have been able to stop, when are you expecting to put all this into operation?'

'Sam, to encourage the media and kill off the criticism which will follow every move, I will be launching our campaign with a codeword known only to the IAEA in Vienna, and the Major, who in dire circumstances, may relay it on to others such as Ana's uncle, Rick. He farms close to the Amazon rainforest and will help the Major in his efforts to prevent any more damage being inflicted on what remains of those magnificent trees growing there.'

'But we are more concerned about your safety, Sir, when confronted by with those hooligans.'

'It should not be a problem, Sam, for most protestors are as brazen as foxes but as stupid as hens when shut out of their coops. When, ultimately, condemned by the world's media for their resistance to the escalating problem of climate change, they will throw in the towel immediately.'

'We admire your confidence, but after what happened on our last visit to Frisco, when you were duffed up by that Armageddon lot, this time, irrespective of your undoubted bravery and because your mercenary is elsewhere, while in the States I am taking over as your personal bodyguard.'

'I appreciate your concerns, Sam, but it will not be necessary. The fellow meeting me at the airport is Mike from the Environmental Protest Group, the same guy I met the last time we flew here. He is tough and has since been raising funds from some of the richest sources in America.'

'Maybe those funds should be spent shoring up those countries who are already suffering from the effects of climate change, for, surely, that must be the first priority, Sir.'

'That's noble thinking, but it is more a matter of what has to come first. The Yanks are the second worst polluters on the globe and therefore, they should first start getting their own house in order before helping the poorer nations who, I agree, are already beginning to suffer dreadfully from the effects of climate change in a frightening way. You must realise, however, that more of a worry is that even should the IAEA persuade such countries to swap their coal fired power stations for SMRs, they will never be able to pay for them.

'That must be the moment for the richer countries of the world to provide their financial support through COP, meaning through the conference of the parties, or the co-operation of nations.'

'That has been worrying us both,' Macey remarked, 'but we thoroughly understand your reasoning. However, being nosey, Sir, so that we can keep our tabs on you, after meeting up with Mike again, where are you going subsequently?'

'He is taking me to meet the governor of California at his official residence in Sacramento, a mansion which looks more like a Victorian-Italianate birthday cake than a centre of government.'

'A surprising building, don't you think, Mr Buckmaster?' The governor said, greeting them both in his capacious office.

'Governor, please call me Bob, a name the employees in my company, Nuklin, have called me since making a few bobs mining and marketing uranium around the world. It was just unfortunate that some countries made bombs with it. And this is Mike from the Environmental Protest Group.'

'Bob, before we begin, as California has decided not to use your dangerous stuff any longer but to revert to natural gas, please tell me why are you back here again so soon?'

'Forgetting the bombs, as my company is now determined to save the world, it is well known that deaths caused by the Chernobyl disaster, including those who may have died of cancer as a result, totalled only six hundred, and after Fukushima, where more precautions had been taken, just one. So why all the antipathy if you compare those figures with the Indian Ocean tsunami, which happened at the same time as Fukushima, when it was estimated that nearly a quarter of a million people perished.

'Or to the thousands who die from lung disease and other complaints due to fossil fuels every year. For what ridiculous reason then is there currently so little appetite for nuclear in the United States, the only form of clean energy now capable of saving the planet?

'Sadly, Governor, it all goes back to World War Two when uranium-235, a highly radioactive material, was chosen as a nuclear fuel instead of its mildly radioactive brother—uranium-233—which, based on thorium, an inexpensive isotope three times more plentiful than uranium, has been side-lined ever since. If uranium-235 had not been chosen, solely because it makes bombs, we would not be facing the terrifying spectre of global warming as we are today.'

'Was there no other reason for side-lining it, Bob?'

'None. Nor is there any point in converting your nuclear plants into more efficient ones. The better option is to invest heavily in the small modular reactors known as SMRs.'

'I know a great deal about SMRs, but they also cost money.'

'Money will be of no consequence, Governor, if no one is left alive to spend it. No new nuclear reactor has been built in this country for over thirty years, and none are planned for the future, which is lunacy. That is unless you, the governor of California, do something sensible about it.'

'Why me is the obvious question, Bob, although, I may already know the answer.'

'Such is the result of climate change already, that together with Australia, California leads the world with the most frightening growth in forest fires anywhere. So, there is no one better qualified than you, Sir, to stand up and back these new factories built SMRs as being the only solution.

'Someone has to lead us out of the abyss, which should be the president of the United States of America. So unless you, Governor, whom I regard at the moment as being of greater influence, are prepared to kick California into this vitally important direction, the world is doomed.'

Bob had left the governor and his "birthday cake" without the reply he wanted. So concerned that he had failed to convince him, he hired a taxi to The Fairmont, the top hotel in town, in order to spend a few hours with Mike thinking through why he had failed so miserably again.

'Mike, how did our meeting with the governor strike you?'

'You did well, Bob, but you may not have hit the right spot with the governor. Why don't we find out more about the guy and then draw up a sensible plan of action to deliver to him as soon as possible by hand, asking him for a second meeting, so that he reads it by tomorrow morning.'

'Not necessary,' said the governor, appearing from nowhere. 'Having thought about what you gentlemen have suggested, I asked my driver to follow you to the hotel here.'

'Governor,' Mike intervened. 'Apologies, but before we start talking again, I should tell you that since we arrived at the hotel, we have been looking up your CV, which has impressed both of us. It states that since your offices were abandoned in 1971, you are only the second governor to occupy the building we have just left, since governor Ronald Reagan was promoted to be president of the United States. It goes on to say you are a family man with three children, marrying soon after leaving Harvard Business School, which you left with a certificate for Disruptive Strategy!'

'Heavens, that will have worried you. You must now think I'm just another of our ante-nuclear nut heads!'

'On the contrary, Sir, it also states that the Disruptive Strategy course is aimed at: Strengthening your capacity to make innovation a reality and unlock your potential to create winning strategies.'

'You are our man, Sir,' enthused Bob, who had been scribbling down some notes. 'And you will be welcomed by everyone with open arms if, as a leading American, you tell them truthfully that only clean nuclear energy, not renewables such as wind and solar power, will provide the lasting solution to climate change, which all of us, who are frightened by the consequences of doing nothing, are praying for.'

'Let's forget all the hype, Bob, and get down to business. For only by working together on a much more international plan will we agree a winning strategy. But that, as I also learned from my time at the Harvard Business School, must be based on innovation and a considerable amount of personal enterprise.'

The three of them had sat down in a room with magnificent views over the city and west across the bay to the Golden Gate bridge.

'That little island of yours over there,' Bob pointed out to the governor, 'which was formerly home to some of the most vicious gangsters and murderers in history, is where I was incarcerated by your ante-nuclear nuts, while on a peaceful visit here only a few months ago.'

'Then, we are fortunate that you are still with us, Bob, for the task ahead must be tackled by all three of us. Firstly, we must perfect the concept. Secondly, we must complete the construction of the first SMR reactor, which, unknown to the White House, we have been working on for many months. Thirdly, we must unlock the unnecessary long-winded business of getting the thorium fuelled SMRs certified. And finally, all fossil fuelled power stations must be shut down once investors have been found to finance the production and deployment of SMRs to replace them.'

'Governor, I am sure that you know about the countries who are already developing SMRs such as China, Canada, Brazil, France, Germany, India and the Czech Republic among them, plus one being built in my country by Rolls Royce. But I understand that there are still problems to overcome, although, at this very moment, the Chinese are about to prove that cooled by molten salt, SMRs may be deployed even in the world's deserts.

'Once, the first standard model fuelled by thorium is certified, I agree with you that the world must start installing them before it is too late, and as it was

risk of being refused entry by his efficient customs officers without being allowed to explain.'

'That will be difficult, but I will give it a try. But tell him to hold on and not to do anything rash.'

'Unfortunately, Sir, that is no longer possible. They must have grabbed his satphone for the line has now gone dead.'

On returning to the meeting, Bob, taking it in his stride, said, 'Governor, we have a problem.'

'Then let's deal with it.'

'I have not yet told you about my mercenary, who, while we are talking about preventing carbon from entering the atmosphere, was heading for the Australian Outback with the intention of activating a significant method for dealing with the increasing amount of carbon entering the atmosphere.'

'You mean that you are paying him to do that?'

'Yes, I am totally responsible for the man, just as I was in Brazil, when he was about to be hanged for killing two Indonesian arsonists who were setting fire to the Amazon rainforest.'

'So who has he murdered now?

'Nobody yet, but it may soon be the two Australian border policemen who have arrested him for entering North Australia with his innovative type of planting machine without permission. He was hoping to replace all the sequestration lost by the destruction of the rain forest within a few years, and now needs your help urgently, Sir.'

'As you know, Bob, we have been sending them firefighters and firefighting aircraft already, and because our dry seasons differ, the Australian prime minister has agreed to do the same for us. So I will say at once that because I dare not jeopardise this important relationship, and the fact he was heading for the Outback illegally, I am not in the position to be able to help your serial murderer.'

'So be it, Governor, but my mercenary is not to be trusted. Make no mistake, he will deal with the men and their helicopter and be back in prison with a noose around his neck, unless you contact their prime minister urgently and ask him to let us get on with our vital mission there.'

'So tell me more about your recent journey to Vienna, Bob?'

'The IAEA has also been reluctant to help us promote the SMRs and limit the amount of CO_2 being released into the atmosphere, but even when they get round to it, as I said, we still have to deal with the important matter of carbon sequestration.'

'You mean somehow replacing the vast number of trees wilfully destroyed in the world's forests?'

'Precisely that, Sir, but trees do not grow fast enough. However, because attempts by man and machine to accomplish such a task on the ground, will never succeed, my mercenary was heading for the Outback to plant millions of acres of carbon eating plants from the air.'

'I'm going to have to leave you there, my time is up and I have another meeting to attend to. Have a nice day, gentlemen.'

'Defeated again, Mike, what went wrong this time?'

'I'm afraid that you English have a different sense of humour to us Americans, Bob. Should you be joking, or not, about your murderer being about to kill those policemen, I could sense that the writing was already on the wall. If only you were able to get a grip of your man and then be able to tell the governor so. But now you have no contact with your mercenary that's no longer possible.'

'OK, Mike, but having hired the Major not only for his ruthless reputation, but for his ability to get out of every situation, our only hope is that he behaves and the governor changes his mind.'

Chapter 19

Hank, USA water bomber pilot.

'Blast it, we're stuck!'

Under a pale moon, the Major, accompanied by Ana and Jeb, who had also jumped out onto the patch of bright green turf he had recognised from the Amazon, was testing the ground ahead carefully, although it was in spitting distance of the shingle beach they had just left. Blotting out the stars above them, the SPOD truly resembled two sides of a sandwich cut from a massive loaf, while below were the two six berth Frontier camper vans stuck up to their axles in deep black mud. 'As dawn is approaching, this could be a disaster, Sir, so what happens next?' Jeb asked.

'All is not lost, Jeb,' replied the Major in a calm voice. 'At least it's still dark. Just get the drivers to replace the drag cable on one half of the SPOD with two ropes tied at each end. Then attach them to the first van and press the button on your remote control to release the compressed helium. We must act fast, so get the drivers back in their vans to drive them out in turn as it does the trick.

'That done, Jeb, once we have avoided the customs in Kununarra, walk back to the airport with the drivers, where, when the rest of the equipment has arrived, you will be in charge of sending it on.'

'That's great, Major, but what will happen if the government refuses us permission to do all this?'

'You will just have to keep low at Kununarra until I contact you, telling the drivers to do the same. Although, my satphone is switched off on Bob's orders, I still have my cell phone to call you on.'

Having raised both vehicles from the mud and re-attached the drag cable, Jeb showed Ana how to compress the helium again, lowering them as close as possible to the ground to resemble the lorry trailers painted on their sides. Once completed and after checking the ropes, Ana wished Jeb luck as he strode off with the two drivers into the distance, returning to the Major with a whoop of joy.

'At last we are alone together, Jimbo, and what is better we are now fancy free in Australia with no one, apart from Barney, Jeb and the two Aboriginals, knowing we are here.'

'That's true, Ana, and don't forget that being nice to the Aboriginals is crucial. Meanwhile, I hope that Bob, after being rung by Barney, is already getting hold of the Australian prime minister. So jump into the other van, remembering that it is not Esmeralda, and we will get some mileage in.'

Towing the "flying trucks" past Kununarra airport while trying not to be seen had been a nightmare. But as they drove on south at a steady twenty-five kph, it gave the Major time to think through the task Bob had set him, only made possible due to his loose purse strings. Bob had told him that once they had permission from the government to operate in the Great Sandy Desert, further SPODs would be forwarded by Jeb to them in a C130 transport aircraft retained entirely for their use, while the tugs and tray lorries would be driven to the site by as many Aboriginal drivers as were needed.

Later, in order to keep as green as possible, any additional tugs and tray lorries required would be shipped to Australia on the N.S. Savannah, a nuclear-powered merchant vessel able to operate without re-fuelling for twenty years.

The 600-kilometre journey ahead was never going to be easy, and because of all the dust being kicked up made them worry, despite their disguise, about being stopped by a police patrol.

As they drove on through sweeping expanses of spinifex dotted with bramble wattle with a few trees of desert bloodwood helping to obscure the envelopes at the low height they were being flown at, they began to feel a sense of relief creeping over them. Not only had they succeeded in eluding the opposition, but even in the early light of dawn. the countryside was beginning to look so stunning that, having passed the small town of Durak, the Major decided to drive off the road to Lake Argyle, the largest man-made lake south of the equator, where he brought out a frying pan.

'Darling Ana, even if we were spotted passing Kununarra, by getting those painters at the airport on Timor-Leste to disguise the envelopes as lorry trailers for the second leg of our journey, was an inspiration. Should we be accosted, I will say that we are about to set them up in the desert as a set for a film crew. One of the best lessons in life is to shoot first and save yourself afterwards.'

'The view from here is stunning,' purred Ana as she sat down to swing her legs over the water's edge. 'Just look at those violet hills rising out to the east. I'm going to strip off and have a swim.' But it was just at that moment, they heard the frightening sound of a rapidly approaching helicopter.

Before they could scramble to their feet, the machine was already hovering over them causing both envelopes to cavort so wildly in the downdraft that Ana's van was thrown onto its side and almost dragged into the lake beside her, blowing the piping hot oil from the Major's frying pan over his injured hand as he grabbed his satphone to alert Sam at San Francisco airport before it was too late.

'We are here to arrest you,' shouted one of two armed men above the noise of the rotor blades, as they leapt from their Bell 429 helicopter with BORDER FORCE painted all over it, while he tried desperately to stuff his satphone into his pants. But his mate, puffing himself up as though he had just won a war, wrenched it quickly out of his grasp.

'So did you think you had got away with it you ruddy pongos? How the heck you believed you could pull the wool over our eyes by towing your coal barges to a place where there is no dock makes me think that both of you are barmy. So what's in those vans of yours apart from your Sheila's knickers? So why don't we go and find out?'

'Go ahead, Captain Courageous, and leave my girlfriend's belongings alone should you wish to search that vehicle you have just thrown on its side.'

Leaving them guarded by his junior, while he poked his nose through the doors of the two camper vans, they were relieved when, after a few minutes, they saw him walking back from his own van without the vital cell phone he had already left hidden under a pillow on his bunk. But then the sat one started ringing.

'So now that you are holding my phone, copper, who is on the line and what's the message? You know that it's a very serious offence to hack into other people's conversations.'

'Just shut your gob and hold out your wrists, you dingos, so we may fix these cuffs on you. We don't need any baloney on why you entered our country illegally, either. So forget the bacon and sausages, you pig hungry poms, for that's the last decent tukka you may ever get to eat.'

'That call, if you had listened to it, could have given you instant promotion, but instead you have shackled us up like convicts. So now, with our hands tied together, if you want it, you had better peg the balloons down, treat my burned hand, and lift the van you blew over, all by yourselves.'

'No, you miserable dags, don't try that on. Let's forget my promotion until you have climbed aboard our chopper and started enjoying life behind bars back at Wyndham.'

The two gas envelopes strained on their leashes again as the helicopter lifted off, but after Ana had looked back to check them and given her Jim a thumbs up, he felt they had survived at least one more crisis, although totally frustrated by failing to get Captain Courageous to tell him anything about the contents of the telephone call, obviously the response to his cry for help.

Without being given headphones, he was finding it hard to hear what the pilot was soon discussing on the radio, for it sounded, much to his consternation, that the border police were being ordered to take their prisoners elsewhere. He was leaning forward listening while fiddling with his hands behind the pilot's seat, but before Ana was able find out what he was up to, Captain Courageous, who had also noticed, stretched out an arm to throw a hood over his head.

As they spiralled up into the sky, the Major's thought at first that they must be gaining height to head for their base at Wyndham. Or were they trying to disorient them before heading off in the opposite direction. Knowing that the Bell helicopter had a range of more than seven hundred kilometres, when they levelled out, he became increasingly suspicious that like some of their police friends in Brazil, they had been given orders to fly them out into the wilderness before shooting them in the head and burying them without trace.

Having already freed his hands by using a tiny length of wire, which he kept hidden in his belt solely for opening handcuffs, he leapt forward and ripping off the hood, shoved it over the head of the man who had just done the same to him. Next, he turned his attentions to the pilot. But hardly had he got an arm round his throat and started to drag him from the controls, when there was a muffled shout of, 'Stop, for Pete's sake stop, you limey idiot, we've been pulling your plonker!'

'It does not look like much of a joke to me,' retorted the Major, tightening his hold around the pilot's neck while shoving him sideways and sliding into the seat behind him. 'You two wisecracks had better behave yourselves before I now start scaring the pants off you!'

'Joking, why?' Ana asked, in a measured voice, but one brimming with anxiety.

'Because, you drongos, that call was from our boss back at HQ in Wyndham, who ordered us to scare the living daylights out of you both, but then to follow the instructions of some nob you may know on Capital Hill in Canberra, who has ordered us to show you where to start your planting operations, however wacky those balloons are, which some smartarse must have told him about.'

'So, Captain Courageous, why don't you allow me to continue flying this American junk heap while you release my Sheila. I found it so simple to get out of your cuffs that you are lucky I did not let her loose to throttle you as well.'

'We are just approaching our refuelling depot at Hall's Creek, mate, so hand the kite back to the pilot, while I undo the ladies cuffs, and then get back to your seat. From there, we will be following the Great Northern Highway until we reach Lamboo Land, from where we peel off south to a creek out in the bundoo, chosen by that wise guy prime minister of ours, as the best place for making friends with those nutty Aboriginals. What the hell does he mean—are you going to teach that tribe to race the dingos, or ride the roos for him?'

'No, we will be giving them joy rides under our balloons, of course. That is why we have brought them here all the way from South America, jackass! How else will we be able to please your prime minister when we are stuck out with nothing better to do in the Great Sandy Desert?'

On arrival at the prime minister's chosen spot, they could see only a meandering billabong edged by a few gum trees set among an endless sea of sand moulded into flakes and fingers of changing shapes and sizes.

'So that's it, mate, right on the grid Tom, our pilot, will now write down for you, if you have ever been taught to read a map. He's been here before and tells me it is where the Aboriginals gather from Lamboo village on the very few occasions when they're not kipping.'

The helicopter was heading north again with few words being said apart from the Major, who asked Courageous for his satellite telephone back.

'Sorry, mate, the boss has told us to hang onto it in case you start shouting your mouths off about how badly we have treated you dipsticks, and how you got past those bludgers in our customs office without being seen, for every varmint in the universe will then try doing the same.'

'So you just having fun burning up fuel when you found us you useless Aussie drug busters. It is your lot that deserves a kick up the ass, not those sleepy nomads. For if you had not been ordered to come and look for us, I expect you would still be snogging it with your Sheila's in bed.'

'As I told you, it was our prime minister, poor misguided fellow, who told our boss to get on his bike. He may no longer be there when we get back. And don't go swimming in that lake of ours, for however filthy you taste, the crocs will have you for supper.'

The light was fading again when they landed, so having again refused to hand back the satphone, and without helping to right the camper van they had knocked over, they lifted off into the setting sun leaving them to go hunting for driftwood and then to huddle together in front of a roaring fire.

'What will happen, Jimbo, when we are forced to leave the flat part of the desert they showed us, and need to move the SPODs elsewhere. For although, the tugs will be useful for topping the snake plants later for their incredible amount of fibre, depending on the terrain, are you seriously intending to abandon them in exchange for those drones you have forced Ud to give us?'

'Yes, I have been planning do just that, Ana, but I am already having kittens about him keeping his word. Although, the Outback continues on for ever, we will look stupid if we plant the snakes solely where it is flat. We must extend our operations to where the terrain is cut to pieces by creeks, or is thick with stunted trees, let alone blessed with low hills like those we are just able to make out, which are some fifty miles away to the east in the Tanami Desert.

'When we start operating all twelve SPODs Felipe will be making, it will make no difference should they be towed either by tugs, or drones, as we will be mopping up more carbon than anyone has previously believed possible.'

'Your plan is incredible, Jimbo, but no more so than your extraordinary feat of extracting the Drones from Ud. As I was in such a bad state at the time, do tell me how you managed to do it.'

'When I approached Ud's hideout after we landed on Komodo, I told you how I was frisked by armed guards before being taken through a tunnel to meet him. I threatened him with the firing squad unless he ceased operations and disbanded his gang of Dragons, who were setting fire to the Amazon rainforest, immediately.

'Only when I saw the powerful looking drones sitting outside his communications centre, which he told me were there to replace his team of arsonists, I realised just how much more damage to the world's forests he was intending to inflict with them. So, I ordered him to hand over all but six of the drones, to be collected by Barney with Bob's yacht later.'

'All but six of the drones, why?'

'Ana, they are last resort weapons for Ud to use, but only if he receives Bob's codeword, in order to save our planet from Australia's increasing production of coal. But we must treat that as top secret. If the Australian government heard about it, that would be the end of us.

'When you were bitten by that Komodo dragon, I only avoided having my throat cut by getting you to hospital. I had warned him that every move was now being watched by the CIA and MI6, with the SAS poised on a nearby island to eradicate him. He thought your death would trigger that.'

'OK, Jimbo, let's forget all our frightening experiences and in between watches tonight, have time for a cuddle. So you have, at least, admitted it! If I had not disobeyed your orders and come to look for you on Komodo, you would now be food for Ud's dragons as a morsel of decaying meat.'

The following morning, after finishing their breakfast, they watched the spectacular birdlife for a time including magpie geese, whistling-ducks, Australian pelicans and their famous black swans take to the air, before heading back to the highway, arriving just before dark in an area of open savanna, where they were to spend the night, although still a long way north of Hall's Creek.

'To continue our discussion, Ana,' he said, as they sat down for a supper of baked beans on toast, 'carbon sequestration is such a wide-ranging subject that we will be only a small, but increasing, part of it. Some countries are thinking of introducing a carbon tax, while others are trying to capture carbon as it leaves the factory chimneys. But think how many factory chimneys there are in the world!

'Also carbon eating machines are being built which suck the carbon out of the air into containers. But the carbon then has to be buried deep in the ground later while ours will be stored by the plants themselves. Meanwhile, the Aussies are hoping to mitigate their loss of carbon sequestration due to bush fires by managing their forests better with more firebreaks. Although, commendable, such attempts are small beer compared with the results we are going to achieve.

'One of the best, more natural, methods of carbon sequestration, as currently being impressed on farmers, is not to plough their fields any longer, but to cultivate them instead, thus to preventing too much carbon being released. They are also being asked to inject fertilisers into the ground and reduce the use of herbicides. Governments should now allow farmers to grow genetically modified crops, saving on sprays and fertilisers, but make them pull back on intensive livestock farming.

'Many people believe that we must re-generate the forests by replacing the lost trees on the same ground. But in Borneo, for instance, where the habitat has been destroyed by planting too many oil palms, it is no longer possible. Also in Brazil, it is out of the question where the topsoil has been rapidly ruined by erosion.

'However long trees take to grow, they play a major part in combatting climate change as illustrated by the Great Green Wall project, inaugurated in Africa thirty years ago, for they also introduce more moisture into the soil. But although, it was estimated over five years ago that the world needed a trillion more trees to replace all those destroyed over the past years, to date less than two per cent of them are known to have been planted.'

They had finally checked the balloons for the night, now tethered to swing freely in the wind, when the cell phone, which the police had luckily overlooked, started ringing. It was Jeb at Kununarra airport.

'All is well here, but you won't believe this. Since being contacted by the coppers in Wyndham, I have managed to persuade one of the customs officers that the paperwork supporting our incoming equipment was signed off,

226

personally, by Australian Deputy Prime Minister. Once the dart trays arrive from the States, I will load them loaded onto the Hercules. I have also found some excellent Aboriginal drivers for the first of the tugs and turn-table tray lorries which were unloaded from the landing craft earlier. Once I know your final location, they will drive them to you.

'To make life easier, I am also arranging for the snake plants to be packed by Felipe, using my multiplier machine, in Rio. Other news is that a fellow called Hank, a US water bomber pilot, who was sent here to fight the bush fires raging near the coast north of Perth, rang asking to speak to you. He says he once saved your life from Colombian drug runners on the island of Montserrat.'

'Fantastic! Did you get his number, Jeb?'

'No, because he told me that because the fires are now largely extinguished, he will ring again in two weeks' time when I should be able to give him your grid number once you know it. He will then fly over to see you again.'

'That's great news, Jeb. For he could be very helpful. This will be our grid number when we get there. Meanwhile, we are about to bed down for the night, hoping to find a good spot in the desert where Hank may land his plane without difficulty.'

'Are we sleeping in our separate vans for ever, Jimbo?' Ana chipped in. 'Or would you prefer I snuggled up to a boomer?'

'Darling Ana, nothing could be better than to be wrapped up in your arms right now, for only then will we both be safe, particularly from the kick of those red boomers, as the Aussies call their male kangaroos around here. Also the desert skinks, emperor scorpions and funnel web spiders, let alone their deadly taipan snakes. However, it is more important that we continue to take turns on watch, not only to look out for them but also for any further assaults on our peaceful way of life!'

'So how many more days do I have to endure this solitude, sunny Jim?'

'Possibly only five more nights, Ana.'

But by the time they had arrived, just before dark, at the spot they were looking for, it was to be seven.

After finally parking the vans and securing the balloons, hardly had they been able to undress and climb into his bunk for their first night without keeping watch, when there was a tap on the door of his camper van followed by a dark face with coal black eyes, a scattering of yellow teeth, and a mass of tousled orange hair tied up in a red bandana, squinting at them sideways through a window.

'Can I help you?' The Major enquired, wrapping a towel around his waist while opening the door.

Bingo. Leader of Aboriginal mob

'G'day, mate,' the man replied in broken English. 'My name is Bingo Nugget, head of the Mulan community here in Lamboo. We need to know what right yer have to bring yer campers and those bloody great balloons onto our property?'

'Your property, I think you must be mistaken, Bingo.'

Whereupon, without saying another word, he took a crumpled piece of paper out of the back pocket of his torn khaki shorts stating in faded black ink that they had been given permission to permanently occupy the land under the Aboriginal Land Trust Act of 1978.

'There you are. An flog a pig's arse, where der yer think yer goin to get yer water, mate? If yer think you will survive here more than the time yer mum had the audacity to drop you into our laps, you are kidding yourself.'

'So would you, Bingo, for we believe there is water in the creek we spotted flying over here earlier.'

'You'll be lucky, fella, for this place is as dry as a dead dingo's donga. We haven't had a drop of rain for as long as it takes a snail to cross over the land of Oz.'

'Then how about a deal, Bingo? I will provide you with all the water you want for those weeds we noticed you were growing over there, and if you can get your people to catch the rain in every receptacle going, they may get enough fresh water to keep them sober from all that Victorian Bitter they are drinking for at least several weeks. In exchange, you will give us written permission to sow the desert far beyond your village with snake plants, which will, in time, will attract more rain clouds than you would believe possible.'

'Fair dinkum, mate,' he replied, leaning forward on his mulga stick with a broad crinkly grin.

'Damn that stretch of desert but what the hell are snake plants? Do they bite?'

Before the magic spell could be broken, 'Of course,' he said, quickly shaking his boney hand.

'OK, mate, but don't you be too hasty. Before we seal the deal, I wanna see the water.'

They were woken up far earlier than they intended the following morning by the loud drum of aero engines and piling out of the camper van, they almost missed the flash of bright yellow passing low overhead as the Canadair Superscooper skimmed the gum trees and touched down on the flat area of sand stretching both ways directly in front of them.

'Top of the morning to you, my old friend. Crikey, you look like a lion in love. Where then is the lioness? How I missed those barrage balloons of yours a miracle. Is this the Third World War, or are they for hanging up the washing, or lifting you up to look for water in this godforsaken place! What the heck are you up to, soldier?'

'Great to see you again, Hank, and your nose must be as sensitive as ever. Who wouldn't be looking for water in this damned desert. Last time we met was when you were crying out for water waiting to have that machine gun bullet extracted from your leg, but that was before you started chatting up the nurses in Vancouver General Hospital.'

'Once a varmint, always a varmint. So, come on, whose the Sheila then, boss?'

'You keep away from her, Hank. You were right the first time, Ana is a lioness, and there is urgent business to be done. We are here to combat climate change by greening up the desert once we have joined those two balloons together and more of them have been flown in here. But the Aboriginals say it's their land and have already told us to bugger off. However, before Ana and I fell into our love nest here, we passed by Lake Argyle, a fresh water man-made reservoir over a thousand metres long, which may solve the problem.

'As the Aboriginals are thirsting for the stuff, Hank, why not drop 'em some over their village, and more on their fields of what they call crops, for I'm sure that the head guy, Bingo, will then allow us to start planting our snakes over what they claim to be their motherland.'

'Blimey, what do you mean by snakes, general?'

'The carbon sucking snake plants we are about to sow from our blimps will cover a greater area of ground than any machines on earth let alone that yellow bird of yours. Surprisingly, they are normally kept in pots by old ladies on their bedside tables, who rely on them for cleaning the air. But growing outdoors under the sun, they behave very differently, and when they are fired into the ground as self-watering darts, the fragments of rhizomes within there points will grow into spiky leaved beauties some two metres in diameter.

'Then, if there is no rain for a time, we can always do some cloud seeding from the Hercules C130 we have on call here, or if not, from some rockets the Chinese are known to use with a reasonable amount of success.'

'So how do those ruddy blimps of yours work then?'

'Let me explain before your brain turns to jelly. Once we have joined the two together, we will shoot the pod darts by compressed air from trays inserted into shoot boxes fixed underneath them. Every evening, Aboriginal crews will then replenish them from the special tray lorries they will be driving. Indeed, they are shorty on their way here.

'To re-load the shoot boxes, we simply activate two internal compressors to lower the SPODs, or Seed Pod Overhead Distributors as I have named them, close to the ground, without expelling any of the precious helium.'

'Clever stuff, soldier, I would never have thought you had it in you! And the Sheila?'

'So who let loose such a renowned lady-killer to prowl around the southern hemisphere, Hank?'

'Better known as a flame-killer, I was invited fly my crate on board the US carrier, Nimitz, with several other pilots of water bombers to join the US mercy mission down under. But no peace for the wicked, as there are so many more fires destroying the forests now, my mission will never come to an end. Therefore, I must fly on to Perth later and be lifted back onto the carrier to return to my native California to fight the fires about to rage again there.'

Together, they watched his amphibian swoop over the village to bring the inhabitants out into the hot sunshine before vanishing over the northern horizon to pick up seven thousand litres of fresh water from Lake Argyle.

'Ana, what an amazing stroke of luck it's been to catch up with Hank again, who, a couple of years ago, was instrumental in helping me to sort out a humane method, devised by Bob, for controlling the world's population. And also how lucky I have also been to meet up with such a clever girl. So before Hank returns from picking up more water, help me decide on how we get cracking with the SPODs afterwards.

'As you know, we are intending to plant the snakes in parallel strips so that the tray lorries don't have to travel too far. But how do you propose we programme them to plant in the opposite direction every day, leaving fifty metres between the strips for environmental purposes?'

'You will remember, Jim, that motoring at forty knots it still took us more than a day to cover the two thousand kilometres from Bali to Timor-Leste on Bob's gas turbine powered superyacht. Then many hours longer towing the two halves of the SPOD across the eight hundred kilometres of the Timor Sea at only sixteen knots. During the first passage, Jeb taught me everything about programming the tugs, and during the second passage, he taught me how to programme the drones to do precisely the same task. So, all is in hand and we are ready to go.'

'Thanks, Ana, I would expect nothing less. But how someone so intelligent should look so beautiful and not have a head looking like an ostrich egg, defeats me. Every day since I was stretchered out of the Amazon rainforest to your uncle's farm by those Indian braves, I have thought how fortunate it was that you were there to save me from dying of malaria while taking a couple of weeks off from training as a doctor in Brasilia!'

But such thoughts were rudely interrupted once more by the sound of approaching aero engines.

Hank was back, and as he flew past at no more than fifty metres above them, Lamboo vanished for a time behind a curtain of water. When the dwellings came slowly back into view, all they could see through the camper van's binoculars, were the villagers holding up tin containers and even their cupped hands to the sky, while dancing like dervishes to such shrieks of delight that they could hear them clearly from almost five kilometres away.

'What are they shouting, Bingo?' Ana asked the gaunt Aboriginal who had returned, leaning again on his stick, to join them.

'Come back, come back they are chanting,' he said, while clapping his hands together every time Hank returned with more water.

'Oh my God, Ana, I never told Hank about the hundreds of fresh water crocodiles the police warned us are living in the lake. What happens if he picks one or two of them up in his scoop, Bingo?'

'Better than a kick in the backside, cobber. Double rations you'd say!'

As the heavens opened for one last time over some crops in the distance, Bingo started hopping up and down while beating his chest, knowing their crops of millet would soon start growing again.

'Now, Bingo, get a few of your ruffians to help us join our two balloons together,' shouted the Major.

'OK, mate, but Boom Ba Ba Hoya. My permo for you poms to hang out here is not granted yet.'

'What the hell does that mean, Ana?'

But she was watching the yellow aeroplane do its final run and failed to hear Jim's question as the din of its two Pratt and Whitney engines slowly faded away until there was a deep silence. 'Great stuff, Hank!' She yelled after him. 'I'm beginning to enjoy Carboneering!'

But she was too hasty.

232

Chapter 20

At the time Bob arrived back in America, the secretary general of the United Nations was doing his nut because the western world had yet failed to concentrate on any realistic solutions to climate change. This also worried Bob greatly, making him feel more frustrated than he had ever been in his life. It was madness that while all his nuclear intentions were poised for take-off, with the International Atomic Energy Association primed for action, the Chinese, behind a cloak of secrecy, were already proving two molten salt-cooled SMRs, fuelled with thorium, out in their Gobi desert.

It was true that climate change was, at last, receiving more attention from the media, but in both England and America that was due mainly to Sir David Attenborough, whose defence of the natural world was legendary, as he continued to warn about the consequences. There were others doing much the same as Greta Thunberg, but none offered any practical solutions. Reducing the emissions from cars and airplanes was now on the agenda, as was the provision of more renewable energy, but such moves were of little consequence when compared with the vast quantity of coal, oil and natural gas still likely to be consumed in thirty years' time by the world's growing population. Those pundits, crowing those renewables and hydrogen would be our salvation, were leading us all astray, for however much of a bonus they were, they would never be able to catch up with the growing demand for electricity.

'The earth is not dying, it is being killed, the folk singer Utah Philips once wrote.' Bob told his pilot as they sped back across the Atlantic. 'But how will we ever bring the murderers to justice when many have been forced to kill by their very need to survive. That is our challenge.'

'Some say, sir, that it is the super-rich and unscrupulous businessmen, who are the murderers, for over just two, or three, decades it is they who are most guilty of swamping the world with carbon.'

'Perhaps, Sam, but the world is becoming dangerously over populated with far too many people trying to kill each other rather than sort out climate change,' Macey joined in, remembering her time working as a nurse for the US Navy Seals while flying in a British Royal Airforce Chinook helicopter with him over war torn Afghanistan. 'No, not just the rich. We are all responsible for arming the atmosphere in the first place, not with bullets or nuclear bombs, but with CO_2, the most dangerous weapon of all. So, surely, Sam, it is up to all of us to clean it up.'

'Agreed Macey, but, as Bob says, we first have to show them how to set about it.'

She knew that Bob, despite his age, was a fighter, who, like his mercenary, had once won a black belt for judo before becoming a national boxing champion while still at school. It was because of his will to succeed that if no one else come forward to lead the battle against climate change, backed by the vast amount of money countries such as Russia and North Korea had paid his company Nuklin in the past, he, certainly, would.

By agreeing to champion thorium fuelled SMRs, Bob was confident that the governor of California would now encourage all Americas to think again about nuclear energy, allowing him, he old Macey, to turn his mind back to the mission he had set his mercenary. But not before he had made another call to the IAEA in Vienna.

'Director General, its Bill Buckmaster here, or you will remember me better as Bob, the name my company Nuklin gave me. On my last visit we agreed that much depended on our American friends changing their attitude to nuclear. Now, as I fly back to England from San Francisco, I am feeling more confident, at last, that we have them in the bag. My reason for calling you, therefore, is that once we agree and I have, personally, sent you the secure codeword, I need you and your IAEA to progress with the promotion of Thunder Power immediately.

'Go ahead then, Bill.'

'When discussing the advantages of thorium fuelled, molten salt cooled, SMRs in America earlier, only their ante-nuclear lobby was being listened to, irrespective of fact that these new reactors no longer require vast quantities of cooling water, leave little nuclear waste and are safe. As you know, the Yanks, largely because of that lobby, have decided to start closing their nuclear power plants and return to natural gas. When they chose to close the infamous Diablo Canyon plant in California, I first held the state's governor responsible, but since

234

he met the head of the environmental group I was with, he has not only changed his mind but will now use his considerable influence to make not just his own people, but all of his countrymen see sense.

At the time I and many others started researching thorium, or u-233, as a better alternative to its big brother u-235, I was astonished to find that although thorium's unique properties have been known about for over a hundred years, once being used in Victorian times for illuminating gas lamps, the element has been totally ignored since WWII, when the US government decided to back u-235 as their nuclear fuel instead—solely because it could also be used to make bombs!

If thorium had not been side-lined at the time, we would not be facing the terrifying prospect of global warming today.

As you know, sir, thorium is one of the most plentiful and least expensive elements on earth. Scientists at the Georgia Institute of Technology have said: 'While considering the overall potential of thorium-based power, the conclusion is that it will result in a thousand-year solution to a huge portion of mankind's negative impact on the environment.

Scientific writer Richard Martin stated recently: 'Thorium will provide a clean and effectively limitless source of power while allaying all public concern about weapons proliferation, radioactive pollution and toxic waste. It should, therefore, replace uranium two three five, which is costly and complicated to process.

While another well-known nuclear physicist made the point: If you wish to have carbon-free energy in the world, I don't see how that can happen without nuclear. And I don't see how nuclear power will be accepted again unless it is safe thorium power.

Some say, director general, that depending on take up, thorium could, in time, become cheaper than coal. It is also said that one ton of thorium can produce as much energy as three and a half million tons of coal due to coal burning being so woefully inefficient and that SMRs will provide the same amount of electricity for a third of the cost of traditional nuclear power stations. But, as it is your job, why are you not totally behind this safe nuclear solution to climate change?'

'Bob' the director general answered, 'do you not realise that there are several companies around the world already working on SMRs, even AMRs, or advanced modular reactors?'

'Absolutely, among them Rolls Royce in the United Kingdom, who already have know-how from building the small reactors to power our nuclear submarines. But they are not being supported financially and Rolls Royce hint that their SMRs will not be in service for another ten years! Meanwhile the Chinese will start marketing their own versions to the world.

Director general, irrespective of the cost, may I suggest that it is now up to the IAEA to launch the most vigorous marketing campaign ever on this safe alternative to nuclear power, ensuring that the free world catches up with China and quickly follows the governor of California's lead.'

'But for most countries converting from fossil fuelled plants to nuclear will be at too great a cost!'

'The cost should be of no consequence for that will be covered not just by governments but by normal market forces. And forget the idea of converting coal, or oil, powered power stations to nuclear. The new generation of thorium fuelled SMRs will be totally independent.'

'Is that generally acknowledged, Bob?'

'Maybe not. But because molten salt cooled SMRs will be factory built, easily transported, and operated without much need for water, they may be installed wherever there is an existing grid, while avoiding normal decommissioning costs due to there being so little radioactive waste.

However, those American's responsible for licensing the SMRs must be ordered to provide a much slicker, bog standard, certification procedure.'

'So, Bob, do you believe that the opposition to nuclear power will now fade away?'

'Not yet. Hold your horses Director General, for first you need to lobby the most likely investors with all the plus points I have just given you. May I suggest, therefore, following the initiative taken by the governor of California, we draw up a list of all those we believe will subscribe to Thunder Power including the multinational oil and gas companies, who, valued jointly at the staggering sum of three and a half trillion dollars, are desperate to fund green alternatives. At the same time, I am hoping that the Californian governor is going to hold a convention attended by every nuclear country on the planet, including China, to choose a standard thorium fuelled SMR, so that it may then be mass produced by those able to fabricate them quickly and subsequently distribute them at competitive prices.'

'So what you are asking us to do at the IAEA is not just to send our members a brief about SMRs, but to ensure they invest in them?

'Yes, for it is better than rich nations giving money to poorer ones to mitigate climate disasters.'

'But your request is not possible, Bob. May I remind you that the IAEA is neither a marketing, or an investment management company. Nor do we have sufficient staff competent to take on such a commitment. Our purpose is to ensure that nuclear energy is used for peaceful purposes. only.

'Then how is such a strategy going to work unless your members are kept up to speed with every new development such at the safe advances in nuclear energy we have just been talking about?'

'I repeat, Bob, that the purpose of most of our two thousand five hundred employees is to monitor nuclear security—not to spend their precious time promoting new, untried, energy concepts.'

'Perhaps. But have your employees ever thought of monitoring climate change and thinking about their family's futures? Knowing how much progress we have made in finding solutions to climate change, will you not feel responsible when they start being roasted alive in a few years' time?'

'That's a ridiculous exaggeration, Bob. Where are you going with all of this? Are you threatening me with hell and damnation unless I change the IAEA's modus operandi altogether?'

'When I send you the codeword, exactly that, sir!'

**

The howl of the Pratt and Whitney turboprops was still resonating amongst the dunes when the Major's feelings of relief were rudely interrupted by a white Toyota Land Cruiser bucking towards them in clouds of red dust with WAPO, Western Australian Police painted on its doors.

Wearing blue shorts and a blue shirt with a large badge sewn on to it, the driver's deeply tanned face was part concealed under a wide brimmed felt hat jammed over his head, but not his voice.

'G'day mate. So, what's on the barbie?'

'It's known as road kill in England where I come from officer, but as you have no roads around here, that roo you have just noticed must have tripped over a sand hill.'

237

'And what the hell is that balloon doing tied up to those rocks over there? Do you know that you are not only camp'n, but shoots for the pot without permo on our West Australian property? '

'Why is it then that the Aboriginals claim this as their land, officer?'

'Are you sure about that, mate?'

'As sure as a fox in a henhouse, Rozzer.' Then taking Bingo's crumpled scrap of paper out of his pocket he read. 'This Act may be cited as the land attenuation restriction act amendment, continuance act nineteen forty-seven. The rights to the aboriginal peoples in Western Australia.'

'Historical crap, mate. You have five minutes to get movin with your ruddy balloon out of here.'

'No, not crap, Rozzer. The Land Rights Act decreed by the Australian National Government later in nineteen seventy-six, entitles traditional Aboriginal inhabitants to claim ownership of vacant areas of Crown land considered worthless to white Australians. So you could hardly say that red kangaroo lying dead over there is a white Aussie, can you?'

'Fair go mate. No worries. I'm off then.' Whereupon, looking totally defeated, the policeman jumped back into his Land Cruiser and sped off towards the distant track to somewhere.

'Having dealt successfully with the last cop we are likely to see, Ana, we may still have to get rid of these rabid environmentalists if they ever catch up with us. However, by planting the strips fifty metres apart, we shall be able to tell them that every living creature in the Outback will be able to move about unrestricted.

But there is plenty more to worry about such as water, although with an average rainfall of eleven to twelve inches here, which we expect to increase after planting, we should be able to grow the snakes without too much difficulty. Far better than having to set up an irrigation system, fed by an expensive solar powered desalination plant we would need to build near the coast.

Tomorrow, when the first two tugs drive in and the C130 Hercules also touches down here, I will get their crews to help fill the shoot boxes with the first of the dart trays. The pilot will then return to Kununurra to collect the next consignment while you programme the tugs for planting the first snakes in two days' time. In due course, it will also be necessary to do the same with the first two drones if they have arrived as Ud promised. We need to have them with us as a backup when the ground becomes difficult.'

'So how about the pilot bringing you a replacement for your satellite telephone, Jimbo?

'Hank, generously, gave me his own, sweetheart, and I am about to use it.'

'Is that you, sir? I apologise for being out of touch for so long, but although I was intending to obey radio silence until we arrived here, we had just reached Lake Argyle when the Border Police swooped down in a chopper, took us for a mystery tour and confiscated my phone, the bastards.'

'Well at least you managed to first get your Mayday call through to Sam at Frisco airport. But how did you get found out?'

'Before Barney sailed us over the Timor Sea, Ana had followed Macey's idea of painting sheets of material on the side of the two envelopes to resemble coal barges, which we then flipped over on landing to resemble lorry trailers. We saw no one when we passed the custom's house at Kununurra, so once we reached Lake Argyle to enjoy our breakfast, we thought we had succeeded.

'The Border Force police took us completely by surprise. Apparently, we had been spotted by them from their helicopter on the previous night as we approached Wyndham. It was sod's law, for they said later that they were not concerned about us until they twigged, we were heading with our empty coal barges to a place with no docking facilities. Something we had, unfortunately, ignored.

'So it was a relief when they told us later that the Australian PM had intervened, believing we would help him tame our Aboriginal mob in the Great Sandy Desert.'

'Well, Major, in that case I should come clean and, luckily for you, explain how that came about.

'I was cursing about flying out of Frisco again empty handed, when the governor of California, on returning to his office from a discussion we had been having with a pro-nuclear group, must have telephoned the Aussie PM and told him about our important project, impressing on him that as his country was already being consumed by wild fires, if he wanted to save it from climate change, he was to allow you to proceed with your seeding trials unmolested.

'All appeared to have been agreed when the PM rang me back to say that because it had been reported by the two drivers of the camper vans on returning to Kununarra, that you had entered the country illegally and were headed for the Outback, he had no alternative but to have you detained.'

'OK, but it is nether his property, or his toes that we are treading on. In fact, it all belongs to the Aboriginals, who are more possessive about their land than any of us realised, or the Aussie PM was prepared to admit. In truth the Aboriginals own the whole of the blasted Outback. And as for entering Australia illegally, why don't we threaten to expose his country's appalling lack of efficient customs and excise surveillance?'

'Before you do so, Major, the governor rang me again later to say that the PM had been on the blower once more. Surprisingly he has had second thoughts saying that because the Aboriginals where you are headed, had once embarrassed him so badly previously through their threatening demands for water, he has since ordered the Border Force to help you bring them to their senses.'

'OK, got it. No wonder we now have their leader, Bingo, eating out of our hands for Hank, an old American friend from the past, has just slaked their thirst with his yellow water bomber.

He was down here helping the Aussies to put out their bush fires when he contacted me through Jeb in Kununurra. When I told him about the plight of the Aboriginals, who were suffering from a long period of drought, he dropped half of Lake Argyle onto them, which changed their attitude altogether. He will contact the governor on returning to California to thank him for saving our project. It's said that twenty-five per cent of the World's carbon is already being captured by plants.

'But what happens if the drought continues and due to global warming, it remains like that?'

'No worries. The Aboriginals are predicting from their magic stones that rain will fall here sometime soon. The alternative is to move our SPODS to the coast and sow seagrass, and kelp there, which grow to a suitable size in three to four months compared to five or six years by tree saplings. Should we have to do that we will need Jeb to contact his father in Salt Lake City and arrange for him to pack the dart trays with seagrass seeds and kelp fragments in a new type of transparent pod dart deigned on CAVX principles to be shot down through water.'

'That sounds sensible, but tell me about seagrass, for it's all news to me.'

'Seagrass, which is the only flowering plant in the ocean and multiplies itself genetically in warm shallow water, is known to be the largest living plant on earth with a history dating back thousands of years. Amazingly, seagrass and kelp are said to capture carbon some thirty-five times more efficiently than terrestrial rainforests and apart from providing a nursery for fish and other invertebrates, although now suffering from substantial die back due to pollution from the land, it has been said to absorb much of the carbon sequestered by the ocean.

Seagrass will be far more valuable as a carbon sink if a more efficient way of planting it is pursued rather than attempting to do so by hand, or attaching it to ropes, which, in such small quantities, will do little to inhibit climate change. Now that we have our SPODs almost ready to go, changing over to planting the oceans will be a better alternative, for a time, to this blasted desert.'

'So, if the drought continues, are you then intending to do just that and move from your base at Kununurra to Port Hedland, which I am looking at on Google Earth right now, Major?

I notice that the port is just south of somewhere called eighty-mile beach and although it has only a small docking area and no airstrip, both the Savannah and the Hercules I have chartered will be able to land there, although probably not the Super Guppy. We must not risk any more planting in the Outback if ……

'Hang on, sir, we have a problem. Some maniacs, presumably a group of those nasty environmental activists I was warned about, have just cut loose our SPOD, which Ana, who arrived at the scene too late to identify the culprits, has shouted back is being blown fast towards the horizon.'

**

Jeb heard his cell phone ring as he finished loading the C130 with the first batch of dart trays. 'A moment ago, we had our SPOD released by a gang of idiots, who must have arrived from nowhere, probably on motorbikes, and left before Ana was able to see who they were. Before going after them, she had noticed men attempting to pull the SPOD down, presumably to puncture it, but on failing to do so they cut it loose from the rocks where we had it tethered.'

'The pilot of the C130 is at this moment preparing for take-off, Major, so I will stop him loading any more dart trays and prevent the support vehicles from leaving right now. Instead, I will ask the pilot to collect you both from your camp near Lamboo, bringing two of their Aboriginal drivers with him, tasked with returning your two camper vans back here to Kununarra.'

'Jeb, we are not going to abort the mission just because of losing our first SPOD, so the camper vans must remain where they are. Please load two of Ud's

241

drones, which Barney should have delivered to you from Komodo by now, and join the pilot yourself, so that once he picks us up, we may all go looking for the rogue SPOD wherever it has gone. Once we manage to find it, we will retrieve it by attaching two of Ud's drones to the tail end of the ropes which, before they were cut, had it secured without a problem.'

The Hercules was already airborne when Ana also picked up the telephone. 'At least, Jeb, she sighed, when you look down on the lake where we eventually spent our first night, it was fortunate, when I dangled my legs in the water, I was not noshed by a crocodile. Thank heavens I'm still able to point the pilot in the right direction as I took bearings on the vanishing SPOD.'

An hour later, after they had left their camper vans sitting in the desert and flown on westwards, it was not long before Ana, who had jumped into the co-pilot's seat, spotted the errant SPOD looking pathetic with one of its ropes snagged in a wattle tree.

'Not exactly like looking for a needle in a haystack, Ana,' the pilot remarked as he dropped the Hercules neatly onto the sand beside it. 'But watch out, I may have disturbed the beast again!'

'You are right. This is getting like a tortoise chasing a hare,' Ana exclaimed, 'for the balloon is always going to escape every time we get near it. I'm afraid it will continue to outwit us in the strengthening easterly wind now blowing unless something else manages to trap it.'

'Jeb,' implored the Major, as he followed the SPOD's erratic progress, 'please search your cell phone for some fields with fences around them along that coastal strip Bob was talking about. The chances of the SPOD getting snagged by its ropes again are virtually nil, but if it crosses anything resembling the arrestor wires on an aircraft carrier we may be back in business.'

'Talking of aircraft carriers, Major, if you have not already done so, why don't you consider adapting the SPODs as rafts and then employ the USA's fleet of nuclear aircraft carriers to replenish them once we start planting seaweed in earnest? But to answer your question—yes, there do appear to be some fields inland from eighty-mile beach, but that is as much as I can tell you.'

But the SPOD had different ideas.

'Watch out!' shouted Ana from the co-pilot's seat, 'the damn thing is going to pass to the left of the fields you see coming into view and is heading straight for the oggin!'

They had been forced to fly in wide circles due to the speed of the aircraft, before altering course to follow it, knowing that once it hit the ocean it was not only going to be the end of their trials for a time, but worse still, the end of any further support from the Australian PM, who would consider their whole operation a fiasco. But then, as if a mighty hand had given the SPOD a push, it headed due south towards Port Headland, the very town Bob had been talking about.

Flying at about five metres above the ground it had nearly grazed the first of the corrugated iron roofs when Ana cried out 'you see that patch of grass this side of the far buildings, for God's sake hit the compressor button and drop the balloon right now, it is our last chance of saving it!'

But just as the Major grabbed his remote control, Bob was on the line again. 'Have you yet caught the damned thing because I need to inform the Australian prime minister immediately if you ever manage to do so.'

'It's happening right now!'

'Hold on to it—breaking news, Major. The Aussie PM has just been contacted in Canberra by an Aboriginal named Bingo, who told him that, together with some others of his tribe, he was the guy responsible for cutting your balloon loose and unless you provide them at Lamboo with more water, he will continue to cause you the maximum amount of havoc until they are satisfied.'

'That's sheer blackmail, sir. If we can get the PM on side again, we will ask him if he is able to help us achieve that for Hank has already returned to the States. Now the fires have been put out for the moment, most of the Australian water bombers have been sent there as well, but I expect he has retained a couple of them. So it will give him an opportunity to improve both his and our own relations with the Aboriginals, if he is willing to follow Hank's lead.

But I am more worried, once we are all properly organised, about that codeword you are intending to send us, sir. So please ask Felipe to contact Rick, Ana's uncle, who farms near the Amazon rainforest, saying that unless I send the codeword to him personally, just as I have told Ud he must on no account launch his own desperate measures, which we discussed earlier'

'Remind me about those desperate measures, before I warn you about a new problem facing your project in the Outback, Major?

'In Brazil Plan A. is to inform their government that unless they reduce their beef production by at least fifty per cent, give up destroying the rainforest to grow more soya, and put a stop to all illegal gold mining, turning to other profitable enterprises instead, we will be forced, much against our will, to resort to plan B.

There are plenty of alternatives to these appalling measures of reducing the national debt, such as growing extensive crops of sansevieria, those snake plants we discovered, well away from the forest. For when drilling for oil becomes no longer acceptable and the world's insatiable appetite for plastic, which is based on oil, comes to an end, due of their high fibre content they join seaweed in being invaluable for producing an alternative to plastic.'

'And beef?'

'Brazil provides over twenty per cent of the World's beef, half of which is exported to China, and that figure is growing. If they don't have enough agricultural land left to raise cattle on, the UN must stop them from destroying any more of the Amazon rainforest. No country should be allowed to lay waste to such natural resources. But sadly, there are too many affluent multinational businesses involved and an insufficient amount of foreign aid available to stop this catastrophe.'

'The plot thickens, what then is plan B, and why have you not discussed it with me previously?'

'Do you remember, sir, at the time of foot and mouth disease we stopped importing Brazilian beef?

'Stop right there, Major, you have said enough.'

'But dealing with plan C, our other measure of last resort will be far more controversial. The devil is in the detail and the devil is Ud, who must be one of the most dangerous bastards on earth. I told you how I threatened Ud with the firing squad, after finding his HQ on the island of Komodo, unless he ceased setting fire to the forests and handed over all but six of his new-fangled drones. With those six, but only when I personally send him the codeword, he has agreed to carry out my other last-ditch mission. Because climate change is known to be largely caused by burning fossil fuels, not helped by intensive beef farming and the destruction of our rainforests, air pollution is already killing more than nineteen thousand people every day, or some seven million every year. So however controversial my plan is, sir, we must stop this madness continuing.'

'I also don't want to hear about this frightening mission you have planned behind my back, Major, but due to your misplaced enthusiasm this is your latest bombshell. When you were investigating your snake plants with that long haired hippy out in the Nevada desert, you failed to quiz him sufficiently on two crucially important facts. Firstly you would have discovered that the plants are poisonous to most animals including marsupials such as kangaroos and wallabies, and secondly, which may put the kibosh on everything, because the plants are known to be seriously invasive, should the Australian PM, who has already been sworn at by the very aboriginals you were expected to pacify, discover what you are about to plant out there in the Outback, you may well find yourself behind bars again. Sansiviera, or snake plant, is regarded as such a pernicious weed in Australia, that even growing it in your back garden is regarded as a crime.

Although my own objectives are not yet in place, Major, even should we ultimately adopt your plan of last resort, you must, somehow, re-organise your planting programme immediately. For we must crack on faster than ever to confront climate change with one last supreme effort. Meanwhile should I also be threatened with gaol again because of your bravado, everything, including our plans to rid the world of fossil fuel, and my business, will fall apart at the seams.

245

So, while I wait anxiously for you to make sense of your project once more, which seems to be in trouble not only with the plants but also with the natives, when do you consider I should press the trigger on my own project by sending the director general of the International Atomic Energy Agency the crisis codeword? From my previous conversations with him in Austria, apart from publishing a safety report on SMRs, it still looks unlikely that he will carry out my suggestions of actively marketing them, so now it may be only the codeword that jogs him into action.'

'Firstly, my thoughts on planting are as follows, sir. Due to what has happened it would be pointless to continue with my plans for the desert and given time to reorganise we will move north from our present location and turn to planting nopal opuntia, or prickly pear, as an alternative to snake plants, in the less hostile and more temperate savannah of the Northern Territories, which stretch across two million square kilometres of Australia. I should not have discounted prickly pear in the first place for it also absorbs CO_2 at night. and being high in fibre will also help to replace plastic. Also, unlike the snake, it will be useful for feeding cattle.

But our priority must be now to seed the ocean, so ask Felipe to design a second SPOD as a raft, and meanwhile arrange for Jeb's father, back at his tissue culture laboratory in Salt Lake City, to start culturing nopal opuntia in a big way. Then, once the pod darts have been prepared, he must create separate trays for seagrass and kelp, for all of which he must be rewarded.

Now to answer your other question, yes—press the trigger right now, sir. All we can do then is pray that the codeword will help to change the director general's mind. But send it only to him yourself in person. There must be no more delays in fixing climate change.' But, as discovered at Bletchley Park during WWII, codes and codewords are never secure, particularly if a clever but dangerous lunatic like Ud is involved. Who, against the Major's strict instructions not to open the envelope detailing his mission of last resort and the bounty he was due to receive, until told to do so, had immediately deployed three of his super-fast 'cigarette' speedboats along the eastern seaboard of Australia, each equipped with two of his remaining six drones.

Then, impatient to get his hands on the five million dollars promised to him by the Major as quickly as possible, and not waiting for his word of command, or giving any thought to the consequences, the night sky over Queensland and New South Wales was suddenly seen to erupt in a storm of eye blistering white light as Ud set about dropping his phosphorus sticks on all of Australia's most productive open cut coal mines, now producing more than four hundred million tons of coal a year—after hacking into Bob's call to Vienna and hearing the codeword "CLIMAX".

———

Saving Mother Earth, The Sequel

United Nations Secretary General

CHINA FURIOUS AS THEIR SUPPLY OF AUSTRALIAN COAL GOES UP IN FLAMES.

But headlines in the world press are often misleading.

It was well known that China, for a long time, had been filling Australian pockets with dollars due to their insatiable demand for coal. Meanwhile, after Indonesia, Australia had become the second largest exporter of coal in the world. So as the direct result of Ud's unprovoked attack on their coal mines, it was not the Chinese economy that was to suffer, whose anger had a very different motive, but the whole economy of Australia.

Ud, determined to claim his reward, acting without orders had found torching the Australian open cut coal mines, which could never be easily extinguished, a piece of cake.

It was not "a piece of cake" for the Australian prime minister, however. Apart from the disastrous effect it would have on their export markets, it was unfortunate that almost eighty per cent of the Australian electricity supply was generated by coal fired power stations. So not only would his people suffer immediate hardship, but much of Australia's booming industry would be brought to an abrupt standstill.

Aware of the advances being made in China, who were already hard at it proving their thorium fuelled, salt cooled, small modular reactors, or SMRs as they were known, next door in the Gobi Desert, he cursed loudly, ashamed by the fact that Australia had become totally reliant on coal by failing to construct a single nuclear power station. Such an oversight had been an endless bone of contention in the Australian parliament since the nineteen sixties, for not only were they sitting on a third of the world's deposits of uranium, but they were in an ideal position to build them.

**

At long last, back in familiar surroundings in England, Bob, having poured himself a large glass of Jack Daniels, was feeling both concerned and elated. Apart from the good news he had received, he knew what hell the Australian prime minister must be experiencing due to his mercenary failing to follow his orders to kill the Indonesian terrorist responsible.

Summoned to meet Bob at his mansion in North Devon, soon after flying back from Brazil, the mercenary and Ana were feeling just as worried for the same reason.

'My failure to kill that bastard will have sent Bob into a towering rage, and we will be lucky to escape with our lives. But by giving Ud that task, I now know I was right. However, considering that our future also depends on Bob's friend, the governor of California, sending Hank and his water bomber down to the Outback again, this must also be a golden opportunity for us to ensure that Bob encourages him to do so.'

'The Aussie prime minister would have provided the Aboriginals with all the water they needed,' Ana intervened, as she also waited patiently with Sam and Macey for Bob to invite them into his study. 'If only that bastard Ud had not acted so stupidly without your orders.'

'But that may not be the only reason for the old man's fury,' Sam added, trying to help. 'He had already been going bananas attempting to get the Director General of the IAEA, better known in Vienna as the International Atomic Energy

Agency, to step out of their ridiculous protocol, and instead of sticking to their primary role of securing the safe and peaceful use of atomic energy, change to promoting thorium fuelled SMRs through their extensive international membership in every way possible.

'Should the director general continue to resist doing so, by spelling out their pathetic mission statement again to justify his argument that marketing nuclear power was not his, or his organisation's, official responsibility, the worry is that the vast numbers of power stations currently burning fossil fuels will not be led by the nose to follow the IAEA's example, and their director general will be accused of preventing Bob's gallant attempt to stop the frightening amount of carbon continually being released into the atmosphere. So watch out, guys!

'But, returning to Ud and the problems of sequestering the great quantities of carbon also reaching the surface of the earth, were you not expecting a man who needs to surround himself with Komodo dragons, known for killing water buffalos, eating putrid flesh and sensing blood with their forked tongues several miles away, to behave like that?'

'I was, team!' Bob interrupted, joining them suddenly, as they leapt to their feet from where they were sitting on some hard wooden chairs in his library.

'However, Major, it was because of the deal that you managed to do with that gangster before he attempted to slit your throat on that notorious island, that, together with Felipe, Jeb and my competent yacht skipper, Barney, you have accomplished considerably more than I ever expected of you. The chaos Ud has created by destroying the Australian economy at a single stroke, has resulted in the most sensational outcome I could ever have imagined in my wildest dreams.

'Now, humiliated as a result by Australia's past failure to construct a single nuclear power station despite their considerable reserves of uranium, and faced by a situation most sane mortals would find impossible to deal with, the Aussie prime minister has had to turn his mind away from mining uranium to the country's significant deposits of thorium, which, totalling some five hundred thousand tonnes, are said to be among the largest on Earth. But that is only the start of a surprising knock-on effect. Now, come into my study.

'You must realise that those sensational headlines you may have read in the newspapers mean absolutely nothing,' he continued, as they sank into his deep leather sofas. 'For behind the scenes, the Chinese have just carried off a coup that leaves me flabbergasted! It's hard to believe it, but the Aussie prime minister has just gifted the Chinese their total deposits of thorium in exchange for just part of the increasing amount of coal they are, as a result, being forced to import from Indonesia.

'So, God help Australia if they have not already converted to nuclear energy by the time the Chinese and the Indonesians close down all their coal fired power stations in exchange for this new and exciting technology. For, apart from flogging them their own thorium fed SMRs, which will have been certified by then, as Rome starts to burn while the rest of the world twiddle their thumbs, the Chinese will, no doubt, soon start selling them to us.'

'Heavens, Sir,' exclaimed Sam. 'If the Aussies fail to install, what you say are likely to be Chinese SMRs, in time, what a catastrophe that would be! So if their country goes bust, knowing how little renewable energy they have to fall back on, presumably we will no longer be able to count on them helping us, when we soon start drilling the plants in earnest with our SPODs. They may not even allow us to continue, which won't matter if the Aboriginals refuse to work for us due to the Aussies failing to provide them with any more water.'

Then Ana took up the cry. 'In that case, Sir, should you have to abandon your valiant attempt to get the IAEA on side, and fail to stop all that carbon rising into the sky until it is too late, it will make a nonsense of us struggling down there in Australia trying to sequester the ever-increasing quantity of carbon still falling to earth you will be asking us to deal with. Surely, you don't expect us to fly back there again, and in utter desperation, continue with our brave attempt to restore the health of the planet's fragile environment to what it was only twenty years ago, completely on our own?'

'I fully understand your concern, team, however while I continue to try and make the IAEA see sense, rather than abandon the idea, I agree with you that by giving their total deposits of thorium to the Chinese, the Australians will not only have jeopardised most of what you have so far achieved in the Outback, but unless we get the rest of the world behind us, your operations down under will start to look increasingly unsustainable.'

'Although, we have always been full of admiration for you, Sir,' Sam followed on, as Ana and Macey stood up as if preparing to leave, 'hearing such gloomy news after all we have done for you is becoming more discouraging by the minute.'

'No, don't leave us now, girls!' The Major implored, 'for I'm beginning to understand Bob's drift. It's high time, once again, for our great country to create a lasting impact in the world and mark my words, he must be keeping something astonishing up his sleeve.'

Bob was in no hurry. Busily lighting one of his favourite cigars, he turned away from them and striding over to the French windows, stood for a while staring out over his garden towards the ever-rising waters of the Atlantic Ocean, where he could see lines of tumbling breakers and gannets diving for fish. Then trying hard to compose himself, he returned to spill them the beans, nonchalantly flicking some ash into his blazing log fire.

'Remembering our great British Empire,' he sighed, 'which has since become the British Commonwealth, and the League of Nations, now known as the United Nations, we should no longer pursue our former, dogged, patriotism, or listen to those once respectable organisations in the way we used to do. Such are the powers which have now been given to individual veto, it is often a mistake to pay too much attention to their more outlandish and politically motivated decisions. But this time it is different.

'While too many of us have been arguing about who is going to win the next football match, the secretary general of the United Nations, a man who has been trying to galvanise the world into taking decisive action over climate change more than any other, including the vital part played by Sir David Attenborough, has made a stunning announcement, which you will read about in a moment.

'Meanwhile, you should no longer be concerned about your own valuable contribution, as it is now all, or nothing. Everyone must realise that the Australian prime minister inherited their lack of nuclear power stations, and being aware of the situation long before he took office, is not as foolish as many think. With all that coal due to be supplied from Indonesia, he will, as you will have guessed, Major, have his country back on its feet in no time.

'Indeed, he has promised not abandon our efforts but says he is more determined than ever to back our intention of establishing enough carbon absorbing vegetation in Australia to replace all those trees lost to the Amazon rainforest within five years. Why? Solely because he appreciates the responsibility, we have already shown in his country by gainfully employing so many Aboriginals.' Then he hesitated as if to make his final point.

'And it is also due only to Ud's outrageous irresponsibility towards our future,' Bob continued, 'which you, Major, instigated behind my back, that this callous Indonesian terrorist has now launched us into one of the great moments in our history.'

Then standing up to his full height of over two metres and drawing a last puff on his Montecristo, while passing them a sheet of paper, he invited them all to take a deep breath.

'Mindful of the fact that the Chinese, are not only facing just the same power and food shortages as ourselves, but also the worry of the Yangtze drying up and leaving them without water, we are, certainly, not going it alone, Ana. Aware of the eye watering sums of money that must now be raised fast and without question by every nation in the world, you and I remain a vital force in what must be the most decisive battle ever seen. Now read this remarkable press release.'

The Secretary-General of the United Nations stated at today's meeting of the UN Security Council, in acknowledging the part played by a small team from Great Britain in defeating climate change, that the following decision has been made:

As a direct result of the economic crisis in Australia, caused when the country's major open cut coal mines were set on fire by foreign terrorists, the Australian prime minister has been forced to sell the Chinese their total deposits of thorium in order to prevent the immediate and catastrophic collapse of their entire economy. To loose such a vital ingredient of our avowed intention to rid the world of fossil fuels, in exchange for clean, nuclear energy, is an unmitigated disaster.

However, such is the progress already being made by the Chinese in the development of thorium fuelled, salt cooled, Small Modular Reactors (SMRs), it has been decided unanimously by the full membership of the United Nations Security Council, that because the clock is ticking in the fight against climate change and we continue to hesitate on developing and certifying our own SMRs, the free nations of the world are now left with no alternative but to join forces with China.

CLIMAX—Addendum
Forgotten Thorium

Thorium is a naturally occurring, metallic element, discovered by a Swedish Chemist, Jons Jacob Berzelius, who in 1928 named it after Thor, the Norse God of Thunder, believing it would be beneficial to mother nature.

Thorium is estimated to be three times as abundant as uranium in the Earth's crust and may be refined largely from monazite sands. It may be mined with less effort than uranium throughout the globe and is found mostly in India, which is estimated to have reserves of at least one thousand tonnes, then in the United States, said to have enough thorium to generate power for a thousand years, followed by Australia, Canada and South Africa. The one notable absentee from the published list being China, whose deposits are unknown.

Once used for lighting gas mantles, its other uses in the past have largely been marginal such as strengthening magnesium or being incorporated in the filaments of some light bulbs. It is said now that one ton of thorium will be capable of producing energy equivalent to two hundred tons of uranium, or over three million tons of coal!

Thorium's more important role was identified during World War Two. For when bombarded with neutrons of recycled plutonium, it became an efficient nuclear fuel, to be labelled u-233. Although, used successfully to fuel a prototype molten salt reactor at the time, unlike its relative u-235, it was rejected by the USA due to its inability to make bombs.

Even though nuclear power is well documented, it is surprising that many of today's nuclear scientists remained unaware of u-233 until well into the start of this century. A nuclear engineer, formally employed by NASA, has stated that if the USA had not discontinued its research into using u-233 as a fuel for generating electricity, they would now be energy independent.

The element thorium is a fertile rather than a fissile material, but when converted into u-233, is now acknowledged to be a better nuclear fuel than u-235, also being well suited to molten salt reactors, such as the new, factory built, SMRs, or small, modular, reactors, which operate without the need for cooling water and leave little toxic residue.

Two of the major drawbacks with previous nuclear reactors is their dependence on substantial volumes of water, plus the dangerous amount of radioactive waste they accumulate, which, because it remains hazardous for thousands of years, is both difficult and expensive to dispose of. The waste from u-233, on the other hand, create no such problems, meaning that the eye watering start-up costs, caused by future decommissioning charges, are greatly reduced.

With China currently facing a serious energy crisis, yet, because of climate change, determined to stop commissioning further coal fired power stations, it is said that they are already trialling thorium fuelled SMRs in the Gobi Desert as a means for generating their growing demand for electricity, although they are unlikely to be blessed with sufficient deposits of the material, yet to be mined anywhere on the necessary scale.

CLIMAX. Postscript

SKY SPOD now equipped with E-Fan aero engines. Operating like a Drone.

My book was already with the publishers when on returning to Bob's gallant attempt to encourage the world to install SMRs and rid themselves of fossil fuelled power stations, and the Major's vital task of saving mother earth by planting its last wild places with carbon absorbing vegetation and its oceans with vast areas of kelp and seagrass—I realised that both had become an obsession.

For an elderly writer, who was not an ecologist and who had little understanding of botany, microbiology, oceanography and plant propagation, let alone of the intricacies of mechanical, electrical and aeronautical engineering, I was so convinced about my SPODs and all they would be able to achieve, I entered my concept in Elon Musk's $100m XPRIZE for the best solution to 'carbon removal'—the largest such prize in history!

To win the prize it stated that individuals, or teams, needed to demonstrate they would be able to sequester at least one thousand tonnes of carbon per year with the ability to sequester CO2 weighing gigatonnes into the future. A tall order, perhaps, for a gigaton is equivalent, it states on the internet, to the weight of 10,000 fully loaded aircraft carriers!

Great balls of fire! what a challenge, I thought in my bath. Already one person, an eminent marine biologist who with his company was busy planting kelp in the heaving Atlantic Ocean along the coast of Portugal, had raised my enthusiasm. 'It needs people like you to think out of the box. Only such innovative ideas like your Seed Pod Overhead Distributor will conquer climate change,' he said, before warning me about the many difficulties lying ahead.

Sea SPOD preparing to plant more kelp and seagrass. Fitted with water jets. Solar panels may be retracted.

So being of a competitive nature I looked up the countless teams that had already entered for the prize and found only one that had put forward a plan on anywhere near the same scale as my own, which was to grow and then sink a vast blanket of kelp in the Southern Ocean, although there was no hope of harvesting it and the benefits of such a plan were questionable. But what surprised me most was the apparent lack of confidentiality for all the ideas were laid bare for the World to see.

'You must patent your SPOD immediately' friends advised, but such is the ridiculous cost and difficulty of patenting anything in Great Britain, plus the mandatory three years it takes to obtain a patent, that all I could do was just apply for a patent though one of my friend's businesses and cross my fingers that no one would try to copy my ideas. For once my book was published "the cat was out of the bag".

With no time to lose I started working on some detailed drawings of Sky SPODs with one planting over endless miles of savannah in Australia's Northern Territories, which I had since chosen as a better bet than the Outback, and another of a Sea SPOD planting the ocean, before calculating the astonishing quantity of carbon they would each be able to sequester.

Starting with the land, while attempting to estimate the amount of CO_2 that would be removed by firing darts containing seeds of deep-rooted sorghum into the ground, my alternative to the invasive weeds which my previous choice of snake plants and prickly pears turned out to be, or slow growing tree saplings, my enthusiasm remained undaunted. So, having moved the operation from the Great Sandy Desert to follow the Gibb River Track through the more temperate zone further north, I calculated that two of my re-designed Sky SPODs travelling at 16 kph (10 mph), being replenished by electric trucks operating from bases moved nightly to land suitable for solar farms and air drops, would plant a fifty-metre-wide strip of sorghum over an area of 1,440 hectares (3,600 acres) during every eighteen hours of reasonable light. When multiplied by a conservative 2 tonnes of carbon removed per hectare, although not comparable to the amounts sequestered by planting the ocean, I was astonished to find that the two SPODs would remove a million tonnes of carbon per year—well in excess of the thousand tonnes stated by the XPRIZE.

Turning to the oceans, as the world's coastline is said to be 1,600,000 kilometres (1,000,000 miles) long, rather than walk it, I found that while a quarter of its length consisted of warm, sunlit, shelving beaches suitable for growing seagrass, a further tenth was of cooler rocky ledges suitable for growing kelp. So determined not to move my newly designed Sea SPODs around the world like grand prix racing cars, or avoid areas already growing the stuff, I decided to deploy six teams, each of two SPODs, to blanket plant seagrass and kelp over the three best areas south of the arctic circle supported by American nuclear powered aircraft carriers. These would not only carry them between planting areas but replenish them each in turn with both seagrass and kelp filled darts to be selected afterwards by sensors according to the underwater terrain.

The result was again encouraging. 400,000 kilometres (250,000 miles) of coastline planted with seagrass in a thirty-metre-wide strip by three teams over a year, would total over a million hectares (about 2.5 million acres) and sequester an average of twelve million tonnes of CO_2. Kelp planted likewise over 160,000 kilometres (100,000 miles) of coastline, equalling some 450,000 hectares, would sequester an average of eight million tonnes of CO_2 per year.

If just a few of my SPODs could remove at least twenty-two million tonnes of carbon from the atmosphere annually, the figure was dwarfed by the amount of blue carbon, possibly running into billions of tonnes, or gigatonnes, which would later drift and accumulate from the seagrass meadows and the kelp forests in much deeper waters to remain trapped, sometimes, for hundreds of years.

Believing that Musk liked tinkering with machinery, I therefore put together the strongest possible case for my SPODs, emphasising the bonus points that would be achieved by harvesting its fibre later for cattle feed and biofuels, or, more importantly, as a vital alternative to plastic.

So, hoping to pass on my ideas to those more able to progress them and to afford the eye watering costs of putting them into practice, I popped my entry into a large envelope and posted it off to the XPRIZE in California, concious that I had been unable to prove any of it!

Sea SPOD being replenished on US nuclear carrier.